The Eagle and the Dove

Death & Grieving With God

By

John J Chaya

*The righteous pass away; the godly often die before their time.
And no one seems to care or wonder why. No one seems to understand
that God is protecting them from the evil to come. [2]For the godly who
die will rest in peace.*

ISAIAH 57:1-2

Printed in the United States of America

ISBN 0-9747190-1-3

Publsihed by VMI Publishers
Sisters, Oregon 97749
www.vmipublishers.com

Author Contact
The White Dove Foundation
www.whitedovefoundation.org

In My Arms

By

John J. Chaya

I savored his tinyness, his gentle face,
His perfectly formed hands, his life blessed by grace,
God's creation, a gift, in my arms I held
Beginning a journey, his season to dwell.
A dream in my arms, one of new life,
not just an infant, but an heir to my throne.
God's sovereign work formed, our creation drawn,
Now our born blessing, to us new hope this dawn.

Nestled deep in my heart, forever secure,
God's whsiper of love, so innocent, so pure.
Our child of destiny, a life and a gift,
To all an eagle, soaring over the mist.

He grew to a man, a warrior, a force,
At times a champion, at times a leader,
At times a lost child, imperfect yet eager.
But always my first son, always a believer.

Alike in God's passion, unique love and a vision,
John, an eagle, giv'n a twenty one year mission.
A warhorse, a sheep, transformed by a dove,
his destiny fulfilled, his calling to love.

Alas, I saw in his eyes early one night,
his Savior come, first dark then so bright.
"Be at peace, he is in heaven." God whispered to me
You stand on Holy Ground, your true destiny.
From my arms to His arms, no dismay, no fright
The eagle and dove became one, lifted in flight.

Prelude

Do You Know Who Your Children Are?

I sit at my desk staring at my computer screen. A gentle morning sun splits the curtains and illuminates the window dressings and casts a golden hue across the room. Outside it is a few degrees above zero with a fresh blanket of snow. It is January 21, 2002, the second anniversary of the death of our son John, who would be twenty-three and a half years old now. It has been two years and it still seems unreal. I finished this book a few months ago, having written about what the first eighteen months was like with the heavy breath of death echoing in our ears. I have read my manuscript many times and still can't make it through a chapter without crying. At times I still can't read the first chapter without shutting down the computer.

Who was John? Why does his death still hurt so much? Why has my life changed forever? Why haven't I found all the answers about life and death? Those questions linger and I'll probably never know the answers.

But there are certain aspects of death and suffering that were never questions. I have never asked why God allowed John to die. Or where God was in all of this? I have not questioned why I never got angry with God, or wondered where John's soul is today. I didn't get outraged wondering why God took my son and why we have suffered so much. I never questioned what I truly believed in, or what God's plan for John was, or what God's plan for me is. Since January 21, 2000, God has used John's death to help me understand real life. I don't fully understand it, but I am able to understand clearly that real life causes you to believe in something real. And when you finally get around to believing in God and what He says in the bible, you realize that is all there really is, God and His plan. He is sovereign and He is real.

John fulfilled God's purpose. It would have been devastating if his death meant nothing or his life had no purpose. It would have been as devastating to me if I didn't realize how God was working in John, in his, and our friends and family, and the events that carried us through the first eighteen months of grieving.

In the midst of wandering through the wilderness of death, suffering and grief, when the whole meaning of life and purpose become dark and there is terror and confusion, God brings His spiritual fruits through His grace. Love, joy, peace, patience, kindness, gentleness, goodness, faithfulness and self-control were all fruits produced by the Holy Spirit during this time and I learned that God does not mock His children or abandon them in times of trial and tribulation.

Many people gave Beth, my wife, and me books about death and grieving and some were very helpful. This book was written to show the raw pain of death and the suffering and grieving, without any attempt to provide the magic formula or the secret scriptural verses to memorize when grief hits. What I hope the book will do is help you see how God works in His time and His way when death occurs. I hope you can understand our depths of pain and the total helplessness we felt, yet how we could sense the presence of God in His own way working to show us hope and mercy. I also want to share with you the hope God gave us and how He worked to create a new career for me. I can look back now and see that God was teaching me how to think and minister and help others in the midst of my pain. He blessed us with insight and guided us through a wilderness, so we can help others who must follow that path.

We certainly weren't prepared for John dying. There are no Bible studies to prepare for dying, or for the death of your child. There are few "death" sermons preached, because our culture doesn't want to deal with death. And too many people walk around thinking they need to know all the reasons why and the facts of how God works. Rest assured, they are rarely revealed. God doesn't work that way.

Americans have learned to find pleasure and evade suffering in our day. Denial goes a long way in coping with situations one isn't prepared for, but when there is only suffering and grief, then you learn to be intimate with God. It is my prayer that this writing will help you get more intimate with God, so that no matter what the situation, whatever the wilderness you walk in, you will see God and know that He is sovereign and loving and there with you. He is real.

But there is more than simply expressing grief in this book. There is a scriptural approach I have learned through John's death that I pray, as it unfolds in the chapters, will help you, in your time of grieving. God has a purpose and a plan for grieving. He uses suffering and pain to get our attention. As C.S. Lewis wrote, "Pain and suffering are the roadblocks on the highway to hell."

But God has a plan of redemption and offers hope in the darkest of hours. Death is part of life. There is no escape. But your attitude toward death and dying, pain and suffering can be a misguided mental state that leaves you empty and hopeless, or it can be a season of renewal, endurance, obedience and spiritual joy. You will come to a point in the grieving process where you will have to make that decision. Which path will you follow?

The questions at the end of each chapter serve one purpose. They provoke you to think about things you normally don't think about, or avoid thinking about. The questions will help you define what are the facts, what are the thoughts and what are the feelings that you may be experiencing, or will be experiencing during the grieving journey. Take them to heart. Ponder the answers. Seek God for His revelations, so you will be prepared to face your own death, or the death of a loved one with an attitude of thanksgiving, love, joy, peace, patience, faithfulness, gentleness, kindness, truth and self-control. These spiritual fruits are produced by the Holy Spirit for spiritual maturity, obedience and perseverance -- all signs of a true believer in Jesus Christ.

Take time and to get to know who your children are. Take time to get to know all those you love. We live in times where everyone is moving fast and are overly busy. Take time to get prepared. When death comes and you try to remember who that person is, you'll realize that you may have taken certain relationships for granted. God did not create us to take love or life for granted. Get to know the "person-behind-the-person" in others as well as yourself. Love them. You never know when they will leave you.

CHAPTER ONE

God's intimacy in the wilderness-Friday night, January 21, 2000

"He is in heaven, be at peace." I heard a voice whisper in my mind as I struggled, kneeling over my son lying dead on our kitchen floor. I looked into his eyes; the pupils were fully dilated and glossy. *It's over, Oh Jesus, I can't believe this! John is dead!*

My wife, Beth, stood in the archway between the kitchen and living room, pressing the phone hard to her ear as she spoke to the emergency dispatcher. "Yes, it's 516 Wood Way, in Burnsville, off Portland Avenue and County Road 42..."

"Jake, how is he?" Beth asked; but went back to the phone, responding to the person on the phone. "Yes, our son has stopped breathing. My husband is doing CPR."

I cleared John's airway, pinched his nostrils together and inhaled, put my mouth over his, then exhaled. His face felt so soft. I checked his pulse. Nothing. I listened to hear if he was breathing. Nothing. I tilted his head back further, inhaled again and blew two puffs into his mouth. *Jesus, he is yours. He is dead.*

I picked his head up again, repositioned my hands and fingers to continue CPR, and looked resignedly at his face. *Oh John, I'm so sad. This can't be happening!*

I leaned forward and exhaled into his mouth, more a loving gesture than a frantic effort to get him to breathe. I looked up at Beth, then back again to John. I almost went into shock with the startling comprehension that he was no longer with us.

Beth continued sharing information requested from the dispatcher. The paramedics arrived. The lead man reached me and I explained what happened. I quickly spoke, "He had the stomach flu for a few days. His breathing was shallow, almost like he normally was hyperventilating; he couldn't relax. We helped him to breathe normal and relax, but then he stopped breathing. So we put him on the floor and started CPR."

"How long was he sick?"

"A few days. He started getting sick Monday, but Wednesday he didn't go to work. He seemed sicker."

"How sick was he?"

"He was complaining of nausea and was throwing up on Monday, then seemed okay, but Thursday and Thursday night he was throwing up more. Then he seemed better. Today, he told me the stomach flu had passed and he just felt weak."

"Did he vomit any more?"

"Not that I am aware of, not since last night. I even asked him today about his stomach and again tonight and he said it didn't bother him, he just couldn't breathe right."

"How long has he been here on the floor?"

"Just about ten to fifteen minutes. I've tried to get him to breathe and I've tried CPR."

"Okay, move aside, let me take a look."

He checked John's pulse, eyes and breathing and started CPR. I stood helpless, looking down at John's glossy eyes. *What can I do? Oh Lord, if it is your will, revive him, but if he is to go, I thank you.*

Time was running out. So was our hope. Beth knew, too, that this could be the end. She went into our bedroom and called our pastor, Roger Thompson. No answer. Beth left a message, "This is Beth Chaya. Our son, John, is very sick and we are taking him to Fairview Ridges Hospital."

"God, heal John. Make him okay," she prayed, her voice tearful.

I looked at his whole body and listened as the other paramedics reached the kitchen and started opening their equipment cases. "Do you want me to help with CPR?"

"Yes," replied the lead man.

I circled around John's legs and began compressing his chest as the paramedic opened the airway and inserted a tube. John was still. His face was turning blue. I felt his arm; it was cool and clammy…still. I peered into his eyes then across his chest, hoping for some movement. Nothing. The other paramedics now surrounded us and I stepped away, seeking out Beth.

I knew in my heart it was over, but kept hoping. I kept watching the quick and deliberate actions as the paramedics courageously attempted to revive John. They inserted an airway, hooked up breathing equipment, set up monitors, and injected needles. As minutes went by and we saw the paramedics, firemen and police working hopelessly to get John's pulse and breathing started, shock set in. *John isn't going to make it.* Again, I heard the voice, deep in my soul. *He is in heaven, be at peace.*

At that moment God seemed so real. I couldn't see Him, but I knew He was there. He wasn't a ghost, He wasn't some feeling, He wasn't in my imagination. He was a life force, present, real, and in control. There were no illusions, no delusions, and no supernatural wishes. God brought peace, calmness, and strength. He filled us with His presence. We moved about the house, almost as if we were somebody else, not grief-stricken parents stunned by death.

We listened and heard the lead paramedic tell the brief words to his team that I shared with him about John's flu and what transpired prior to them arriving. Other voices flowed together as I heard excerpts of "his blood sugar is high,"

"He's still not breathing,"

"Go ahead, get the bag, start respiration,"

I stepped into the kitchen along side the workers, "Is he responding?"

"No, not right now."

"Is he breathing, does he have any pulse?" I got no response, just polite, courteous silence. We all knew. But no one wanted to shatter the faint hope that maybe he would come back. I forgot what the paramedics were saying as they worked so courageously, but somehow it kept sounding like John may have been diabetic and the flu weakened him so much that his heart stopped.

Beth interrupted my thoughts, warning about our bulldog. "You'd better get Champ. He may snap at the paramedics."

"It's okay, Champ. Come, let's go." The doge only looked at me and John, then followed as I led him to our bedroom. Our other dog, Deacon, hid under the bed in our room.

A policeman asked if we would answer some questions about John. "Was there any chemical abuse? Any alcohol abuse?"

We answered in the negative. He took down the facts of John's name, age and address and went back to helping the paramedics.

John was blue, lifeless. We were stunned, knowing the inevitable, but somehow hoping for a miracle. "How could this be happening? He only had the flu."

As the team prepared to take John down the steps, we knew there was no hope. They covered him with a simple blanket. We knew that if there was hope, they would have been wrapping him up warmly, treating him for shock. But by now, at least thirty minutes had gone by and we knew what they had conceded. John was not with us any more.

"Is he responding to anything?" I quietly asked.

"No."

The team worked quickly, securing him to the backboard, then to the stretcher, then covering him as life support equipment surrounded his head and chest. He was lifted up and he departed from his home accompanied by the medical team.

The policeman and a paramedic started cleaning up the floor and packing away used equipment. We watched the gurney being carried down the steps; we looked at the empty kitchen floor. We were in shock. Our 21-year-old son had died in our arms and they were taking him to the hospital, not to revive him, but to make the news official.

Why didn't we take him to the hospital, or to the doctor earlier? What did we do wrong? Was there something more we could have done? Did we not care enough? Did I not care enough to want to help him earlier in the week? Thoughts raced through my head. Guilt, regret, remorse, and sadness filled my heart. *What a poor father I am! Why didn't I take him to the doctor? But I asked him if he needed to go, I asked him if he was having too much pain, I asked him what I could do. Why didn't I just do something more?*

My thoughts rattled around in my mind, attempting to grasp what was happening, searching to understand that John was now dead, quasi-analyzing what went wrong. *Could the flu be that bad?*

The house grew dark and quiet and the team removed John from the house and the remaining paramedic and policeman finished straightening up the kitchen.

"Follow us to Fairview Ridges, drive around back to the emergency entrance. Take your time. We can have someone drive you?"

"No, we're okay. We'll drive over."

Beth and I prayed as the front door was closing.

"Oh Lord, don't take him, don't take my baby. Please, bring him back. Let him live," cried Beth.

"Father, whatever Your will is, help us accept it. We would like him to be okay, but let Your will be done."

I prayed half-heartedly, still hearing the echoes from the moment I knelt by John and heard in my mind, "He's in heaven, be at peace." The holy God who took John by the hand and led him to heaven was extending His hand to us, to lead us into the valley of the shadow of death. I knew the prayer was not a real prayer, but a wish. John was already in heaven and God had given me a deep peace and joy. I looked at the VCR clock.

It was 8:10 p.m., January 21st, 2000.

I went into the bedroom and called my twin brother, Paul. "Paul, it's Jake. Please pray for John and us. He is sick and stopped breathing. They took him to the hospital but it doesn't look good." I spoke those words but I didn't believe them. I knew.

My mind seemed to be flowing in mega-slow motion. "John is in heaven. Thank you Lord," I said to myself, not wanting to upset Beth more. We got our coats and the car keys and walked out the door, almost in a zombie-like state. *None of this is real*, I thought. *This can't be happening. How can this actually be happening?* I struggled with my mind and emotions as I started the car. Tears filled my eyes in the cold night air. My heart and mind grew heavy with grief. *What do we do?*

We slowly drove the mile or so to the hospital, not really saying anything, both of us deep in our thoughts and sadness. There were no people outside, just stillness, darkness, parked cars and loneliness. We walked into the emergency room and I approached the nurse's desk. I could tell by their faces that they didn't want to be the first to break the news.

"Hello, we're John Chaya's parents. He was just brought here. Can we see him?"

A nurse approached us and told us the emergency room team was working on John and we were to go to a room and wait. Beth was talking with a different nurse, asking for a phone book to call the pastors and our three children.

A nurse brought us water as we sat waiting. A woman entered and introduced herself as the doctor. I was watching to see if I could tell by her body language if there was any hope. A split second later, her eyes told me what I already knew. She slowly tried to tell us what the emergency team had done, finding it more and more difficult to tell us the inevitable. Finally Beth interrupted her; "Our son is dead?" she sobbed.

"Yes."

I sat down next to my wife and we held each other tightly and cried. I smiled weakly at the doctor as if to say, "thank you, it's okay, we know you had to tell us and we understand."

She put a box of tissues on the desk and Beth and I pulled tighter to each other, letting reality pierce our hearts as we heard someone else confirm what we knew. John had died. Emptiness filled the room. It felt like a black hole in outer space.

We sat in shock, disbelief and hopelessness. We looked at each other. Our deep relationship of twenty-five years of marriage strengthened us as we knew at this moment, neither of us could go on and handle this on our own. We both felt God's presence, but we needed each other to feel the other's hurt and loss and strength and faith. We knew John was with God, but his physical departure, so sudden, so final, so unreal, shook our logic, our senses, and our emotions. At that moment we had lost a precious life.

Together we had held him the first moments of his life and now we realized, just minutes ago, we had held him in our arms in his final minutes of life. *How does one explain that feeling in words? How does a mother and father articulate to each other, or to our children, or to friends or pastors, or doctors and nurses, that our first born is our first dead?* No one could ever prepare us for those moments, and slowly we realized we had nothing but God to get us through this. Our eyes saw John die, but our minds couldn't understand it, our hearts couldn't believe it and our words couldn't audibly articulate what we saw, thought and believed.

We regained our composure as we sat and cried. "Can we see him?"

"Yes, you may," replied the doctor. "He is in the room next to us, the door on the left."

Beth called our daughter and broke the news, "Adrienne, you need to come now. Your brother has died."

I stood up, feeling incoherent, but knowing I had to see John. I walked out the door with Beth and twenty feet in front of us, sitting in the waiting area, were Don and Monica. They had been long-time friends and missionaries and ministry partners and were faithful companions. They stood and looked at us in anticipation and we looked at them in stunned silence. *What do I say?*

Beth walked over to Monica, "John died," she said, as she hugged Monica. I stood there, bewildered at those words, but knowing they were true. I looked at Don we walked towards each other. I couldn't say anything, nor do anything.

There was THE room. I proceeded to open the door. A sign on the door said, "Knock before you open," and my cynical thoughts leapt in response, *why?*

It was barren with a cabinet against the narrow room wall. There lay John, blue, eyes closed, shirtless, face covered with tape, an inserted airway, and the fluid and blood smeared on his face and neck. His stomach was now huge with a blanket covering him from his chest down. I cried as I walked to his side and I put my hand on his shoulder and stared at his face. I had no feeling. I just sank deep into my soul as I looked at his face.

Finally, I spoke to him. "John, I love you. I am so sad. John, you are with God now." I placed my other hand on his forehead and ran my fingers through his hair. He was cold and stiff. Death seemed so complete, so unreal, and so final. I cried softly as I looked at him, not wanting to leave him. *John, I'm so sorry. I wish I had done more to help you. I wish I had shown you more love. I wish I had taken you to the doctor. I'm so sorry.*

I wish I wouldn't have tried to be so strong and not show I was afraid when you were afraid. Maybe I would have done something differently. I'm so sorry for sounding impatient and frustrated as I was trying to help you relax and breathe. I'm sorry. I didn't love you more and have more compassion. I wish I had taken better care of you. How could you die from the flu? It was my fault.

Beth came in alongside me and cried as she looked at her firstborn. We tried to be strong for each other, but the sight was too shocking, too surreal, and too unimaginable for comprehension. She talked to John but I couldn't hear her words as my grief and guilt pounded inside me. *I should not have sounded so insensitive, so callous. He was dying and I was frustrated that he wouldn't relax and try to breathe normally. Why did I ask him to get up and walk around? Why didn't I rush to him as Beth did and comfort him? Why did I sit in the chair and not pray?*

I cried in my shame, believing in my heart I always showed him I loved him, but confessing that my words were "not always loving" words. I was angry with myself. *Why didn't he ask to go to the doctor? Was he afraid I'd get mad? Why didn't he tell me he was in pain when I asked him? Was he really hurting and he just didn't want to show me he was weak? He told me he was sick and I told him he had the flu. Maybe it was more? Did I really know? No I didn't really know!* What I did know was that I had the flu also and had called urgent care to learn about the symptoms, and was told what I should do. Only after I pressed for an appointment (because I was leaving in a week for a short-term missionary trip to India and Vietnam) did I get one. And I got the usual tests and antibiotics and was told to rest, drink liquids, and that it will take a good ten days to recover. So John had the flu, and I could take the same advice and apply it to him. *But did I really know? No. And now look. He is dead.*

Beth walked out of the room, yet the guilt and conviction of how bad I really was, stunned me. "John, I am so sorry. Please forgive me. I love you. God, please forgive me. I was afraid and I tried to be strong, but some of my words didn't show strength, they showed my fear, pride, anger and frustration."

Although my attitude was one of helping and I tried to give him encouragement, I knew deep inside, a few times that evening, I was not helping and encouraging. I knew I had read John wrong. I knew over the years, there were times when he over reacted and was dramatic. I had thought this might be the case now. *It was too late. I had misread him. I had misinterpreted the situation.*

Memories flooded my mind, of the final minutes as John sat (at his spot) in his chair at the kitchen table. He was struggling and his speech became garbled as Beth covered his shoulders with a blanket. He tried to look up to the ceiling but couldn't completely lift his head up. He stiffened his arms trying to push up from the table. He looked at Beth in wonder and said, "Everything in the room is going around, but I see it up there. I see him."

He strained forward and slowly a look of peace drifted across his face and his body relaxed. He breathed normally and it seemed the crisis was over. He had mentioned earlier that he wasn't in pain, but that he felt he was having an anxiety attack. He was afraid he couldn't breathe. Now he was breathing normally. He was at peace, no pain, no struggle, no fear.

I remembered feeling so encouraged at this turn of events. As I saw him relax and be peaceful, I softly spoke, "Good John, good, Buddy you're relaxing, that's it. Everything is okay. Just rest, you're doing well." As I saw him trying to hold himself up, I spoke, "No John, it's okay. You're tired, close your eyes and sleep. You haven't slept much, you've been sick. Put your head down on the table and close your eyes and sleep, everything will be okay."

We were happy and felt close and loving knowing he was relaxed and at peace and breathing normally. He tried to open his eyes again and I said, "Just relax, Buddy, you're okay, everything will be all right, just put your head down and sleep." As he started to lower his head, he slumped forward and Beth and I held him. I looked at his peaceful face and the sheer terror of something seriously wrong struck me like lightning. He wasn't breathing now. I checked his pulse; it was shallow and weak. I lifted up his head and the brownish clear liquid dribbled out of his mouth and down his chin and chest...

The emergency room nurse came and asked if we were considering donating any of John's organs. Beth and I acknowledged that we were. The nurse said she would contact the Red Cross as she placed an ice bag across John's eyes to save them. She was extremely gentle and compassionate. Our children arrived, and some of their friends arrived. I walked out of the room, hugging Beth and crying with her, then with my children, not knowing who knew what or where they were coming from, but we were all together now. None of it seemed real.

Adrienne arrived, getting a ride from her boss's wife. I met them in the little waiting room. Adrienne was crying and upset, because she and John had had an argument earlier that day and she hadn't been able to reconcile it with John. Finally, I asked, "Adrienne, do you want to see your brother?"

"Yes."

I walked with her into the room where John lay. Adrienne wept and talked to her brother. She asked for forgiveness and I could see God moving, strengthening and comforting her. I cried and prayed for her, thanking God that He was strengthening her, giving her peace.

We walked out of the room and I stood outside the room as my boys, Scott, then Ben arrived. They cried in their anguish. They had lost their big brother. Scott leaned against the wall, then we hugged. Ben came, we hugged and he leaned against the door. We walked back in to see John. I watched as they looked in silence and cried.

Everything became a blur as Roger Thompson, our pastor, arrived. In minutes more pastors arrived. I turned and was surprised to see Scott Peterson, John's youth pastor, standing alongside John, then comforting Scott and Ben. The room filled with more pastors. What strength they brought! God's men were there, and somehow we were going to get through this. We knew we couldn't get through this on our own.

Beth comforted some of Scott's and Ben's friends. I was humbled as I watched their grief and sadness. I walked out of the crowd and stood against the wall adjacent to John's room, away from the people. My heart was broken, I was in shock. I struggled to breathe and I coughed and blew my nose as my bronchitis and sinus infection ravaged me. The stress, the crying and the pain seemed to be exacerbated by my physical ills. I slumped against the wall. *I'm so sick I can't even stand. I can't talk, I can't see right. I'm a real mess. God, please help me. Give me the strength to make it through the next hour.*

I walked to the first room and met with the doctor. "What did John die from, the flu and high blood sugar, diabetes?"

"We aren't sure, but his blood sugar was high and the flu could have led to complications."

"I'd like to have an autopsy performed," I interjected. "I want to know for sure."

"Yes, because he was so young, an autopsy is required." responded the doctor.

"When? When will it be done?"

"Tomorrow, probably in the morning. We'll have the coroner or deputy sheriff's office, call you with details."

Meanwhile, Beth had been on the phone with the coroner's office. An autopsy was required but we could request that it not be done. She told them to do the autopsy and asked to be informed of the details.

Eventually it was time to leave. I didn't want to leave John. I didn't want the quiet of the dark night to tell me again about death. I had experienced glimpses of heaven in the past during short-term missionary trips, but now I had seen a glimpse of hell and I was defeated and devastated. Nothing could be so bad as seeing my son die and feeling the guilt and shame of not being able to help him when he needed me the most. I was totally alone in my world.

We gathered in the waiting room for a time of prayer. The doctor came and I gave her a hug. Jesus was there. Our friends and pastors surrounded us as Roger prayed. His words were so loving, comforting and soothing at a time when nothing seemed real. His petition was for God to protect us against Satan at this time of vulnerability. It was so profound. I realized that some of the earlier anguish, guilt and shame were from the enemy. Roger had spoken the truth and the heavenly host must have responded, as the peace and joy of knowing John was with God surrounded us. Although we may look defeated, we had victory and the enemy wasn't going to steal it away. Suffering reflected the depths of love. I held Beth's arm and we walked out the door, past the nurse's station. It was over.

It was after ten p.m. as we slowly walked through the parking lot to our car. The dark, still night reflected our situation. "What do we do next?"

"Who do we call?"

"Who can we talk to? How do we go about making funeral arrangements?"

"Where should we have him buried? In Pennsylvania? Where is a cemetery near us?"

We sat in our car without any answers. We didn't know what to do. I slowly drove back to our house. Disbelief, shock, sadness, peace, joy, and grief mixed into the dark. Emptiness is so confusing, yet so real. Silently we got out of the car, almost moving in slow motion, trying to grasp what needed to be done next. I stood in the driveway, gently closed my car door, took two steps and reached out to a red Grand Am. John's car. *Was he really gone? He couldn't be. Here is his car.*

I sobbed as I leaned against his car. I smiled as I saw all the junk in the back seat and floor. *Typical John*, I thought. Sadness filled me as a wave of grief crashed through my memories. *I miss him so much already.* I cried,

"I love you John." Beth tugged at my sleeve, "C'mon, let's go inside."

I nodded and trudged inside after her. I removed my coat to be jolted by a second reminder. The new black leather coat John got for Christmas was draped on the banister. I stood staring at it. *Oh God, help me. Everything reminds me of John and he is dead. How can I go on?*

I peered into the kitchen, again stunned by the aftermath. Kitchen stools sat in disarray, the dining table and chairs askew, a trash bag filled with discarded medical equipment and supplies on the floor. I stood as if in a sanctuary, picturing John's body lying perpendicular to the counter. *Did this really happen? It must have. I wouldn't be so sad and confused if it was just a nightmare.*

Beth and I stood in our bedroom and hugged; *What were we to do next?*

I picked up the phone and called my brother. "Paul, it's Jake. John died. They think he had high blood sugar, maybe was diabetic and the flu created complications that stopped his heart."

There was silence. I didn't expect to hear anything. "An autopsy will be done tomorrow. I don't know what to do. We need some time to think and plan. I'll call you back in the morning. Please pray for us." We exchanged a few words and we hung up. I lost my composure and sat on the bed, dreading the next call. *I am helpless!*

I called my mother. "Mom, it's Jake. I have bad news. John died tonight."

"Did he? ..."

I interrupted, "He had the flu and was having a hard time breathing. Tonight it got worse and we tried to help but he died at home. The emergency team worked hard, but we knew he was dead before they got there."

She responded through her weeping, "Okay, well, I am so sorry. Call and let us know what you're going to do." I hung up crying, knowing my mother had now lost three generations of men in her life in the past eight years: her husband, (my dad), her father—my grandfather— and now a grandson, —my son. I felt the same strange eerie losses she did. Life seemed so empty all of a sudden. *I can't believe I'm calling people to tell them John died. I just can't believe it!*

Beth lay on the bed crying. Now it was her turn. She called her two sisters and shared the grim news. We walked out of the bedroom, having spent a few moments in prayer.

Minutes later, we had visitors. Klaas and Mary Van Zee, a couple we'd shared ministry with over the years, arrived to be with us. We had been in Bible studies together and Klaas and I often met over breakfast or lunch to just talk, share perspective and ground each other in the scriptures. More often than not, Klaas did most of the grounding. But tonight, I didn't want anyone around. I resigned myself to the facts that I didn't know what to do and I needed help and that we needed someone to get us through these hours. They had lost a newborn baby many years earlier, and I found great comfort in knowing that they had been there and knew what we were experiencing. A short time later, Paul and Linda Emanuelson arrived. Paul was the children's pastor at our church.

The evening drifted away as we recounted the previous weeks, days and hours and how we could feel God at work. John was gone and no matter what we shared or prayed, wished or hoped, nothing was going to change that fact. As we relived the past events, we sensed God's hand revealing His perfect timing and master plan for John's life. We were comforted as we talked through the events and started to see that a loving God had His hand on all the details leading up to this evening. Our heavy grieving was interspersed with revelation. We thanked God for being so merciful, and being so real in this difficult time.

We realized we had been blessed with John for 21 years. We were humbled and thankful that we were with John in his final moments. We had held him when he was first born and we were there to hold him in his final moments. God had allowed me to be home. I wasn't traveling on business, or on a mission trip. We were grateful John didn't die alone, afraid with no one near, perhaps in his old apartment, or a college dorm, or in his car.

We relived the final hour of how obedient he was as we tried to help him relax and breathe. In his last hour, he was the most obedient and "willing-to-listen" son. We rejoiced that he was with God, in heaven. I shared how it seemed like a split second after we realized the look of peace on his face and his relaxed breathing, that he had passed from this life into heaven. We reflected how critical the decision he made was at age five accepting Jesus Christ as Lord and Savior. Now, in the most crucial moments, that decision was the most important thing he ever did.

It dawned on me that even as I struggled with the flu and bronchitis and a sinus infection, I was happy, since it caused me to stay home from work and I was able to spend time with John. Only later did I see God's sovereignty. John and I stayed up all night, because we were too sick to sleep. What a blessing! I had spent John's final night on earth with him, just hanging out in the living room, watching television, viewing the Praise channel, channel-surfing, talking, napping and just having a slow comforting, drifting late night. We had each known the other was sick and it had been good just to be in misery together.

God was taking care of John. We knew He was in control and He would not forsake us or abandon us at this time. As the night grew on, fatigue set in, but there was peace and joy in knowing God had been so gracious by bringing people into our lives for comfort. We embraced the two couples that had come and their words, prayers and tears.

Several times during our time together, we were interrupted by phone calls. A missionary colleague and friend, Kathi, called, audibly upset over the death and the pain. Somehow we got through the conversation and I asked her to contact people from my team at work and the members of my foundation. Another good friend, Mark Ledson, (after getting the message from Kathi) called and once again I relived the details. Mark and Joan had followed John throughout his high school athletic career and had named their new baby, Jake, after me.

I felt like he was a brother as I shared my soul. He had given us his English Bulldog, Champ, after his son (Jake) was born. John and Champ were made for each other. Now Champ watched as everyone began to leave the house. He couldn't find his buddy John.

A final call from the deputy sheriff's office confirmed that John's body would be taken to Hastings and the coroner would perform an autopsy mid-Saturday morning and hopefully have results by afternoon. I thanked the caller, relieved that someone had taken care of the logistics for that procedure.

It was after midnight when Beth and I climbed into bed. We talked and prayed, cried and stared at the darkness. We still couldn't believe what had happened. Our prayers gave us comfort, yet there were the gnawing questions. Could we have done something more? Could we have gotten John help sooner? Were we too slow? What could we have done to keep him alive? What did he really die from? Those and many other questions shook us, and then the guilt and self-accusations filled me as they had done earlier in the hospital. The short night was filled with crying, shame, restlessness, worry, and fear, tossing and turning. Our hearts were as dark as the night. The greatest fear a parent could have was now real and we were experiencing death.

REFLECTION

None of us are prepared to go into the wilderness of death. How prepared are you? The wilderness can be a long journey, a time of barrenness, confusion, bewilderment, pain, guilt, anger, terror, and surreal adventure. The wilderness can be dry, dark, lonely and empty. The journey is one of humility. You can't go through the wilderness by yourself. But very few people can go along with you. Most journeys in the wilderness will either lead you to a new intimacy with God, or turn you away from God in anger and bitterness. The wilderness is the place to learn who you are. You will never be the same once you come out of the wilderness. You may have avoided the wilderness so far, but eventually we all will journey into it. How will you respond?

Chapter Two

Lost in the wilderness -- Saturday, January 22, 2000

Morning came with very little rest. The shock hadn't lessened. Beth and I held each other and prayed. We felt God's presence, His peace and joy. We felt assured again that John was with God in heaven; there were no doubts, but the incredible pain of losing a child and the physical emptiness strained deeper into our souls.

Beth and I labored as we weren't sure which day to have the funeral. We weren't sure if we were to have John buried or cremated. Finally we decided to have him cremated. I called the funeral director, John White, and found soothing comfort in him as we started the planning process. We'd meet early in the afternoon to make all the arrangements. Klaas, who has been with us the night before, had volunteered to accompany me to the funeral home.

The director comforted me over the phone and arranged getting John from the coroner's to the funeral home. I felt safe and secure, knowing that my son was being taken care of. Even though I didn't know what to do, a steady guiding hand was there.

I called Pastor Roger and gave him the latest news. He was very empathetic and down-to-earth, taking away the discomfort of uncertainty. He prayed for me, wished us well and I promised I'd call later.

My brother, Paul, called and informed me that he was in touch with Mom and they were all coming out from Pennsylvania.

The phone started ringing mid-Saturday morning and as people called, we saw God's love manifest itself through an amazing display of deep sympathy and caring. Plants, flowers, baskets of food, acts of kindness and love, filled the house. One couple, Darrell and Marge Sanborn, came over with bags of items, but they brought with them a love and comfort and an authority, for they had lost their son Jeremy, at age 23, in an airplane accident.

I had watched from afar for years as they grieved their loss, yet this man and woman of God had a special grace about them. Their son had coached our John in the church league Stockade basketball program and he had a tremendous impact. Darrell provided a profound statement that grew to be a great comfort over time. He said, "You know, if God were to ask Jeremy and John if they wanted to come back, they'd say no." I froze when I heard that statement. *Cool, that says it all. Why WOULD they want to come back here? What comfort!* I thought.

Darrell continued. "And if we knew what they are experiencing now in heaven, we wouldn't want to ask them to come back." *I thought through his words. If I really believe in God and eternal life and what Jesus did on the cross and how John invited Jesus into his heart, then I must believe that they wouldn't want to come back and that I should never feel like I should ask that question.* From that moment on, I understood the depths of faith during death. My son had a champion's heart, he was a winner, and his ultimate victory was in heaven.

That Saturday morning, women from our church came over and helped clean the house and ran errands. Food arrived and they made sure that family members ate and were cared for. I sheepishly thanked them as they came and went, embarrassed by the attention and gifts. Slowly I surrendered to the humbling situation.

The morning shifted into afternoon, as the house grew full of shocked and caring people. They helped us grapple with arrangements. People from our church, neighbors, friends from work, from the foundation we established, Beth's choir partners, my sons' and daughters' friends and parents led a never-ending stream. We felt awkward, realizing that for so long we were the ones who would give comfort and help. It was much more difficult to receive than to give.

I struggled once more as I sat with the people in our living room. Reliving John's last days was painful, yet I kept searching to relive moments. A wave of joy surged over me as I coughed and sneezed and blew my nose. Although I was having the worst case of flu I ever had, I was thankful for it in a strange way.

For the past week I had been to the doctor and had tried to work, but eventually had to take two days off. I was home Wednesday when John came home early with his stomach illness. We talked a bit and relaxed, doing nothing but being sick together.

I had gone to work on Thursday because our newly organized work group was having dinner that evening and I wanted to be a team player. I returned home that night, feeling feverish and weak. John was sleeping when I got home. I went to bed, hoping to get some sleep.

I woke up around midnight, sick and aching; I arose and went out to the living room where I reclined on my lounge chair and channel surfed. A few minutes later I heard John downstairs in his bathroom. He vomited a few times and I was praying for him. He then must have taken at least a 45-minute shower. He emerged at the top of the staircase drying his wet hair. "Hey Buddy, how are you feeling?"

"The shower made me feel better." he replied. He didn't seem overly concerned, as if something was seriously wrong.

"That's good; how's your stomach now?"

He didn't answer. He lay down on the large sofa and watched television with me. We channel surfed, snoozed, and talked about us being sick; about him needing to relax and try to breathe normally as he sounded like he was hyperventilating. We watched the Praise Channel. We didn't say much, just small talk every now and then. A few hours later, I asked him how his stomach felt and he said, "Better."

"Any pain anywhere?"

"No, just I feel sick."

"Well, probably we should try to go back to bed and get some sleep. I'm staying home today."

"Yeah, me, too."

John struggled to stand, looking stiff from lying in one spot too long and he slowly made his way down the steps to his room. "See you later."

"Good night John."

I turned off the television, went out and got the just-arriving newspaper, and went to bed. It was 5:30 a.m. Friday, January 21st. Only now, two days later, this Saturday morning, did I realize that John had spent his last night on earth with me. I felt overjoyed that God, even in this painful time, had provided me with such a special blessing. I was glad I had the flu. If I weren't sick, I never would have been able to spend that last night together with my son. God was taking care of even the smallest details. Shortly after that, the guilt crept in. *Why didn't I try to comfort John more, or pray with him, or do something to help him more? All we did was lie around in the living room. Maybe I should have probed for more answers! Maybe I shouldn't have assumed he only had the flu. Since when do I think I'm a doctor? Maybe God had him come upstairs so I could help him and I blew it.* Tears filled my eyes as a crowd of people mourned with us, but none of them ever knew what was going on inside of me.

Beth seemed strong, even in her tears. She was sharp in her thinking and chatting with our friends. Adrienne seemed to be doing better; sad, yet like a rock, steady and solid. Ben and Scott were in and out with their friends and I knew the hurt they were experiencing, but they wanted to hurt with their friends. Both came home mid-morning and it was good to have us all together.

Beth and I discussed who might be pallbearers "Let's try to get some of the football players and wrestlers that played with John," Beth suggested.

We interrupted our thoughts trying to decide what clothes John should have. Clothes? We decided on his khaki slacks, a white shirt and his only tie. Klaas came and he asked us a few questions so we could make some decisions with the director. We decided to have the funeral Tuesday morning, following the advice of Roger after he told us not to worry about anything, the church would provide a luncheon and take care of whatever needed doing. Beth decided she would stay at the house and greet people, answer the phone and take care of the deliveries as food, beverages, fruit, plants and flowers were arriving frequently.

Klaas and I went to the White Funeral Home. It was a cold sunny day as I rode in his van. I was so preoccupied and numb with grief that I don't remember anything we talked about. We arrived and I sat down uncertain of what to say. John White, soft-spoken and patient, explained the choices of memorial cards, scripture verses, caskets, obituaries, costs, services, memorials and times for the viewing and funeral. I found myself unprepared and sought to take notes. Klaas was writing things down and in a much better mindset than I was. I chose a memorial card cover, a design background of blue sky with ice-glistening on trees and the bright sun shining through. The scripture overlay was, "I am the Resurrection and the Life."

I felt at peace making decisions and discussing the many details until one small term –dream team— shook my emotions and I wept.

"Have you selected the pallbearers?" asked John.

"Well, Beth and I discussed them, but we don't have all of them. I'm not sure who all to ask."

"No, problem, take your time. I won't need to know until Sunday about 6 p.m.," John responded.

"We're going to track them down, since most of them are in college. It would be great if we could get the three other players who were part of the co-captains of the football team, and we'll see if we can't get some wrestlers from the 'dream-team.' "

DREAMTEAM…as soon as I said those words I lost my composure. That team was a state championship team that went 31-0! What an honor, to have members of the dream team as pallbearers. I cried as I thought about those days and their many achievements and John being such a great part of it. What a blessing to have a son start at heavy weight and be a part of a high school wrestling team considered the best team ever in the history of Minnesota wrestling! Sadness crashed through the memory.

We finalized plans on the cremation, costs, and whatever else needed to be done. Monday would be the visitation, from 4 p.m. to 8 p.m. I was to finalize the message on the memorial, get the names of the pallbearers, determine the scripture, bring the clothes and make sure my tasks were done by 6 p.m. Sunday evening. The funeral would be Tuesday at 11 a.m. with an open casket viewing at the church at 10 a.m. I was relieved to be finished with the arrangements, but dreaded the outcome of our plans.

We returned home to see the house overflowing with people. Word reached a close friend, David Pierce, a missionary who had been like a brother to me for twelve years, introducing me to the missionary world and mentoring me in times of struggle and spiritual growth. He was going to try to get connections from New Zealand. My younger brother, Tom, had talked to Beth earlier and he and his wife, Lynn, were going to try to make it from Florida.

News came that all the pallbearers were confirmed and God blessed us with the three captains, John's linemen buddy, Cliff, and three of the "Dream Team."

The assistant to the coroner called. She explained, "I'm not a doctor so I don't have all the medical understanding or details of what we found but I want you to know that your son was an amazing young man who had a high threshold for pain or wasn't a complainer. We thought when we went in, we'd find what the paramedics thought, possibly diabetes, a high sugar count and heart and respiratory failure from the flu. We were shocked to see the devastating damage."

I sat, stunned, listening intently. "John died from a rare and fatal virus. His death is termed Acute Hemorraghic Pancreatitis. Basically he was sick for a while with the virus. It attacked his pancreas. Being so strong and healthy, his body fought the virus, even after the pancreas shut down."

"Mr. Chaya, how long was John sick?"

"Well, he came home early from work on Monday, but worked Tuesday and Wednesday. He vomited often on Wednesday night and Thursday. Thursday he slept and was sick but we thought it was the flu. I have been sick, also."

"The tissue in his bowel region was black and dead, leading us to believe he was sick 2-3 weeks, maybe longer than a month."

I quickly thought about the last few weeks. *No way, he wasn't sick that long,* I thought. "We were back in Pennsylvania for Christmas and he was fine. We had a good time, he had a great appetite. We went bowling; he seemed normal. We had a great Christmas vacation. He didn't appear to be sick at all. For the past few weeks, he was doing well, eating, working, and getting rest. It was just the past week and really only since Wednesday night that he seemed very sick."

She asked, "Did John complain of any pain?"

"Yes, Wednesday and some on Thursday. But Thursday night when we were up I asked him if he was in pain and he said no. Friday night during his last hours I asked him if he was feeling any pain and he said no, that he was sick and uncomfortable, but feeling more like he was having a panic attack. I asked him what he was fearing."

John responded, "I'm afraid I can't breathe."

"So we thought he was hyperventilating, because he did have an anxiety attack a few months ago. He said it felt the same and he had gone to the emergency room. He received a battery of tests and X-rays and the doctors found nothing other than bronchitis. They gave him an inhaler and said he should see a doctor and gets some medication for the anxiety attack."

The coroner's assistant listened then reiterated her earlier comments. "Well, he is amazing because the devastation to his organs was traumatic. If he wasn't feeling much pain, he either had a high threshold for pain, or the virus had destroyed the nerve endings and nerve tissue in that region."

"He had been a football player and wrestler in high school and college so he did handle pain well, but something this serious, I knew he would have told us."

She continued. "There was a cascading effect. Once the pancreas shut down, the gall bladder, liver, stomach and kidneys failed. The pancreas hemorrhaged and filled his stomach and abdomen with dead blood. You can be proud of your son. His body fought the virus. His liver was the size of two footballs, thus compressing his lungs. That is what caused him to have shallow breathing."

I felt so miserable, listening. I started to cry. "Mr. Chaya, she continued, "John died from a rare virus. He could have been in the hospital and the virus wouldn't have been detected. No matter when you brought him in, it wouldn't have mattered. You couldn't have saved him, the medical team couldn't have saved him, and the ER staff wouldn't have been able to do anything. He died from a rare fatal virus, a natural enemy which can't be diagnosed or treated."

"Thank you for your report. It is comforting to know we didn't do anything wrong or were negligent or too slow."

"Oh no, this virus can't be treated. It is swift and fatal. You weren't at fault for anything." A huge weight was lifted off me. For nearly 24 hours questions and guilt and shame had tortured me. Now the soothing voice was telling me the facts and I didn't have to think of the awful thoughts I was dwelling on. We spoke for a few minutes and I gave her information as to which doctor should receive the coroner's final report. I hung up the phone, shocked by what I heard.

Beth nearly descended into a state of shock, realizing our son had fought hard against impossible odds. He had the heart of a champion as an athlete and now we learned, at death, he still had the champion's heart. Relieved, we cried and comforted each other, affirming our faith that God's timing was perfect and He was merciful. Also, the regret and guilt washed away. This was John's time to go home. We had done nothing wrong and no one could have changed the outcome. All that mattered was that God was merciful, sovereign and omniscient and His timing is always perfect.

We walked out of the bedroom, deeply saddened by the news, but very much relieved. God had given us the truth and the spiritual fruits of joy and peace, something that couldn't be manufactured on earth. Grief mixed with joy and peace. There weren't any words to fully describe that dichotomy.

As we shared the news with the mourners in our house, you could feel the sadness and grief build. We could also feel the questions being thought. Why did John die so young? How could he have been so sick for so long? Where does the virus come from? How does one contract a fatal virus? Why is there no way to diagnose it, or treat it? We had experienced the same questions, but God had given us a grace and a peace. We learned what a sovereign God really meant.

Somewhere around nine p.m. our house grew quiet as guests and friends departed. Our children had gone into seclusion with their friends and Beth and I sat in the stillness of a darkened house. Overwhelmed by the outpouring of friends, neighbors and people from our church, we were humbled by how the spirit of God was at work and how gracious and merciful He was.

I called Pastor Roger and explained the coroner's report. Roger assured us that John was in heaven, that His plan is perfect and that he, Joanne, his wife, and our church family at Berean Baptist loved us and were constantly praying for us. I was comforted as we made plans to meet on Sunday afternoon to discuss funeral arrangements.

Beth and I stepped deeper into a silent living room, miserable from our failing physical health, wounded emotions, heavy grief and the sadness of knowing John had died from a devastating virus. It had been a long day. It had been a hard day. It had been the saddest 24 hours of our lives. I remembered Roger's prayer at the hospital, that our family would stay united and the enemy wouldn't be able to create disunity and hardship among us. His prayer was being answered.

The night grew late, and my brother called. "Jake, I had to call you about something I heard tonight. I lifted John's death and your family up in prayer tonight in our small group. I basically explained the coroner's report to them. Afterwards, a fellow in the prayer group approached me. He is a medical doctor who specializes in infectious diseases. He concurred with what Paul reported about John's death and stated that the coroner did a good job explaining what happened. He added, "Tell your brother that God is a merciful God. The illness your son had because of the fatal virus is devastating. It is 100% fatal. Usually 85% die the first day it is diagnosed. The other 15% die in 2-3 weeks after life support systems, transplants and dialysis are performed. There is no way to track it. John could have had a blood test the day before and no one would have found it. God is merciful. John didn't linger. The virus moved quickly. We can thank God for His grace and mercy. If John would have been normal size, he probably would have died sooner, but because of his great health he fought hard and lived longer. We can thank God for His mercy and His love."

We cried together over the phone. I told Paul, "John was a champion athlete and to hear how he fought, he will always be a champion. Ask your church tomorrow to praise God for being so merciful and for John being such a champion. We Chaya's were champions and you, Paul, helped me and helped John, so let your flock pray for the champions."

We were so proud of John, not because of who he was, but because of who God made him. This was tough, but we knew John would always be a champion. I shared our conversation with Beth and as we held each other and prayed, our sadness mixed with the ever-present joy and peace, knowing now just how God's hand had been at work.

Although neither of us slept much, the night passed with only small waves of grief. Memories flooded our minds of moments when John was born, throughout the many adventures, events and words over twenty-one years, right up to the final moments.

Beth was holding up well. I was slowly sinking into the conviction that my words throughout John's life were sometimes critical and frustrating and unloving. As I relived his last hours, my mind dwelled on the negativity, fear, frustrations and impatient words I had said, not in anger, but in a blend of my own fear and my desires for John to try harder to relax and for his breathing to return to normal.

My guilt changed from not doing enough to save John or help him and comfort him, to the many times I was loose in my words, critical, hardhearted and insensitive. I conceded over the years that we had had a few rough episodes of rebelliousness and disrespect, but now I was blaming myself for all the problems because of things I wished I hadn't said. I was convicted deeply that it wasn't just with John, but with Adrienne, Ben, Scott and Beth and many others over the years to whom I had spoke with conditional words. Remorse and regret grew as I realized I could make up for those harsh words with my family and others, but I wouldn't get another chance with John.

REFLECTION

Being lost is the ugliest feeling I can experience. The next ugliest feeling is being helpless to do anything about it. The wilderness calls each of us. We live to avoid the wilderness. It is ugly when you get lost in a beautiful wilderness. Nothing looks good. The birds, and flowers and rich greenery, the moss and the animals darken and melt into the background. The sun dims, the fresh air stagnates, the clear cool shadows fill with distorted images and swarming gnats. A peaceful walk in the woods transforms into panic. Does anyone really know what to do when you're lost? Does anyone really have the answers about death? Only God. Ask Him. He'll tell you.

CHAPTER THREE

Voices in the wilderness -- Sunday, January 23, 2000

Getting very little sleep, I tossed and turned, filled with grief, fear, shame, and confusion, weird dreams and rambling thoughts. One question percolated through my rough night. "Did Satan win?"

For eleven years I had been going on mission trips. I always ran into spiritual warfare prior to the trip. For a few years, the attacks were focused on me. For the past six years, the warfare was pointed at my family. Although nothing had happened to them, the attacks began to escalate and get more intense.

My most recent trip in April to Singapore and India in 1999, found an attack on my daughter, Adrienne, while I was in Singapore. The crisis was resolved but I was concerned that the enemy did get to my daughter. A few weeks later I was in an auto accident which totaled my car and could easily have been fatal. God protected me. Regardless of the near misses, I had put my faith in God and saw him victorious in every battle.

I was scheduled to go to India and Vietnam on January 30th. I had my plane tickets, visas, funding and materials ready for Goa, New Delhi and Ho Chi Minh City for the 17-day trip. But now all that changed as I immediately canceled the trip. Was there spiritual warfare occurring and with the death of John, was I effectively neutralized? Did Satan finally win? Knowing God is victorious over the enemy but not having that sense of victory, I wanted God to answer my question.

Sunday morning dawned brightly, but I lay in bed praying, tainted with guilt. I couldn't get the critical words out of my head that I had said to John over the years, especially over his last few hours. I brushed aside the many great talks we used to have and the fun telling jokes and being bizarre in our stories and perspectives. None of that mattered as I could only dwell on what I shouldn't have said. I detested my behavior, knowing so often my words weren't fruitful or soft. Somehow I didn't want to remember the many fine things I had said.

I had made it a point never to say anything bad about any type of performance in sports, music, or academic competitions to my children and I was very sensitive not to embarrass my children in public. Yet it was my disappointment in the small details, the minor issues, the frustrations of missed expectations; it was then that I was cutting and hurtful. Sometimes I didn't perceive myself doing it, other times it just happened and sometimes it was my pride and anger that overcame my discretion and I said words I shouldn't have. But now I could only think of the negative words, the lectures, and the sermons that did no one any good. I was a conditional lover in the words I spoke. I wept in shame and guilt.

Beth awoke to my sobs of sadness and helplessness. We held each other and prayed. No matter how she tried to comfort me, I wouldn't let go of the guilt and regret. Those struggles cast such a pall over my thinking that I couldn't remember reality. Her words didn't help as I heard her speak. I was preoccupied with my self-disgust. We prayed again and suddenly there was a breakthrough.

I cried to her that I missed John so much and that I had always wanted the opportunity to coach him as a champion. I watched his football and wrestling coaches coach him on six state championship football, wrestling and track teams. I watched them coach him to All-State status twice for wrestling and All Conference for football and I was proud of him and his coaches. But having coached high school football, wrestling and gymnastics for twelve years myself, my one desire went unfulfilled. As I cried my heart out to her, her voice became more deliberate and instead of trying to comfort me, she was stating what really happened that Friday night.

"Jake, you were coaching John. You coached John his entire life and many times you did it in a very productive and loving way. Yes, there were times you shouldn't have said some things you said. They weren't only spoken to John, but to all of us and you do need to change. But much of the time you said the right things and we listened and John listened. They may not have followed what you coached them to do, but you were always there for them. Your heart was always right, even if your words sometimes weren't and they knew that. You were always there for John." I listened now, keenly aware that she wasn't trying to simply comfort me, but get me to look at the big picture.

"Remember all the games. Ever since elementary school, he would come over to us after the game and give me a hug. Then he would shake your hand and talk to you about the game. Win or lose, he always sought us out. And you always complimented him, win or lose, good performance or bad and he needed that. How many times on the wrestling mat, when the match was over, was he looking for us? Remember when he was a freshman and the Apple Valley football team won states in the Dome? Everyone was celebrating and he was looking for us. And when he won that match to win the state team wrestling championship as a sophomore, after that mob scene, he came over to get a hug from me and listen and talk to you about the great win."

She was right.

"You coached all your children. They are good kids because you were coaching them. And John was a champion and you helped him. You were more of a coach and a friend, you were more than just a father. We were both coaching him on Friday night. We were coaching him to breathe and relax. You were coaching John in his last moments."

I was filled with a renewed peace and joy. "You're right, Beth. Sometimes I can't see the obvious. But we did coach him." I could feel the comfort in recalling the facts, pushing away my distorted emotions to what really happened.

Beth continued. "John was a champion."

I cried, "John really had a champion's heart. He was a champion in everything he had a passion for: sports, art, and music. And you know it seemed like after he got hurt in college and was later diagnosed with arthritis in his knee and ankle, I thought he lost his focus and some of that champion's heart. He so identified with sports, that when it was taken away from him, he lost his identity and struggled."

Beth agreed. "That's why he struggled with jobs, a career, college education, girls, cars, money and independence. He lost his focus."

"Yeah, but you know, the last six weeks, when he was back with us and when we went back to Pennsylvania for Christmas, I had some good talks with him. Thursday night when we were up all night, we were talking about what he was planning. It seemed like he was putting it all back together, making good decisions and he was even talking about possibly making a comeback over eight months to get himself in good physical condition to go back to collegiate wrestling. I thought he was getting that champion's heart back again"

"John was a champion Friday night. As you coached him and we talked to him, he did everything we asked him to do. He tried so hard. Remember all the times when he wouldn't listen, when he thought he knew better? But Friday night he was so obedient, so coachable. He did listen and he did everything we asked him to."

I cried at that memory because Beth was right. He had fought the good fight as a football player and wrestler. Friday night he fought the good fight as a Christian. Then it hit me, as if God spoke directly to me through Beth. "You coached John into a new life. You did get the chance to coach John as a champion. You coached him through the minutes of life and death and then into eternal life."

I interrupted her sentence. "We did! We coached a champion. He had a champion's heart again and no state championship, no all state award; none of those could compare with the newly crowned champion in heaven!"

God had spoken through Beth and comforted me. I wrestled with the grief, but the guilt was gone. I climbed into the shower and cried. As soon as I turned the water on, it reminded me of the long showers John took which made him more comfortable during his last two days. Grief didn't wait for the most ideal moments, waves crashed down on me as the water flowed over me.

I had not slept much either Friday or Saturday night and the deep hurt made me drowsy. I lay down on the bed. I was reveling in the twilight of Beth's earlier words but the guilt crept back in. *I wish I had shown my love more through my words. I am sorry John. I love you so much.* I closed my eyes, then opened them and looked at the bedroom ceiling. Drained of joy, I could only remember what I wished I would have said.

Suddenly, I was interrupted by a mental image of John. It wasn't a vision or some dream, or super spiritual experience of seeing John in heaven. It was a mental image of a memory I had seen so many times in real life. It was the face of John, from his shoulders up, looking over his left shoulder, wearing a black T-shirt. He was smiling, a look I had seen so often when we were talking about sports or grilling steaks, trading cynicism and sarcastic jokes and comments. I was awestruck that this memory came at this exact moment. My mind told me, "It's okay, Dad."

I smiled at his memory and his words. We had many great conversations, many great moments, many memories I hoped I would never forget, but at this moment, his smile was all I needed.

The house was quiet with the others still sleeping as Beth and I discussed the funeral. We thought of scripture and music and how we wanted God to be glorified. Our dialogue was a mixture of anticipation and sadness. *How do parents plan a funeral service for their son?* We knew we had to get some ideas together, as I was meeting with Roger that afternoon at 4 p.m.

"Beth, I'm not sure what scripture to use, but I need to find verses for the memorial card at the funeral home, as well as provide Roger with the same scripture."

Beth spoke up. "John really loved the Book of Revelation. Since he was a little kid, he was fascinated and drawn to the imagery and mysterious words. You should look in there."

I knew immediately upon her mentioning Revelation what verses we should choose. We didn't want a funeral talking about death, but about life and hope and who God is and who John is and most of all, what heaven is. I searched the Bible and found the words. Beth read them and concurred.

Revelation 21:2-7: And I saw the holy city, new Jerusalem, coming down out of heaven from God, made ready as a bride adorned for her husband. And I heard a loud voice from the throne saying, "Behold, the tabernacle of God is among men and He shall dwell among them, and they shall be His people and God Himself shall be among them and He shall wipe away every tear from their eyes; and there shall no longer be any death; there shall no longer be any mourning, or crying or pain; the first things have passed away.

And He who sits on the throne said, "Behold I am making all things new." And He said, "Write for these words are faithful and true."

And He said to me, "It is done, I am the Alpha and the Omega, the beginning and the end, I will give to the one who thirsts from the spring of the water of life without cost. He who overcomes shall inherit these things, and I will be his God and he will be My son.

I reread it and decided it would be the memorial card verses. I added a paragraph defining our belief in knowing who Jesus Christ is and who our son is and our prayer:

By the grace of a loving and merciful God, John has overcome death because he thirsted and drank from the spring of the water of life. It would be his desire and our prayer, that through John's death, others will thirst and come and drink the water of life from the spring.

I decided to write a eulogy. The words flowed as I reflected on what I had been thinking over the past months and now they seemed to fit. I wrote: "

A Champion's Heart-Our Son' s Character"

Each of our children has inherited a fourth of their dad's heart. But each child has taken that portion and personalized it into who they are. Scott has his dad's heart for rock music and has taken that portion and become a musician who writes and performs. Ben has his dad's heart for football and has taken it to become a star high school athlete. Adrienne has her dad's heart for missions and she has taken that portion to become a passionate short-term missionary with her sites set for the future. John has his dad's heart for being a champion and took his portion to become part of a state champion football team and three time state champion wrestling team while gaining awards as an all-conference and all-state athlete.

An injury in college stopped him from continuing his athletics and it looked like some of John's heart as a champion had died then. For the past two years he struggled and lost focus on who he was. In the past six weeks though, John seemed to be regaining focus. In John's last days, as he struggled with a virus that could not be detected nor treated, God gave him back his champion's heart as he fought and suffered valiantly. Hearing from the coroner how amazing John was in his fight with such a massive failure of his pancreas, kidneys, liver, and gall bladder, we remember the look on his face in his last moments. It was of peace.

We held John in his first moments of life and his last moments of life and God held John in every moment of his life. As we remember his look of peace, it was the same look he had standing on the wrestling mat at the state wrestling tournament and the Metrodome at the state football championship. He had fought the good fight and he had won.

The twenty-one years of blessings God granted us with John, and John's great achievements, all pale to the decision he made when he was five years old, when he and his dad prayed and John invited Jesus into his life. We remember the look on his face then as he was so excited by what he had done, remembering him with his eyes closed and head bowing, praying to accept a new life in Jesus. Friday night, in his last moments, after the pain and the struggle and the fight, he had that look again, as he closed his eyes and bowed his head, and passed into that new life. He had fought the good fight and won.

We watched for years as others coached John to become a champion. We didn't realize until Friday, we had been coaching a champion all John's life. As we look back in peace, by God's love and grace, He had us coach John into that new life. We praise God as John's in heaven this day, a newly crowned champion and we know he has that same look. Now we must continue his legacy, to fight the good fight and win.

I sat staring at the words on the computer screen. They may not have meant anything to anyone else, but to me I felt as if God had showed me how to capture the essence of John in those paragraphs. I showed them to Beth and she silently nodded whispering they were beautiful.

"Do you want me to add words about you? I feel it is only from me. I want you included."

"No, this is perfect," she concluded.

I finished the rest of the tasks I needed to do for John White at the funeral home. I slipped into a surreal trance as I looked at what I had written.

John Edward Chaya-
In loving memory of:
John Edward Chaya
Born: June 16, 1978 in Berwick, Pennsylvania
Passed Away:
January 21, 2000 at his home in Apple Valley at the age of 21.
Funeral Service:
Tuesday, January 25, 2000 – 11:00
Berean Baptist Church
309 East County Road 42
Burnsville, Minnesota
Officiating: Reverend Roger Thompson
Survived By:
Parents: John & Beth
Brothers: Ben & Scott
Sister: Adrienne
Grandmother: Jean
Pallbearers:
Cliff Bailey
Ricky Crone
Mike Cubbage
Chad Erikson
Tony Gunderson
Mike Henrickson
Gary Josephson
Memorials: Contributions made be made to the Apple Valley High School Athletic Department to supplement the wrestling and football programs and/or Steiger International, a youth outreach evangelistic ministry.

I felt as if I was writing someone else's obituary; that these people weren't us and this funeral was someone else's. I shared it with Beth. We talked about music and hymns. We wanted everyone who attended to see the glory of a living God and His promise fulfilled by His son. John was with God. All we had to do was acknowledge what we believed.

We decided upon *On Eagles Wings* by Michael Joncas, a victorious hymn; *It is Well with My Soul* and three contemplative contemporary songs by John Michael Talbot; *The Hiding Place, Confession,* and *I Will Lift Up My Eyes.*

I sent emails to everyone around the world. I typed through tears, growing more frustrated and sad because I couldn't get the communications done properly. Simultaneously, my good friend, Mark Ledson, dispatched a note of his own to my colleagues at American Express. It read:

Subject: John Chaya - Open Immediately

This is probably one of the hardest notes I have ever written. John Chaya (Jake Chaya's oldest son) died on Friday night. For many of you this will be just an update. For some, this is probably the first opportunity to get the news. John died on Friday night from a massive shutdown of his liver, pancreas, and gall bladder. John was only 21. The condition is called Acute Hemorrhagic Pancreatitis. It is a virus that apparently was at work for a month at least. Basically his pancreas shut down; his liver enlarged to the size of two footballs. Because John was so big and strong, his body fought the virus by functioning with other organs until the damage was so great that he died.

Apparently he had much suffering for 1-2 days until the disease ruined the nerve tissue, then he felt no pain. The final two days he had a hard time breathing, but the pain went away for the most part, although John may not have shared how much he was suffering.

He was a champion who handled difficulties well. They found massive amounts of dead tissue and dead blood in him signifying he was sick for awhile. A coroner and doctor concurred that no one could have diagnosed it and no one could have saved him medically. It is a 100% fatal virus.

The doctors said John was an amazing person and his body fought hard. In life John had a champion's heart in everything he did. I personally saw him play football from the tenth grade, up to graduation. He was simply amazing! He was a great player and a tremendous leader on the field. He was also a great wrestler as well, but most importantly he was a wonderful young man who loved life and his family.

A viewing will be held on Monday, January 24 from 4:00 - 8:00 PM at the White Funeral Home. (It is located at 14560 Pennock Avenue in Apple Valley. The number is (612)432-2001.)The funeral will be on Tuesday, January 25 at 11:00 AM at the Berean Baptist Church in Burnsville. For those of you who know Jake, he needs your support as his family goes through this difficult time. I know that I am just scratching the surface on all of the people who may want to know about this. Jake is beloved by so many people. So, if you could help me out by passing this note on to anyone who would like to know, I would be very appreciative.

Mark Ledson

Feeling at peace, I decided to drive down to Crystal Lake and pray. For the past eight years, I used to go down to the secluded wooded area on the west side of the lake and pray, think, meditate and listen to God. This past year while I was on a four-month sabbatical leave, I found myself spending much time there and had learned how to listen more deeply to God. I wanted Him to reveal new truths to me.

It was sunny and probably 10 degrees below zero as I walked from the parking lot to my lake sanctuary. My clouded thoughts focused on the last time I had been here. It was a week before Christmas, about a month ago. Beth's sister had died suddenly a few days earlier. Since there was no viewing or funeral for her sister, and only a private memorial by her husband, Beth was encouraged not to come out to Albuquerque to mourn for her sister. As we struggled with the hurt and disappointment of not being able to bring Leslie's death to closure, I decided to perform a funeral service at the lake with Beth.

It was a cold snowy day when we went down to the lake, two days before Christmas. We were leaving for a family Christmas vacation the next day and I knew Beth had been grieving. We weren't sure if her sister had invited Christ into her life and it was dreadful thinking about it. There may never be a second chance for her again.

I brought a page of scripture, lit a votive candle and Beth held a flower as we prayed and lifted our words to God, memorializing Leslie and helping Beth close the chapter on her older sister. I gently set the paper aflame stating the words were fire of the Holy Spirit which would warm us and that love Beth had for her sister would continue to burn brightly. Beth walked to the edge of the lake and tossed the frozen flower onto the ice as big snowflakes descended, making us feel like we were in a dream.

Now as I stood near the snow-covered bench remembering that funeral, I couldn't believe John was gone. It was a beautiful quiet morning. I looked out over the frozen lake. There must have been twenty ice-fishing houses with a few trucks and cars parked on the ice. It was clear and still. *John is in heaven. He is gone.* My thoughts snapped back to the snowy lake, hearing a few snowbirds. It sounded for a minute like spring. *I can't believe it; John died two days ago. John is dead. My son died. Father God, what do I do? How am I supposed to feel? How do I go on?* My mind started to spiral downward and my emotions built.

Then I cried out loud. "God, please help me. I loved John so much and now he is gone. Please help me go on."

I heard nothing and felt only a growing heartache. In my pain I cried out again. "John, please forgive me for all those words over the years. Father, Lord Jesus, Holy Spirit, forgive me for all my sins and critical and harsh words."

Because of my worsening illness, I felt like a hopeless mess. I approached a narrow bush inhabited peninsula, merely wide enough to walk on. I looked at the footprints and snow mobile markings, then focused on a three-foot tall scrub bush.

"Lord Jesus, I ask for forgiveness and I ask that I can be pure and strong. Help me be a comfort and support to Beth and my children. Help me bring You glory. Somehow, let Your Name be honored and Your kingdom advanced during this time. Help me, for I can't do this. I'm not ready to be strong or to lead. I am a nobody, a loser and I can't go on."

I cried again, yet joy and peace filled me. I thought back to the many wonderful moments we had, his great athletic feats, his humor, our family vacations, my helping him out of a financial jam this fall, swimming, going to Disney World, fishing in Florida, watching him play middle school football. There was the Ribfest, and chowing down ribs with hot sauce, and the Taste of Minnesota.

I smiled through my tears and sorrow knowing that our 1999 Christmas vacation had been so special. Every Christmas was special. But this one had been the best.

I thought about the short-term mission trip he and Scott had gone on with me last summer to Poland and Germany. I thought of the times when he helped me roll logs into our basement when he was four years old.

My mind bounced to Friday night and seeing him dead, lying on the kitchen floor, then seeing him in the hospital after being pronounced dead. Then the peace and joy came back as I remembered hearing a split second after he died. *He is in heaven. Be at peace.*

The Master, the Creator, the God who was sovereign, omnipotent, omnipresent, and omniscient not only had His hand on John, He also had His hand on each of us left behind. I learned what the spiritual fruits of peace and joy are. They are so much deeper, so much more intense and penetrating than a joyous happy moment of peace I felt when I was comfortable. Those were good feelings. But spiritual fruits, these were different. They were gifts from God.

I slowly walked through the snowy powder, looking at the scenery around me, hearing the fishermen, the vehicles, the children and their pets and crunching snow beneath my feet. *The world goes on. Very few people, if any, know my son has died. No one else's life has changed so dramatically, but my life will never be the same. And no one here knows.* I felt so alone, so sad, and so insignificant....so dead. It really didn't matter what the world thought or what I was thinking. It didn't matter that I was alone, or that no one knew. All that mattered was that John was in heaven. Somehow I would cope with the loss and the rest of the world would move on.

The left side of my face was beginning to throb. My teeth and jaw hurt and I could feel my left eye watering more than my right. I sensed a sinus infection was growing. The pain of John's death coupled with being so sick with bronchitis and the flu seemed to drop any self-confidence and assurance that I could be strong and get through the next few hours, let alone the funeral. I drove home.

Darrell, the warrior, came by to drink his coffee. "People will come in and see you and know about John and they won't know what to say. They will feel bad and you won't know what to say and you'll feel bad and awkward as well. But it's the one's who won't know yet. They will treat you like nothing happened and you won't feel good and when they find out, they will feel worse. It's good not to go to church this morning."

Darrell was very enlightening as he talked about officiating John and Ben's football games as well as the loss of his son, Jeremy, two years ago. I asked what was one experience he had which we needed to be prepared for.

"The flowers... When we walked into the funeral home, all the bouquets of flowers just blew me way." Darrell confided. I pondered his words, preparing for that moment tomorrow.

The overwhelming generosity of our church family, neighbors and friends drew us closer to the unending reminder that God was working through many of His people. At one point in the afternoon, there were four couples sitting in our living room, all of whom had lost sons at a young age. They explained how they relied upon God to help them during the walk through the valley. I felt so sorry for them, still not comprehending that I was going through the same experience.

Late that afternoon, I drove into the church. A rush filled me when a memory of John and his youth group band played during a Sunday evening celebration and how proud I was of John playing bass. The next celebration was going to be quite different and as I walked to the church,

I quickly asked God to help me not "lose it" when talking with Roger.

I met Roger in his office. We hugged and sat at the table. We talked about how my family was doing and how I was handling things. Then in my awkwardness and nervousness, I laid out the paper with all Beth and I had been planning for the funeral. Roger was very patient and understanding. I think he knew that I needed to put all my thoughts down and then we could sort out what we should do. We talked about the choir, the special music, the hour visitation before the funeral, how Berean people were going to provide a luncheon and what the scriptures were and that I wanted my brother, Paul, to speak. Roger suggested we ask Scott Peterson, who used to be John's youth pastor to speak, also, and read my eulogy.

The pastoral gifts of Roger surfaced. He talked about "clean grief." It was profound. Our family had its usual ups and downs raising four children and we had our critical experiences, conflicts and regretful times, but we also had a very stable family and in our time of grief, Roger explained our situation. We weren't grieving about past dysfunctional behavior or terrible relationships. We didn't have the guilt or shame of abuse, broken relationships or conflicts, which led to grudges. We had been a fairly strong family by today's standards.

We were grieving over the loss of a loved one and there wasn't any baggage. It was pure grief, "clean grief" as he put it. Those words were so comforting because I did see that our sons and daughter were handling John's death well. We were a strong family built on the foundations of God and we were together, having shared the struggles but rejoicing in the great achievements and experiences of a family well blessed. "Clean grief" so completely described our situation that I felt God was going to be glorified during the next few days.

"Jake, what is important is that we be authentic Christians. There will be many people at the funeral. We will be watched and people will be struggling with John's death as well. But we need to let them see clean grieving, tears, and sadness and we must let God be glorified and His light shine."

At the conclusion Roger prayed, Then it was time for me to walk out of his office. In a few moments, I was able to experience all that Darrell had mentioned earlier that morning. I didn't make it out of the receptionist area. Three women began to cry as I said hello and we hugged. I couldn't say much and neither could they. It was okay, yet I knew Darrell was right on with his warning. It was a difficult time. I smiled, mumbled something and went to my car. *I just planned my son's funeral.*

Word of John's death had made it to missionaries from Steiger International all over the world. Emails were coming from India, England, Poland, Germany, Vietnam, New Zealand, Thailand, Holland, Austria and the states.

I could hardly fathom all the condolences that were coming from them. Having known some of these people casually and some very deeply from our missionary and professional work, the comforting love from every note filled us. No matter how empty, how lonely, or how discouraged we felt, we weren't alone. God made sure of it.

Our church was shocked by the news as Roger and other pastors shared at the beginning of each of the four services. Directors from my non-profit group, The White Dove Foundation were among the first to know and slowly all of our neighbors knew. In two days, it was as if everybody in the world knew. The phone calls and e-mail proved it.

I started hearing questions like, "Why would God take John so early?" "Why did John die at 21?"

And I heard comments like, "This is the wrong order in life and parents aren't supposed to bury their children." These questions came up often and I thought through them, not so much seeking an answer to their questions, as trying to understand what it was that made people ask these questions. For some reason I didn't have any "why" questions. I didn't have any "why" answers, either, but I was okay.

Late in the evening the fatigue set in. John's old high school girlfriend visited, obviously very distraught. We shared with Julia pictures from our living room table. Our coffee table and television were covered with John's pictures, athletic awards, newspaper clippings and childhood keepsakes. He still had his baby blanket, and Vince, a ragamuffin stuffed dog he got when he was four. The blanket and Vince had made it to high school and college and now we were holding them for one last trip.

Someone handed me a clipping. I had not read it, but now as the day grew to an end, I picked it up in the midst of all the pictures. It was our son's obituary. My heart sank lower as I read it. I couldn't believe my eyes.

Chaya
John, age 21, of Burnsville on 1/21/00 suddenly at home. John was a student at Normandale College. He was a 1997 graduate of Apple Valley High School where he starred in football and wrestling. Survived by his parents John Sr., & Beth, and brothers Ben and Scott and sister Adrienne. Funeral service 11 a.m. Tuesday, Berean Baptist Church 309 East Cty.

Rd.42 Burnsville. Visitation 4-8 p.m. Monday at White Funeral Home, 146th and Pennock Ave. and also one hour prior to service at church. White Funeral Home, Apple Valley, 612-432-2001.

I put the obituary on the table, not even mentally acknowledging where the announcement came from and not aware if anyone else was interested in reading it.

One of John's best friends, Cliff, showed up with John's high school football game jersey. The head coach had given us "John's number 74" which we would place at the casket. Cliff also got his hands on a football helmet. .

As the evening wore on, we were down to one couple remaining in our house, Ron Crakes and his wife Haeja; members at Berean and parents of a son John's age. Ron had followed John's high school athletic career. He was deeply grieved by John's death. We talked about John, and my trips to Vietnam. We relived Friday night over again and talked about our plans for the visitation and funeral. They departed and finally our day came to an end in the dim candle light of our living room. It was quite an amazing display of generosity scattered throughout our house, but the pictures of John and his scrapbook lured me into spending some tear-filled moments reminiscing great moments. John certainly had a full life.

I closed the scrapbook and looked again at his pictures, medals, and newspaper clippings adorning the room. The dogs were asleep, Beth was in the bedroom and as I sat in the stillness and darkness of my house, I looked again to John's place where he sat at the table. I looked at the floor again where I gave him CPR. There was no escape from reality.

No matter how much I was still in shock or deemed this moment as "not really happening," the room betrayed me. Nothing was going to change this situation. I dreaded going to bed. I knew I couldn't sleep and the night would be long. And in the dawn, I would rise, knowing the wintry night in my heart and mind would not leave.

I wandered into the kitchen and looked around. There pushed to the back of the counter, I saw the Gatorade bottle; the one John asked me to get him Friday morning when I asked if he needed anything. It had about two inches of water he had refilled the bottle with, probably many times that day. I had gotten him exactly what he wanted, *Citrus Cooler*. As Beth went into the bathroom, I took the bottle and placed it on top of the mirrored mantle of my dresser and covered it up with a Minnesota Vikings hat John had bought on our Christmas trip in Philadelphia. The hat hid most of the bottle; I didn't bother emptying it out. I stubbornly wanted to save something from him.

I went to his bedroom and sat on his bed. "I'll miss you, Buddy. I love you."

"Thank you Father God. Your timing is perfect. We love You. We are so sad and hurt so much, but we know he is with You. Father; let your grace and mercy flow. We can't go on without you. We need You. Tomorrow we see John at the funeral home. I don't know if I can handle that. Then we have the viewing for four hours. It is going to be so hard. We need your divine intervention. Please, Father, help us through this difficult time. We pray this in your Son's most precious name."

I couldn't sleep. I was reliving Friday night. I remembered the coroner's report, trying to figure out if I had enough life insurance to cover the costs. I wondered if there was something I didn't know about John that I should have known. I thought of my mother who now had experienced three generations of men, her father, husband and grandson die within eight years and how our meeting tomorrow morning in the airport may be very unsettling. I thought again about our happy family Christmas vacation and how only a few weeks later, it was now less than happy. I only had questions and no answers, yet I had the peace of God and the knowledge that He was in control. I seemed to keep drifting back to the funeral arrangements. *Can this really be happening?*

The most significant learning I had about this grieving process was that God protects you and only allows as much as you can handle, occur at any one time. As I looked back over the past two and a half days, I saw how He worked. First there was shock. It was pure mental and emotional chaos. I couldn't think, or understand what was happening. My emotions were numbed. All the facts seemed skewed. I was totally focused on myself. I tried to hold myself together, hold my family together and keep some form of sanity, while being totally engulfed in confusion. Yet God was there through it all. I could feel Him. I never felt alone other than for a few minutes. He was faithful.

I knew He was there with us because through all the confusion and shock and chaos, there was a peace in knowing the truth. I learned early on, stay focused on the facts and truth, not on my thoughts or feelings. The thoughts and feelings will come and go. They will change. But the facts are constant, never-changing. The truth is the truth. When I felt overwhelmed and in deep despair, I recounted all the facts and I prayed and read the scriptures. The truth was the stabilizing factor. It still is today.

REFLECTION

Hearing voices in the wilderness is comforting, haunting and frustrating. People care but don't know what to say. But their words are always welcome. I never knew what to say to families of loved ones. Now I was addressing hundreds of voices, including my own. The voices were real. But deep in the recesses of my mind and heart, I heard the still soft voice of God. He was there and He was with me and my family. And his words were heard above all others.

I now listen for God's voice all the time. I listen for the truth and the facts. I listen to other people more as well. Being a believer doesn't always mean you have to talk. How about you, are you a listener or just a talker? Do you focus on the facts first? Or are your feelings and thoughts dominating your inner self? My advice...focus on the truth and the facts of what is truly happening.

CHAPTER FOUR

A view from the wilderness -- Monday, January 24, 2000

Monday was a sunny, cold Minnesota day. Our families would begin arriving at the airport that morning. There was joyful anticipation of a reunion, something that none of us could ever put together. God would be honored and glorified in a way we had never honored or glorified Him before. I also dreaded seeing John's body in a casket.

Later that morning, I found myself standing at the airport gate watching my brother, Paul, and my niece, Jennifer, walk out of the jet way. We smiled, hugged and let the love and grief flow. I hugged Jennifer and waited as my sister-in-law, Debbie, appeared and we hugged. My brother's wife, Jean, and other daughter, Sarah, and my mother came next. I stood watching them, hugging them, then approached my mother as she began to cry. I hugged her and prayed to myself, *Oh Lord, hold me together, I don't want to lose it in an airport and create a scene.*

We drove home with little dialogue and had another round of sad greetings and dog welcomings. The house was full of family again and as they surveyed the food and assorted flowers and plants, they began to settle in. We told the Friday night story again and shared what had transpired over the past two days.

My bronchitis was getting worse as the medication and cough syrup seemed ineffective. The left side of my face throbbed with pain as a full-blown sinus infection progressed with a swollen left eye constantly draining and red. I had to handle the grief and sadness and ill appearance. I couldn't even look strong. I felt so weak and humiliated.

We got everyone to their hotel and prepared for the funeral home. I dressed in a suit, wondering how I was supposed to act and feel. I couldn't imagine what the viewing would be like. My pastor's words, "that all we could do was be authentic and not to try to act or prepare to be a certain way," popped into my mind. We prayed together and as Adrienne, Ben and Scott got into the van, it hit me that we were now a family of five.

The drive to the White Funeral Home was slow and quiet. We were about to embark on the most difficult hours as a family in public, and none of us were sure what to do or what was going to happen. We had John's remembrances, which we'd place, on or near the casket and we'd have an hour to spend with John and get ourselves prepared for mourners.

John White met us at the door and escorted us to a side room. We talked about our son's items and the memorial cards, flowers, and other details, yet the only thing on my mind was what did John look like and could I see him. As I looked into the chapel, Darrell's words hit me, as there were baskets and bouquets everywhere. They were overwhelming expressions of people's love and sympathy.

Beth and I walked arm in arm as we approached John. We cried as we saw him. We stood in disbelief. *This is John, our son, in a casket. This can't be real.* I felt lost and alone, empty and helpless. I stood close and scrutinized him. He looked so much better than the last time I had seen him in the hospital. I was thankful for the preparation John White had done. Our John had a peaceful look with even a touch of a pleasing smile, faint but still there. He was a big man but somehow he fit into the casket. He wore his khaki slacks, a new white shirt Cliff had bought him, and my favorite red tie. I stared at him, then at the full length of the casket, back at his face and then to the flowers.

Tears welled up. Standing there in my physical and emotional misery, I cried to myself, *"Lord Jesus, I can't go on. I can't make it through this. This is so incredibly hard, I can't deal with this pain."* I looked at my watch and it was 3:15. I turned to see my boys were setting up John's pictures, wrestling and football awards and his senior high school graduation picture collage in the back of the chapel.

I walked to the cards on the bouquets. It was humbling. Moments before we entered the chapel, I was thinking there were only going to be two bouquets, the ones I ordered. One was a spray over the casket that said *Son* and the other was a white bouquet to the left with *Brother*. But now as I looked, there were over twenty bouquets and plants. Friends, family, colleagues, and missionaries from across the country and all over the world had expressed their condolences and I cherished each remembrance. God was comforting and strengthening us through the love and support of others.

I looked carefully at each bouquet, preoccupied with seeing John, and fearing I'd unravel. Someone had put his baby blanket in place. His 74 jersey hung over the casket lid, his football helmet was on the casket's corner near his head and across him on the other side of his head was Vince, his lifelong stuffed dog. I cried hoping I could mentally capture all the details for future memories. A small Penn State banner rested near his left hand, as he was an avid Penn State football fan.

Paul, his wife, Jean, and his daughters, Jenn and Sarah, paid their respects. My mother approached. I reached out, held her arm and escorted her to a position where she was closest to John. She cried and stood, staring. It was so hard to believe. John's grandmother was at her grandson's viewing.

I wanted so much to go home. I hadn't ever been this sick with the flu and on top of that, I knew the next hours would be so hard emotionally. But I had to do it. It wasn't something we could postpone.

Ben, Adrienne and Scott paid their respects. I was so proud of my children. We had always tried to raise them not to get too high or too low emotionally, but I didn't know what to expect. Who teaches their kids how to think and behave when their brother dies? They were very sad, but I was comforted by their response. They commented on how good it was seeing him now, compared to last Friday evening in the hospital. I cried as they expressed their love for their brother. *Father God, use John's passing to bring fruit in some way to my kids as well as all of us who knew and loved him.*

After a few minutes I turned and wandered around the room. Plants and flowers continued to be set near the casket. It was after 3:30 and I was dreading my sickness and the amounts of people who would be coming. I had this strange fear that no one would show up because they forgot John, or people would be too busy to come. I wanted John to be remembered and given a last tribute, but other than family and some close friends and church people, I wasn't sure who would remember him.

I talked with Beth, Ben, Scott and Adrienne individually. I spent a few minutes here and there with my brother and his family, Mom, Beth's sisters, and niece, and a few early arrivals who were setting up a private area for refreshments for the family.

I don't remember four o'clock coming as some magic moment to start the visitation. People started to come, and I stood to the side about halfway down the room from John. Beth joined me as people approached. Klaas and Mary were there and a friend and ministry colleague, Kathi, came. It was comforting to see people come, and to see more flowers and plants arrive. Moments of dread passed as a long line started to form. People were remembering John.

There were many of John's teachers and coaches, teammates, and Ben, Scott and Adrienne's friends who decided to come early. We did our best to comfort people and say something meaningful. It was humbling to see teachers and coaches and even the friends and their parents whom our children hung with; ones we never knew, express sympathy.

People didn't know what to say and we didn't know what to say, but there was a spirit there of people caring in their shock and disbelief. God's hand was upon us, comforting us and my early inclination of leaving and not coming back was replaced with a humble love and compassion for the visitors. They really cared, and we wanted them to know we appreciated them.

I was crying and hugging them, knowing they were really hurting for us and themselves. God was bringing His grace and deeper peace, strength and encouragement by having so many people come to us. Beth and I no longer stood side-by-side, as friends hugged and talked, cried and tugged us gently into their worlds. We were ministering to them now, comforting them, as they were at loss for words. They didn't know how to respond and once they saw John, the reality hit them.

My twin brother brought much attention. He and I are identical twins. Very identical. Most people didn't know I had a twin. Others who did, couldn't tell us apart, so there were quite a few embarrassing and awkward moments as grievers approached Paul, thinking it was me. Words of sympathy, hugs, tears and all flowed, often with no reservations, to my brother. Paul would politely reveal the truth to them, which my children thought was comical. Those who experienced him, found it a relief to share their experience and felt more comfortable to talk to me after they became aware that there were two of us.

The afternoon darkened to evening. The line of people kept lengthening. *People didn't forget John. People weren't too busy. They came in large numbers.*

How word had reached so many people and spurred them to visit us in the cold of winter was hard to imagine. Students, athletes, and their parents hugged us. Church members, pastors, deacons, people from Beth's workplace and my workplace filled the room. I was more conscious of my facial appearance as people would look at me directly, then to my left eye. I knew I was not a pillar of strength and I looked even worse. I would talk, hug, cough, blow my nose, wipe my eye repeatedly, then greet the next person. God loved us through the love of these people. It didn't matter what I looked like or how I felt. What mattered was that even in the shadows of death, deep in the valley, God was bringing His glory.

We saw John's kindergarten teacher, his Sunday School teachers, fellow classmates, and his boss. We saw our children's friends, neighbors, and people we hadn't seen for years. We hugged and thanked each one. The line didn't appear to be shortening. People congregated in the back, along the wall, and in front near the casket.

Our immediate family members were flocked by sympathizers as well. There was a lot of shock and sadness and much love shared. It was a fitting tribute that people would get together and linger, talking about the past, John, old memories, and catching up on the whereabouts of people. It would have made John happy to see all those people visit.

Sympathizers would wait patiently next in line and when it was their turn, open their hearts to us. The outpouring of love and support seemed to energize us and sustain us. God was at work as my dread and grief would melt and my strength and joy would grow. I wasn't living in the past anymore. I was living for the future. *People may be here to remember John and the past, but the present will be such a beautiful memory.* The more I talked with people and shared my heart, the more real God felt and the stronger I grew in knowing John was in heaven, and people needed to know I knew that.

Two wrestlers from another high school came and shared their tribute. "We didn't know John personally, but he wrestled against us and he was very good," one said. "We wanted to pay our respects."

The other fellow I recognized as the heavyweight who had wrestled John for a few years. John had never lost to him. He spoke, "I wrestled John and he always won. He was a great athlete. I'm sorry for your loss."

I was struck by the warrior spirit they had. "Fellows, I appreciate you coming here. I know there is a special respect athletes have for one another, because they have done battle and know what it takes. You both are class athletes. Thank you for paying tribute." We shook hands and they moved along.

It was somber as people passed by the casket. Men and women cried, some simply stared, others prayed, some wouldn't look at him, but they wanted to do their best to pay their respects. As the people passed us by, the shock was apparent. Some people just looked and shook their heads, others mumbled, hoping not to be heard. My heart went out to them. We tried to be the first to speak, the first to hug and the first to comfort. I felt awkward if they felt awkward, so I took the initiative. It comforted both of us. I was tiring and getting weaker, sweating, and my bronchitis and sinuses were working against me. God showed His love through the hugs and words, handshakes and tears. *How could I be so sad and joyful at the same time? How could I feel so much anguish and be at peace?*

I remembered when John stood on that wrestling mat after his team won the state championships. I was overjoyed. It was hard to contain myself. But spiritual joy is different. It is deep and fulfilling, more intense

---

in presence. It was the joy of love and thanksgiving that touches every area of your being. And it lasts. All joy, no matter how satisfying on earth, paled in comparison. *He has gained the final victory.*

John was in heaven. It was God's perfect timing with His perfect master plan, and we were experiencing it. What an honor, to be privileged to be part of His revealed plan at His perfect time. I desired to sustain this condition because it is perfect joy. Perfect joy originates from God. It can't be manufactured by humans. It can't be replicated. Spiritual joy is foreign until it is produced by the Holy Spirit. Then it is an unmistakable acknowledgement that God is present and has gifted you with a fruit that can only come by abiding in God. I was nearer to Him than ever before. Suffering had brought that joy. He was teaching me much.

We greeted the final visitors and said our good byes and thank yous. I sat down on the sofa and watched the stragglers chat with my family and friends. My shirt was wet with sweat, I could hardly see out of my left eye and my voice was almost non-existent, hoarse and raw from talking and coughing spells. I felt as if I had passed through the shock and devastation to the hope and understanding of eternal life. I looked at the casket, about fifteen feet away. The front of the room was awash with flower bouquets and plants. I absent-mindedly wondered aloud, "I wonder how many bouquets are up there."

Paul heard me. "Wait, I'll ask mom. She'll know."

"Hey mom," Paul asked, dryly, as Mom was standing in the middle of the room. "How many bouquets are up there?"

Instantly she responded, "Thirty-four."

I looked at her, puzzled, and then at Paul. He interjected. "That's Mom, she keeps track of everything. You know how she is. That is her way of handling these things."

As the viewing concluded, I walked up to John. It was time to go, but I wanted to talk with him and pray. I stood in silence, thanking God for being so merciful, for fulfilling His promise, for the joy and peace He had blessed us with, and for the outpouring of love as so many people came to visit us. I cried as I looked at him, but I was at peace. *I'm going to miss you, Buddy.*

Beth and my family gathered around me. We prayed, spoke a few words and leaned over and kissed John's forehead. I looked over his body, glanced at Vince and his jersey and helmet. "I love you, John. I'm so sad and I miss you so much. But I thank God, you're in heaven. Lord, thank you for taking John to be with You. You are a merciful and gracious God.

I love you, Father. Thank you for the beautiful evening. Thank you for the comfort of so many people; for showing Your love and encouragement through them. There were many good memories from many good people. Thank you for loving us."

My eyes filled with tears as my sadness grew intense. Now, I didn't want to leave, but there was nothing else to do. Even if I stayed, I wouldn't know what to do. I couldn't fathom how much I missed him already. I wanted to hear him talk about sports and joke about pro wrestling and hear him laugh and tease the dogs. I wanted him to walk through the door and in his own patented way, let us know he was home from work or school or wherever he had been. I longed to hear him tell me his latest scheme for getting me to pay for something. I wanted to get mad or get happy, or be frustrated, but mostly to be proud of him by being with him one more time. All I could do was be sad and empty. *Father, this is so hard. I'm so thankful he is in heaven, but I thought that joy would take away some of the pain and the loss. It's two different things. The joy is immense, but it is totally separate from the anguish.* I cried and was ready to explode inside with sadness.

We gathered our belongings and headed for the cold night. I felt a sense of accomplishment; I had made it through the visitation evening. It had been a very fulfilling and memorable night. The Master's hand had been upon us. Not only was God's hand upon John when He took him home, His hand was on us, on every detail. He did not forsake us, He did not walk away in our most difficult time. His presence was so real and intense. I never felt Him so close to me. I was in awe, knowing at my toughest moment, God drew the nearest. I saw God in Beth, in my children, my mother and brother, in my nieces and sisters-in-law.

I felt Jesus in the tears and embraces from the multitude of mourners, from John White, and from the flowers. God was magnificent. I was intrigued and captivated by God's presence; then the waves of grief would crash over me.

I couldn't appreciate Christ's presence totally, yet I wanted to so badly. At the darkest time of my life, the Creator came to me and showed Himself to me. I was honored and humbled that God would care that much. I had hoped for many visitors to come and show John how much they cared. I didn't realize God would visit us, too. He had come to me on Friday night as He took John and He made His presence so strong. I was focused on God while I did CPR, while I held John, while we watched the paramedics, while we gathered as a family in the hospital. He was with us every moment on Saturday, and we knew He was with us. He drew even nearer to us this Monday evening.

How could I feel so sad and so happy at the same time? I was on both ends of the emotional spectrum. The sadness was because of losing John and knowing how much we missed him. The happiness was because of his future. He would never be sick or in pain again. He would never be disappointed, or fail, or be worried, or fear. He would never experience defeat, incompletion, imperfection or grief again. John would never grieve over me and my death. He would be happy when I died, because he knew I'd be coming to meet him. He would only be filled with joy. I was so thankful and joyful that John was in heaven.

Our house was dark and quiet. Champ and Deacon met us at the steps. I took the dogs outside before we called it a night. As I stood outside with the dogs, I looked at the black night and John's red Grand Am. I felt thousands of miles away. I had helped John buy that car. I had helped him in so many ways over the years. I dreaded the thought, *I'll never get the chance to help him again.*

I walked back into the house, oblivious to everyone and everything. *What was John doing now in heaven? Was he talking to God? Did he meet Jesus? Was he having fun? Did he get to see my dad yet? I wonder if he is sad leaving us, or if he is so busy with the cool things in heaven, that he doesn't remember?*

Beth and I changed and relaxed in bed, holding each other, filled with sadness, unable to talk, but our kindred spirits wept. It still seemed so unreal.

"I can't believe how God brought so many people to the viewing." Beth finally spoke.

"I can't believe how God gave us the strength and courage to get through the evening." I replied.

"So many people, so much love; it was a very good time. People really cared for John. They really cared for us."

"There were so many people that didn't know what to do or say, and it seemed after awhile, I felt better when I tried to comfort them."

"God was at work in us tonight."

"I feel like I've turned a corner. Instead of pure shock and grief, I feel a newness, a hope, a sense that God wants me to move forward and look at Him and know He has John and we must go on. He wants us to pass through this season of mourning but He wants us to live life to its fullest." I whispered to Beth.

A warmth in our spirits grew, knowing God drew very near to us this night. It started out so difficult, but it finished very well. God was so incredibly "there." He was there with us as we drifted off to sleep.

Having learned to focus on the facts surrounding John's death and the truth from God, it became easier to grieve. I wasn't getting as lost in my feelings. I wasn't struggling, trying to make sense of it all and organize my thoughts. God was revealing to me a way to grieve. First, focus on the facts. Next think about the facts, utilizing your own thoughts as well as other people's thoughts. Finally allow your feelings to surface. Within a few days, I was learning what worked for me. It was the reverse of how I used to handle issues. Previously it was all about me being immersed in my feelings and determining my thoughts and finally looking at the facts and what God might be doing. I had always been an individual, thinking about my feelings and thoughts first. God was showing me a different side of life. I wasn't an individual now. I was part of His creation and He was in control. He was showing me how I was to cope and grieve.

REFLECTION

Never underestimate the importance of a viewing. It gives you a deeper perspective on people as well as your own death. It makes death real. It proves death is the final fact, an absolute truth. Never expect answers or people to understand. Their thoughts and feelings usually center on themselves and not on God or on others.

What I realized is that God used Beth and me to minister. I don't know why-we certainly didn't plan it- it just happened. Allow God to work in your most difficult times. He may use you to minister. Be aware of what is going on, also. It can make for some very intriguing memories. How will you respond at a viewing of a loved one? Will God be glorified? Will you simply obey the promptings of the Holy Spirit? You really won't know until you are experiencing it. Just remember, even when it feels like a time of total self-absorption, you may be used as a saint.

CHAPTER FIVE

Walking through the shadows of death -- Tuesday, January 25, 2000

Tuesday morning broke into another sunny cold day. I walked out into the living room and the flowers smelled so strong, but sadly like the funeral home. I had a warm afterglow from last evening's visitation. I also had a new emotion, and a new mindset. Something was lighting me up. Instead of dreading the funeral, I had a joyful anticipation. I tried to think when I last felt that way. It was a vaguely familiar feeling but I couldn't place when I had felt that way. It was a long time ago.

I was still very sad, yet I was so looking forward to the funeral. I showered and cried as I stood under the water and the flowing memories. *John had taken long showers especially in his last two days; sometimes he fell asleep in the shower.* He told me he felt most comfortable in there. I had gone so swiftly from feeling a joyful anticipation to being crushed and empty.

As we dressed, I broke the silence. "I have this great sense of joy. I am excited about the funeral." I wasn't sure how Beth would respond.

She looked at me and continued dressing. "I feel better, too. I have this deep peace."

I thought for awhile. "You know, I feel like I did the morning of our wedding. I was so fired up, wanting to get married. Our friends, family; everyone was there. And I feel the same way now. I can't wait to see the people and know God will be there. I think God is going to bring a lot of people to the church and they are going to hear a powerful service and see God honored and glorified. People are going to have a tremendous time with God."

Beth agreed. We had sought for John's funeral to be special, to be a time where people would know who he was in Christ and who God was. It wasn't going to be a time of lamenting or realizing John wasn't perfect. It was a time to thank God that although John had flaws and imperfections, none of that mattered, for Jesus had taken care of the imperfections and flaws, not only for John, but for all of us who believed.

The five of us Chaya's assembled in the driveway as we prepared to ride to the church. It was 9:45 a.m. By 10 a.m., we'd have our last opportunity to see John before the casket was closed. Sadness filled us again, but there was joy. Before we left the house we decided to get one last thing for John. Over Christmas, our close friends, Joe and Louise

Thear had given us a small gorilla mascot adorned with a Penn State jersey. When you pressed his hand a recording of a Penn State cheer played.

We walked into the commons area of our church as a family. John White had the casket surrounded by flowers and everything arranged for a final hour of visitation. We put the gorilla in the casket next to Vince. I spent a few minutes talking to God and to John, embraced Beth and watched as each of my family stepped forward for their final respects.

I couldn't take it any more. I turned and walked into the sanctuary and prayed. This was overwhelming. I stared at the huge wall hanging, to the right of the platform, next to the illuminated cross. It said, "Each one a gift, life." It had been a banner hung to commemorate Sanctity of Life Sunday a few weeks earlier. The platform was filled with flowers. I felt I was in a dream.

Beth and I regrouped and we stood next to the casket again, as visitors started to trickle in. The trickle grew to a steady stream. We instantly fell back into our visitation mode from the previous evening. Coaches, teachers, friends, neighbors, church members, my team from work and hoards of Apple Valley-jacketed high school students; some whom we saw the night before, some new, all entered the church.

Finally it was time to say our final good byes to John. The mourners were directed away from us. I stood before John, crying and sick. "Thank you Lord, for giving John eternal life. Thank you for taking him to heaven." We had repeated those words so many times, but they always seemed fresh.

"John, I miss you so much. I love you." I cried again, then leaned forward and kissed his forehead. My lips felt the cool skin and I lingered a few seconds knowing it was the last kiss. "Good bye, John."

Beth and my mother next stood before John. Paul put his hand on my shoulder and kept saying, "Good coaching, Jake. You coached a champion! He's in heaven, he's a champion. Good job."

We moved to a prayer room across from the sanctuary as the pastors gathered us together. Roger and Scott had a few words and prayers. It seemed like we would never start the funeral. John Michael Talbot was music was playing in the sanctuary and I listened intently to the words being prayed, but now it was all melting to a blur.

Beth and I were led out of the prayer room. The casket was closed, the jersey was on it with flowers and the pallbearers stood behind it. Our children lined up behind us and we began the slow procession to the front of the sanctuary. As we broke into the entrance, the church was flooded with people and music and sweet fragrances. The sanctuary was crowded. As we slowly walked forward, people would touch our arms or shoulders in comfort. My mind slowed, almost as if I was going to fall asleep. *I can't bear this. I can't do this.*

The casket was positioned perpendicular to the pulpit. Number 74 hung draped over half the casket and flowers on the other half. Beth entered the first pew as I followed. Our children came after us. We slowly sat down as the soft music continued. I struggled to understand the moment. I was preparing to worship at my son's funeral. *How do I worship at my son's funeral?*

I looked at the casket, then down the pew at my children, across the sanctuary to where the pallbearers were sitting, then to the many students, then finally to the cross with the life banner beneath it. I looked back at the flowers, at the casket and I stared at the jersey. *There were so many good memories of John in that jersey. I loved going to those games. He made me so proud.*

The choir was poised and as they began the first verse of *His Grace is Sufficient*, the sound became majestic. The song was so fitting, for it talked about sorrow, and grace and the thorns and revealed that His grace was sufficient for me. *Wow, those words explain it so clearly! God will bring us through this by His grace. He had done it before and He was doing it for us now.*

I looked at the choir members, most of them good friends of Beth and although I didn't know most of them as well as Beth did, this moment was as if they were there only to minister to us. Some smiled, some acknowledged us with non-verbal expressions, some steadfastly held back tears and others wouldn't look at us for the obvious reasons. We were a family at this moment and they were praising God for us. Our worship pastor, Greg Dirnberger, a great guy and fishing buddy had begun the funeral with great love and compassion.

Roger stepped up to the podium and welcomed the worshippers. The magnitude of this moment was unbearable. We were closing a chapter on physical life and to hear the words, "we are gathered here to pay our last respects to John Edward Chaya," I instantly felt like a lone voice crying in the wilderness. Somehow I was able to sit upright, but the heaviness seemed too much to bear. Beth nudged closer to me and I caught myself slowly drifting away and I held her hand. I stared at the casket and listened to Roger as he concluded his opening remarks.

Greg led the church in two hymns, *It is Well with My Soul* and *God*

Will Find a Way. I loved *It is Well With My Soul* and tried to sing but my voice was too distorted from being sick. But Beth sang.

We listened to a taped song *Confession* by John Michael Talbot and then Scott Peterson came forward to speak. Scott had been John's youth pastor for quite a few years. He had gone on a few youth trips, summer camp and a few out of state ventures, but John and Scott had moved on. Scott, a professor at Bethel Seminary, was visibly shaken as he initially spoke but he grew very strong in his message. Scott read my eulogy, "A Champion's Heart-Our Son' s Character."

Pastor Scott then preached. He included John's brothers and sister in his words and I gained a tremendous amount of relief when Scott stated that John blew right by death and was in heaven. His message was strong as he was showing John as a strong fellow and a champion.

Paul approached the pulpit and with his humor breaking the ice, said, "No, I'm not Jake," began to preach about fighting the good fight, having a champion's heart and finishing strong. His message transformed from talking about John, to the true Champion, Jesus Christ. He finished talking about John having a champion's heart, because it was the heart of the champion, Jesus. His words were powerful. I was proud of John, proud of Paul and proud that Jesus was glorified. Paul had captured who Jesus was, who John was and who we were, children of God, loving our Father. My son Scott slouched forward, and I reached across his shoulders, to comfort him. *God, comfort us.*

Roger spoke after Paul and he comforted me greatly with his words that John, on earth was incomplete, but now he had been made complete in heaven. He talked about heaven and that John was there, because at five, John accepted Jesus as his Lord and Savior.

I remembered that day. It was a Sunday evening in the summer. We had been over to Beth's friend's house for a picnic with her family. John had been misbehaving much of the day and I was pretty frustrated with him. We came home from the visit and I talked with John. My heart softened as I realized he was just a child and my words could either bring new life, or destroy his feelings. We talked about God and how He loves us but we need to believe He loves us and ask Him to come into our lives and help us live the way He would want us to live.

We prayed, and I asked him if he wanted to invite Jesus into his heart. He said he did. I was blown away by his faith as a little kid. He didn't say anything spectacular but I could see he was sincere and he knew what he was doing. I told Beth that John had prayed with me and he was now a born again Christian. I felt that was a wonderful day in our lives, and this day changed his life forever.

That event was a humbling experience for me. I had always loved my son deeply, but to see him pray the prayer of salvation thrust me into a different light. I had helped John fulfill God's purpose. I never looked at John the same way again. He was a new creation. Old things had passed away and new things had come.

Beth had always been a fine mom and she raised four children who all invited Jesus into their lives and that was so special. Now we were assured of how precious those decisions were. I had grown less appreciative of that moment and perhaps had taken the salvation decision for granted. Now, at this moment, I realized how serious a decision John had made and that a five year old had taken the responsibility into his heart for fulfilling a destiny.

I sank in the church pew, listening to Roger and looking at the casket. Roger was an outstanding speaker, easy to understand, very wise and not afraid to tackle the truth head on, as well as deal with difficult life issues. He proceeded with his message, focusing on aspects of heaven which were found in the Bible. I was comforted sitting in that first row, reassured that heaven was beyond my greatest expectations and one day I would be there and see John again.

As Roger gave a benediction and a final prayer, he gave two invitations. One was for everyone to join us for a luncheon in the fellowship hall and the other was an invitation Beth and I wrote.

Invitation:

John and Beth, Adrienne, Ben and Scott extend an invitation over the next few weeks to stop by our house and share some of your memories and stories about John. During this time of our grief and yours, we'd like to get together and share the joy of God's blessing us about John. We would also like you to write us a note about something John may have said or done over the years that helps us know who he was and how God had used him in the lives of others. Our hearts and doors are always open.

The service concluded with music from John Michael Talbot. Beth and I walked down the aisle with our children close behind. I saw a mass of people. The church was overflowing and many high school students wore Apple Valley brown and gold letter jackets. It was surreal. One or two gripped my shoulder as we passed by. I looked straight ahead, feeling the horror and anguish build.

We walked out of the sanctuary by the overflowing standing throng who watched intently as we made our way across the commons and to the front door, where the casket slowly rolled. We all cried as the pall bearers picked up John and placed him in the back of the hearse. A cold wind blew as we watched the proceedings, standing just outside the doors. The fellows struggled as they lifted their buddy, fighting back tears, sadness, emptiness and the cold noon wind.

The hearse door closed. Truly we all felt the loss, but there were no words or gestures to capture our heartache and sadness. I didn't want to leave. Beth turned, crying, and moved back into the protection of the lobby. The pall bearers stood staring; my children stood staring, no one knew what to do or say. The pastors, funeral director, and mourners watched, tears streaming.

The wind picked up and chilled my face. The hearse proceeded through the parking lot very slowly, now about ten feet away, then twenty, thirty feet and then a hundred yards, maintaining the same speed. The most piercing heartache I ever experienced, filled me at the realization that this moment was the last time I'd see him. The pall bearers and pastors started to break up and head back inside for the luncheon. I just stared. The hearse made it to the street entrance and slowly turned left and proceeded down the hill. I stared until I couldn't see it anymore. He was gone. His last departure crushed my heart. *No way. What I just saw really isn't happening.*

"It's over. I lost my son. I love you, John." I mumbled to myself.

Completely empty, numb and barely able to stand, I conceded it was over and walked back into the commons area. Beth found me, as others guided us to proceed to the fellowship hall for the luncheon. I shook hands and hugged people from work and from my church. I didn't realize how much these many people cared. They came and paid tribute to a champion and I couldn't believe the mass of people who shared their love and grief. "Thank you Lord, You show Your love through these people and I am so thankful for Your love and strength through them."

I found a seat at a table with Beth, but I wasn't hungry. People stayed at a distance as we nibbled, but a few friends came to the table and the sorrow and tears poured out again. Beth seemed to be holding up well emotionally as well as physically and Adrienne, Ben and Scott spread out with their friends and families. I could tell that Beth was beginning to have the same flu-like symptoms I had, yet she was a pillar of strength to me and our friends.

I looked around at the guests. I saw football coaches and wrestling coaches, Apple Valley teachers, administrators, friends and neighbors, John's old girlfriend and her family, fellow athletes, cheerleaders, youth group members and people I didn't know, but they certainly knew us. It would have been a great social gathering if John had been there to enjoy it with us. I couldn't see the magnitude of what was happening until weeks later.

I walked back into the sanctuary, still filled with the flowers. It was empty now, lights dimmed. I slid into a pew and cried. "Oh God, this hurts so much! I am so sad but I thank You for taking John to heaven. You are a great and mighty God and I thank You for Your perfect plan and perfect timing." I sat there with praying hands and a broken heart, embarrassed that someone might see the physical and emotional state I was in.

God and I were in communion and I listened intently. I heard nothing. Thoughts of John in my arms as he slowly left this world, to the nightmare of seeing his body in the hospital, to thoughts of Beth's heartache as a mother whose worst fear came true, flooded my mind. I thought about what the pastors said. Each of the three had something very prophetic they had shared and it strengthened me. I thought about the viewing, about the coroner's report, the phone calls and e-mails coming from all over the world and then I heard a calm, soft voice, "Remember who you are and who John is, and remember who I am and not what I do. It's not what you did right or wrong, or how I bless you, it's all about our unity. I am in you and you are in me."

"Wow, I heard from my Father! But why should I act so surprised, it's not like this never happens!"

I felt a deep joy and peace fill me as I sat leaning forward. I began to cry again as my good eye caught the wall-hanging. That said it all! John had been such a gift. I loved watching him play football, throw shot, wrestle, play bass, talk sports, talk music, talk about careers and college and jobs and money decisions and cars. He had a dreamer side to him as well, sometimes outrageously so, to the point of absurdity, but that was John.

I lost my son and a good friend. "Thank you God for giving us John for twenty one years," I whispered. "It truly was a blessing! And it will always be a blessing." I walked out of the sanctuary. It was well with my soul.

People wished us well and began to exit the luncheon. Beth wanted to thank everyone, but that would be impossible. She did express our appreciation to as many people as she could and she was doing well.

Volunteers helped us gather up all the bouquets and many were put in the administration offices, some were kept in the commons and the sanctuary and we decided the rest would go to hospitals and rest homes.

We gathered all the cards, notes from the flowers, and John's items and slowly walked out the church doors, following John's last exit. I felt a twinge of pain as my mind declared, *everyone else can go back to their worlds; for them it's finished, but for us, our lives will never be the same and we can't go back to the way it was.*

As soon as I thought it, another thought overwhelmed me. *They hurt, too. John did impact others' lives and many will miss him, because many will always love him.* Peace and joy blanketed me as I focused on what I was doing in the physical, trying to drive out of the parking lot.

Our families returned in the evening as well and other friends came and went, delivering food, cards, fruit trays and meals. More flowers and plants arrived throughout the evening. I was glad so many people were continuing to visit. God's hand was on every need, but also I could see how He was providing the caring, love and support as He brought His sheep to gather around us. God revealed His presence and His love through other people. They were instruments of His grace, comfort, love and mercy. Somehow we were going to be able to go on with our lives.

I was beginning to realize He had a circle of intercessors, mourners, comforters, encouragers, and healers gifted for a special moment. I was humbled by their compassion, and filled with a deeper understanding that God does not give up on conditions and it's never over until He says it's over. Most of all, I remembered from a pastor's message, the light of Jesus shines brightest during the darkest times and in the darkest places.

REFLECTION

There are no words to explain what goes on in your mind and heart as you walk in death's shadows. You know the facts and you know your thoughts and feelings, only to lose sight of the facts, thoughts and feelings. Grieving wasn't a set formula. Grieving didn't have a process. At least not at this early stage of mourning. There was very little that was predictable.

You yourself feel like a shadow. Nothing will ever prepare you for that walk into the sanctuary or that walk out of the sanctuary. Seeing the exiting hearse brings a multitude of distressful thoughts and emotions. It is more than emotions, it is more than a symbolic departure. Part of my life went away with the hearse. Expect it. It will happen to you. Will you be willing to surrender a part of you at that moment, or will you fight God and His plan?

CHAPTER SIX

Going deeper into the wilderness -- Wednesday, January 26, 2000

I tried to get a night of sleep, but between the illness, difficult breathing and the constant flashbacks of the past few days, I tossed and turned without much more than a combined hour of sleep. I watched as Wednesday's dawn lit up the bedroom. Lying in bed, I could hear Beth's labored breathing. She was struggling as the flu broke full force in her. I prayed for her healing and comfort, and knew she, too, needed to see a doctor as her sinuses and lungs were sounding bad.

My slumber was broken by Champ's half-bark and grunt. That was his signal that he needed to go out. I rolled out of bed, put on some sweat pants and a hood, slipped into my shoes and said the magic words, "Which dogs want to go out?"

Deacon crawled out from under the bed, barking, and Champ stiffly strained his pudginess into a rugged turn and rumbled ahead of me to the living room, then down the steps.

As I opened the door, the below-zero cold hit me and cut through my sweats. A cloudy breath lingered in the air.

I stood in the driveway, frozen in mind, body and thought. Everything seemed so crystal clear, but nothing seemed real. There sat the red Grand Am, silent; a memorial which flung my thoughts back to Friday night. *John isn't even dead a week.* Yet so much has happened and so excruciating have the days been, that though my heart still was full of peace and joy, disappointment and loneliness was infiltrating my being. I stood crying in the driveway. "Lord, I didn't know what suffering meant until these past days."

The dogs plowed a path through the snow and didn't waste any time getting back to the porch. Dejectedly I opened the door and looked back at the car. *This really couldn't have happened.*

I stood at the top of the stairs in the living room and surveyed the acts of love and support from so many people. In the dim of the dawning light, it was serene, as if God was sitting there. The house was swamped with sympathy. John's sports albums, scrapbooks, and cards sat over the surface of the coffee table. I looked at some of his awards and medals and sank in heaviness. "Help me, God, to get through this day." I whispered.

I knew physically I was in trouble, as my health worsened. I went back to the bedroom and sat at my desk, reading scriptures and praying, reflecting and sorting my thoughts. Beth was up making coffee and the afterglow of the funeral filled me. We talked a bit as the kids were still sleeping and I could see the grief and sadness in Beth but, also her worsening health. "We certainly are having the most difficult times, aren't we?"

An hour or so later, I decided to go down to the lake and talk with God. I had received so much peace and comfort there in the past and I was feeling restless and growing deeper in my anguish. I got out of my car and retraced my footsteps to the ice. All alone at the lake, I walked across my frozen sanctuary and stood at the bush that I had singled out as a reminder of John. Guilt and shame overwhelmed me. Every wrong I had done John, rough times, anger, reminders of unloving words, hit me as if a demon was striking me with a stick.

I stood and wept intensely for about fifteen minutes. Then perhaps the lowest point of my life came when I tried to cry out to God and I realized I could make no sound. My hoarseness and illness took away all my abilities to just release my hurt and cry and sob. *I can't even mourn completely! I can't even express to Your creation how ashamed, how guilty, how sad, how hurting I am. No one can even understand how I feel and I can't tell them , I can't even tell You. You've taken my son, You've taken my passion, my life, my spiritual walk away from me. And now You've taken my expression of woundedness away. I feel like I have lost everything.*

I felt so small, so lost, so insignificant, so defeated. And I felt God wasn't there. I felt abandoned, shocked, and confused. *Why did God leave me? Why did You leave me now, when I need You the most?*

All the crowds are not here to support me, I know. Now, it's going to be very tough, because once the days melt into weeks and months, people will forget. They will go on with their lives. I can feel it already. This feels like the Garden of Gethsemane. I am alone with You, but I can't sense Your presence, God. Where are You?

This was a scary revelation. God had been so close and we had followed Him these past days and He was glorified. He had comforted and strengthened us, always present. Now, at this moment as I stared at the snowy woods beyond the lake, He seemed gone. I was alone for the first time since Friday night, really alone. *Please God, come into my life. I need to feel Your presence. I need to know that my life didn't end with John's life.*

I grew panicky. Unable to let any words or expressions out because of my sickness, too stiff to even collapse from the deep discouragement, I stood brokenhearted and helpless. I had felt my insignificance before God many times, but now I felt my significance without God. I was alone in the world. Totally alone. *God, what fruit will come from John's death? What was his purpose during his short life? What will I do now? How will you use his death as a redemptive gift to others? Oh Lord, don't just let his death be a memory. Please Lord, it doesn't matter now how sick I am, or how much I hurt. It doesn't matter if I feel so alone and forsaken. Just use the death to change people's hearts and minds. Please, in some way, use John to impact the lives of those who knew him.*

I grew angry with myself because I couldn't do anything but stand there and attempt to cry out, attempt to grieve, attempt to recover from a spiritual attack. *How can this be? I am unable to do anything but stand here in the cold and snow. God, please, help me.*

I wandered about on the lake, looking at the scrub bush. I turned half way around as I looked at Buck Hill over the tree line. Skiers were descending the slopes. I looked at the lake, the geese walking across it, and the glistening snow on the trees and shoreline. Empty. No feelings now. Just emptiness and loneliness.

Be at peace. He is in heaven.

I heard those words in my mind. It wasn't a dramatic voice from the heavens. It wasn't a trumpet, or a thunderous word, or the rushing wind, or an earthquake. It was a soft whisper of a voice. I listened for more. Comfort came with the whisper. My achiness and stiffness from the cold were penetrated by a smoldering fire deep inside. The warmth came from the words. Then the thoughts rushed through my brain. *John was a champion! He had a champion's heart! He is experiencing the glory and presence of God! He is in heaven! Nothing you could have ever done, or planned as a father for him in this life could be better than what he is experiencing now in heaven. I wonder what he's doing now up there? I know how fascinated he always was with Tom Clancy books and maps and how he read so much. He must be totally enamored with heaven and God and all the angels and saints. My dad met him already in heaven. Grampy was there to welcome John in. And from the description of heaven in the book of Revelation, John must be so caught up in the new sights and sounds and surroundings. He is probably very inquisitive, asking questions and searching out his new home. I wonder if he sees any of this. I wonder if he is aware of how people loved him so and how they paid tribute to him. I wonder if he was able to hear my cries and prayers and words. Does he know how much I love him?*

My thoughts felt like gentle waves on a lake shore on a warm sunny day, flowing up to the beach, then receding, and my questions fell back as a low tide. Peace and joy slowly returned. God had given His assurance......

God had assured me He was there; He had not abandoned me or forsaken me. In the cold wintry day, He was faithful. His words were so calming, so liberating. The sadness, deep pain and travail persisted, yet it wasn't overwhelming. It was as if nothing changed in my mind or in my grief, but my emotions calmed and my heart strengthened. I was learning about Elijah's oil. The oil was only enough for that day, but it never ran out.

I trudged back to my car, thoughts bouncing off the inner walls of my brain, some rebounding, some dissipating, but no sequence, rhyme or reason. Some were of John; some were of the previous few days, a few were seasoned memories of John's athletic feats. I couldn't concentrate as I reached for the car door. I climbed inside and sat stunned at the events, my emptiness, and my pain. I was mesmerized by the clean grief. I tried to think back at the sequence of events, but my mind was playing tricks on me. "I can't go on. I hurt so badly. What am I supposed to do now? No one has a secret formula or seven steps to perfect grieving. No one knows how I feel."

Into my mind popped the memories of the movie *Braveheart*. Mel Gibson played William Wallace, a Scot freedom fighter. It was one of my favorite movies, as well as John's. I relived the scenes of when William Wallace's wife died and how distraught he was, how grieved and wounded he was. I relived his inspiration of setting Scotland free and how his love for his wife never went away. Her loss was devastating, but instead of giving up and quitting, his loss drove his passion to live for freedom. I couldn't remember all the details, but the scenes provoked my thoughts to not quit or give up. I remembered the compelling term from the movie that William Wallace used, describing him and his soldiers as, "warrior poets."

John's death has to have a redemptive blessing, so others can know their names are in the book of life if they believe in the cross and what Jesus did for them. I can't give up. I need you, Lord, to show me what his death means in your great plan. O Lord, what was his purpose on earth? It had to be more than sports.

I drove from Crystal Lake to my house. It was cold and sunny, a bright clear blue sky, a great day for a Minnesota winter. I turned into the driveway and looked around. The memories of a black Friday night with flashing red and blue lights from emergency vehicles floated through my mind.

I made it into the house, greeted by our two barking dogs. The fragrances of flower bouquets and Beth met me at the top of the steps. Our children were sleeping and the house was quiet. Beth and I prayed together. I looked around at pictures and photo albums, cards, flowers and plants. I stared at John's graduation picture, then walked into my bedroom and lit up my computer to send some e-mail.

Beth informed me that I had a doctor's appointment and she had scheduled one for herself as well later in the week. Death and grieving didn't take time off, even for sick people. My sinus infection and respiratory flu worsened and I could tell Beth's same illness was building. I prayed as I waited for the internet connection, "O God, bring your peace and comfort. Bring your healing hand on us. Heal Beth and me and keep Adrienne, Ben and Scott healthy. Bless them; bless their friends and parents who You are using to help them in their pain. We love you, Lord. Thank you for the time this morning at the lake. (That time hurt so much.) I had never felt so empty, lonely or broken. It was a time of cleansing. Thank you for speaking to me and comforting me as I stood on the lake. I love you, Lord; thank you."

The rest of the day was uneventful. My emotions fought my logic. It was great to have family in our house, but the purpose was heartbreaking. Other friends came and went throughout the afternoon and evening. Fighting to stay engaged in conversation, and expressing gratitude for the many acts of sympathy, eventually I gave up and retreated for a few moments of solace in my bedroom. I kept being reminded of the agony of seeing John breathe his last, remembering his body in the hospital, experiencing the viewing and funeral and the sullen finality of watching the gray hearse proceeding slowly through the church parking lot. Yet God was ministering to us with each new knock on the door, phone call and casserole.

These couple of days were being filled with surprises, some funny, some humbling, some sad. I watched my mother handle her days-recording cards, monetary gifts and addresses. It didn't take long to amass cards and letters. Over four hundred had come so far and it was comical watching how thorough she was. It was also becoming apparent that we needed to identify where memorial gifts should go as nearly every card included a memorial check.

We had decided that half the gift would go to Apple Valley High

School athletics, split between the wrestling and football programs. The other half would go to Steiger International, the evangelical ministry focused on youth. We found that memorials were also being designated to our White Dove Foundation. Other memorials were designated for our church, Berean Baptist. It was humbling to see the generous outpouring. I never would have imagined that so many people cared so much and were so willing to share their love with us. But I also never imagined that I'd be writing about John dying at age 21.

Throughout the day, family and friends arrived and departed. Food, bouquets, cards and letters arrived almost hourly. I wanted to get on with life, to feel normal, to be happy again, but I didn't want to give up any memories, or details, or cherished moments. God was blessing us mightily and though there was so much hurt, there was a newness about life. Things were different. Things would never be the same and no matter what we wished, hoped for, or dreamed about, the facts were the facts.

The day revealed more sympathizers as the Minnesota Twins radio announcer, John Gordon, a member of our church, called us to tell us that a local radio station had taped an interview as a tribute to John with John's high school wrestling coach. I wept when I heard about the tribute. It was so humbling. People wanted to remember who John was and they wanted to tell others. I thought to myself, *if I died, what would people remember about me? What would they want to tell others about me?* My heart sank when I thought, *what would I want people to think and say about me after I died? Had I made a contribution to the lives of those around me?* I wasn't sure. To hear that John's wrestling coach, Jim Jackson, was doing a live tribute to John on the radio sports show the next evening, again, pierced me with humility.

People wanted the community to know that John meant so much to them and that they valued his contribution to the sports he participated in. A major newspaper, the Star-Tribune, called and told us there would be an article in the sports section the next day. I pondered the irony of the newspaper article. Only a few years ago we repeatedly saw his picture, read his name and glowed over his football and wrestling feats as well as his team's achievements. Now it would be a tribute to his past. There would be no more athletic achievements, no more pictures. The obituary and the article would be documentation of finality.

Wednesday evening was a quiet time. Mom and I sat at home, she tending to the myriad of cards and I answering an occasional phone call. Mostly we chatted about small stuff, each keeping the other company, but too drained to discuss anything significant. It was a time when a mother and a son only had each other, nothing pressing, nothing profound, nothing noteworthy, just the understanding that we were of the same blood, same genes and same heritage. Only she could be my mother at this time and only I could be her son.

REFLECTION

So when it is supposed to ease up? When is it you begin to accept what happened? When do you simply accept the facts? How deep into the wilderness will you go? There are no straight answers. But one thing is certain, funerals don't bring closure, they simply take you another step along in the process of grieving. Thoughts, feelings and facts intermingle with no rhyme or reason, no starting or stopping points and as a believer in Jesus Christ, you simply persevere through the suffering.

God doesn't bring closure, either. He knows it hurts as the shock slowly wears off. It's not like He gives you a certain amount of grieving time, then tells you to get on with life. Not yet, anyway. It felt just as bad one week after as it did at that deadly moment. Will you allow God to work through your thoughts and emotions? Will you cling to His truths in the scriptures that He will never leave your or forsake you, even in your darkest hour?

CHAPTER SEVEN

Stumbling in the wilderness -- Thursday, January 27, 2000

So many memories, and as many "should-haves, what-ifs, would-haves, maybes, if- thens," kept me wide-awake. I welcomed the dawn. Emotionally and mentally tired, and now this being Thursday morning, I looked forward to my doctor's appointment.

Daybreak brought another bright clear and cold day. But I awoke with the same dread. Catnapping throughout the night, I felt fatigue and uncertainty. John's death was sinking in, as were all the events that surrounded it and I wasn't feeling much better physically. I had made plans to pick up Paul at the hotel after my doctor appointment and we were to meet the rest of the family at the bowling alley. It was to be our planned way to ease back into the world of reality. We needed to be together and try to have some fun.

The infection and respiratory woes were in full throttle, so physically I looked and felt defeated. I had grown used to never feeling rested and pain-free due to my long illness with Lymes Disease. But now I was concerned that all that was coming down on me would take me down once and for all. I felt panicky knowing it would be so unbearable if Beth and my children lost their dad so soon after losing John. But the panic intensified with an alternate scenario. I switched my thinking to how sick Beth was and what would happen to my children and me if she died. Nonsensical thinking at any other time of my life, but for now, it was a concern. There was also a concern no one said anything about, but we all thought "did we have the same virus John had?"

The doctor's visit brought a new series of thoughts. I entered the medical clinic for my appointment and I felt the staff and nurses were all watching me, as if they were expecting me and determining how they should respond. I wasn't a stranger, having been a regular over the years, but something was different this day even if I was making it up in my head. It was the first time I was out in public doing an ordinary chore, yet it seemed so magnified.

As I walked into the clinic for my appointment, I felt as if everyone knew my son had died. At the same time I felt no one knew and life was going on and everyone had no idea of the pain I was experiencing. The moment I mentioned my name and the appointment time to the front desk, I knew they knew. I had gone to this clinic for so many years. My entire family had been there more times than I could count. Now it felt like we were a family and they felt the loss as well.

I paid my fee, received my receipt and took a seat in the waiting area. I eagerly looked forward to some relief for my draining sinuses, hoping for some magic the doctor was going to provide. The waiting area was bustling, mostly with little kids and their mothers and I silently watched, feeling the sadness grow as I thought back to John as a little kid. He had been a healthy child and other than a few athletic injuries and strange viruses he picked up from wrestling mats, he had been well. He was a happy kid and he had a great sense of humor, but he was mischievous and a purveyor of antagonism with friends, siblings and opponents. Now I couldn't imagine how our lives would ever be the same without him.

Those were moments it felt good to be a parent, knowing he was supported and we were providing him the medical care he needed. But as the little children fussed in the office and jabbered impatiently, the emptiness throbbed in my heart. I held back tears, smiled faintly at the children and looked beyond to the walls, pretending I was only sick.

My name was called, and I made my way to my doctor's examining room. My thoughts shot back to over a week ago when I was coming down with this virus and John was sick as well. So much had changed in such a short time. The nurse took my vitals and I sat for a few minutes in the quiet room. I couldn't fathom that any of this was real, as Dr. Lynn Koch greeted me. She attended my church and had been my doctor for quite a few years. I could see in her eyes the sympathy and sadness. She checked me out and we talked about my condition and the treatment. She ordered a comprehensive battery of tests as a precautionary measure. Since John had died of a virus and I had been performing CPR, she wanted to make sure we didn't overlook anything. I concurred and was somewhat relieved. For a second I had a thought that it would be an honor to die as John did and I would be with him. I came back to reality, knowing Beth and my children needed me dearly at this time and I couldn't take the easy way out.

I had the tests done and returned to the examining room. We chatted about how I was doing with John's death. Dr. Koch was very empathetic and eventually brought me back to why I was there, but it felt good knowing people on the outside cared.

She told me part of my treatment would be administered by a nurse who specialized in this procedure. Connie Braun came in and we proceeded further with some respiratory procedures. Then, with her eyes filling with tears, we talked about John. I was impressed by her expertise and professionalism, but also by her heart. I had never met her before. She held my hands and asked if she could pray with me. I was comforted in her gesture. Knowing I was in good hands medically was one thing, knowing the Spirit of God was working through those hands made it special, a divine appointment of sorts.

My appointment ran about 90 minutes longer than I had planned. I drove over to the Holiday Inn to pick up my brother to go to the local bowling alley and meet our families.

"Hey, sorry for being late...." I apologized, "They did a battery of tests. They wanted to see if there was a tie with my virus and John's virus."

Paul looked at me and remarked. "I was praying that God would provide you or the doctor wisdom so you'd have tests done to see if there was any sign of the same virus John had. I didn't want to say anything, but I was hoping that you'd get thoroughly checked out. No need to apologize, God answered my prayer." he concluded calmly.

We were driving to a new experience as Paul and I pulled into the parking lot of the bowling alley in Apple Valley. The past Christmas vacation when all of our families were together had been a special time of fun and fellowship. We had spent only sporadic periods together as a family since we were scattered across half the country, but when we did get together it was memorable. That Christmas of 1999 was special, particularly the day all of us went bowling. John, as I remember, started out rusty but powerful. Yet by the end of the day, his scores got progressively better and his power remained as he destroyed the pins. He certainly had authority, if not great skill. I remember watching him progress during each game. I had watched all the offspring and nieces and adults. It was special. It was fun to be a family.

I snapped back to the present. This day, as we got our shoes and bowling balls, I sat alone fighting grief as I remembered the fun we'd had with our families bowling at Christmas. I fought the clutching of my throat and eyes, remembering big John progressively getting better with each game and crashing pins. No one knew, or let on they knew, of my struggle. For about 30 minutes, I wasn't sure if I wanted to be in the bowling alley.

I was just a sad father, not wanting to be there, yet knowing it was the right thing to do. As we got our bowling teams organized, steadily I sank further into a dreadful period of depression, thinking back to the previous Christmas. Ben and Scott were already going through their antics and the customary whining and mockery had started, but I couldn't get into it. I tried but then held back, filled with memories and then guilt. *John hadn't been dead a week. Was it wrong to try to have fun and laugh and smile?*

We finished bowling and returned home to more people dropping off food and flowers, cards and treats. I surveyed the covering of food, beverages, boxes, baskets, plants and bouquets that blanketed every flat surface. My mind relived the meal times we used to have as a whole family. I looked at John's spot and his chair. Inwardly I mused on how John could pack away the food, and it was entertaining watching him enjoy himself. Only now as my thoughts melted, I felt lonely and empty. Our table would never be the same, ever. There would always be the times when we gathered for special occasions but then, too, nothing would ever be the same again, knowing we were short one from being complete.

After dinner we remembered the radio broadcast tribute for John was minutes away. We listened to John's tribute on the radio. Somehow we made it through the segment, although there weren't many words spoken in our quarters after the coach's remarks. As the announcer introduced the story of how the head wrestling coach, Jim Jackson heard about John's death, we were silent and relived that night.

Jim had been at the hospital with his wife who just had a newborn. Our son, Ben, saw him there. Ben told Coach Jackson the news and the coach stated on the radio how he went through a gamut of emotions, the full extremes of joy and sadness as he was a new father, yet had lost a wrestler. The wrestler who had been part of the Apple Valley wrestling family for so many years. I fought back the deep pain in my heart and the tears in my eyes as I sat in my lounger unable to comprehend hearing someone say anything about John. *How could I be in so much disbelief?* I felt for a moment as if this was the first time I heard the news about John. I fought back the tightening in my face and throat and finally cried. Anguish filled me. I was looking around at the others knowing each one of us were crying in some way, but not sure how to go on.

The tribute lasted a few minutes and I was filled with pride for my son. It was good that so many others respected him that much. No one had to give John this tribute. I hardly knew any of the people who made the tribute happen, but I was strengthened, knowing God had put into the hearts of these people a desire to show us love and respect and sympathy. They in their own way were being a support and they did just that, encouraging and giving us a sense of dignity during a loss. Quietly I thanked God for this special moment.

I gently reopened the scrapbooks and newspaper clippings about John that filled our coffee table. People had perused that literature endlessly over the previous days, but I hadn't really paid much attention to them until now. These articles and pictures and awards, portrayed the athlete John was. I remembered how proud I had been as I relived some of those journal stories going back six and seven years.

I watched television for a while as Mom continued recording cards and memorials. We talked some and I answered a few calls, one from the "Rock Priest" from New Zealand, David Pierce, who was calling me daily and was a huge support. He had called nearly every day and sometimes more than once a day since he first heard the news. I felt God moving. David knew exactly what to say and when. He would pray, he would encourage, he would ask questions and he would joke. What mattered to me was that he was a brother in Christ who cared. We had tough moments, silly moments, and an occasional profound moment.

He apologized again for not being able to be there for the funeral, but we knew he'd be coming on a planned trip a few weeks later and he promised he'd take a few days out of his schedule and spend time with us. It was good to know someone so far away cared that much.

Unable to sleep much that night, I thanked God again for how He was bringing us comfort. Others were his instruments of love, compassion and peace. I lay in bed thinking. *Every night now, I lay awake looking at the ceiling thinking and meditating. My heart would break every time I thought about how often my words didn't show unconditional love to John.* The broken-ness spread as I was convicted over and over again how my loose tongue was so critical and conditional to John, to Beth, Scott, Adrienne and Ben, to others around me at work, church and in ministry. I regretted those moments and promised myself that was one area I needed to repent of immediately. I mentally punished myself, with a little help from the devil, so I alternated between wrestling with myself, wrestling with Satan and wrestling with God.

I had loved my son and worked hard to love others, being loving and accepting, but my tongue was a long-time struggle. Then the words of the Lord came as I remembered James 3:5-9.

Likewise the tongue is a small part of the body, but it makes great boasts. Consider what a great forest is set on fire, a world of evil among the parts of the body. It corrupts the whole person, sets the whole course of his life on fire, and is itself set on fire by hell. All kinds of animals, birds, reptiles and creatures of the sea are being tamed and have been tamed by man, but no man can tame the tongue. *It is a restless evil, full of deadly poison. With the tongue, we praise our Lord and Father and with it we curse men, who have been made in God's likeness.*

REFLECTION

Do you want to be an unconditional lover? Learn to control your words. Nothing is proof of love as your words. My biggest struggle with pride is my words and after a death, for some reason, you remember moments you wished you had said things differently. I was often too proud. How about you?

Don't wait. Are there people in your life today, that if they died, you'd be filled with excruciating pain because of your conditional words? I am learning that you must act on what you believe to be a believer. You simply can't think about what you believe or tell others what you believe. You need to do what you believe. Death has a way of making us honest. More honest about what we believe than at any other time during our spiritual walk.

CHAPTER EIGHT

One week in the wilderness -- Friday, January 28, 2000

I only slept for about an hour that Thursday night. In all I hadn't slept more than ten or twelve hours in total since John died. But my time wasn't wasted. I prayed for Beth as her doctor's appointment was the next day. I thought a lot about heaven and played out scenarios in my mind of what John might be doing. I wondered if he had met great men and women of God; saints, apostles, high priests and angels. I wondered if people slept in heaven, if John had gotten to see all of heaven, and if he still wanted to listen to his type of music or read his favorite books. I wondered if his type of music was heard anywhere in heaven. I thought about him meeting Jeremy Sanborn, my dad and other deceased family members.

As the night wore on, I increasingly started to think about everyone leaving on Friday afternoon for Pennsylvania and how empty it would feel. I thought about what it would feel like on Friday night from 6 PM on, as we remembered the last moments with John.

The sun came up on Friday morning and with it brought another bright but frigid day. It was January 28th, a week to the day of John's death. *Unbelievable, one week. It seemed so long ago and yet so recent. We had experienced so much; yet somehow time really didn't mean anything.* I picked up the newspaper and opened to the sports page where the headlines on the back inside page of the Sports section read,

Apple Valley grieves for former star wrestler.

"Last Friday, Apple Valley wrestling coach Jim Jackson went through the complete range of emotions at Fairview Ridges Hospital in Burnsville.

After dropping off his wife June, who would give birth to their first child the next day, Jackson parked the family van and ran into a brother of the former Eagles wrestler, John Chaya.

Chaya, 21, was dead, Jackson was told. A viral infection had attacked his pancreas.

"I went from the highest of highs to the lowest of lows," said Jackson whose baby girl is named Taylor Anne. "John was a three sport athlete and a wonderful human being."

Chaya was Apple Valley's heavyweight for three years. As a sophomore in 1995, he won the deciding match when the Eagles beat Simley 27-23 in the big-school state final.

The next year Apple Valley took second place and Chaya fourth as an individual. And as a senior, Chaya was a member of another state championship and was state-runner up at heavyweight.

"He was a big guy with a gentle heart, a kind polite, caring person," Jackson stated.

Chaya also played varsity football for four years and was a member of the track and field team.

Services for him were held Tuesday.

"The church was packed.....The Chaya's are very good people," Jackson said.

A moment of silence will be observed for Chaya on Saturday when seven teams compete in the Valley Invitational starting at 10:30 a.m. He also will be mentioned in the tournament program.

We had received an earlier call on Wednesday, telling us this article would be in the paper. Word came from the athletic director at Apple Valley that the coaches were dedicating the Annual Invitational Wrestling Tournament to John and they wanted us as a family to attend a short program prior to the finals on Saturday afternoon. I cried as I heard the news, humbled by the respect shown to John and I dreaded having to attend something so painful so soon. My sequestering in my house had been comforting to me. It was my sanctuary. I felt too vulnerable to go out, but I knew I must.

Something was beginning to take place in my emotions and thoughts. I sensed God was at work more and more. In spite of the sadness and anguish and pain, I was beginning to also experience the awesome wonder of God. I felt Him in a new way. All the events that were now taking place as tributes and reminders of John, were taking on a sense of this was how God was comforting us during this time. He was using others around us. Their acts of love and sympathy were taking on a deeper purpose. God was using them to help us get through the hard times.

I wasn't experiencing sadness as much as I was experiencing a deep relationship, a new sensitivity of God at work, a satisfying peace that He was not going to leave us or forsake us. He was going to show Himself to us more than ever before. It was becoming a privilege to see Him working during this week and He was telling me He wasn't done yet.

My tears were mixed between mourning, sadness and overwhelming love for God. I never had felt anything like this before. I knew God was real but I never had felt Him the way I was feeling Him now.

We were ending the latest chapter of our family events as my brother and his family and my mother prepared to depart for Pennsylvania. First we wanted to go over to Apple Valley High school. The trophy case and wrestling room were shrines and John had made his mark there. Beth had called the school earlier to make sure we could visit the wrestling room and we were granted access. We met one of the administrators in the visitors' area and gained access to the school. The trophy case was in the cafeteria.

The students were on lunch break as we met one of John's football coaches. We stood and viewed John's pictures on the football and wrestling plaques. We saw the accolades and were filled with pride. We slowly moved up the steps to the wrestling room.

The yellow and brown décor was the backdrop to a multitude of record boards, pictures, championship bracket charts, individual and team championships and statistics. We strolled around the perimeter of the mat and looked for John's name and picture. He had a few pictures as an all-state wrestler and his name was on the career wins board. He was ranked 29th all time in wins with 73 career wins. I stood and let the tradition sink in. John may not have been one of the best wrestlers Apple Valley had and he wasn't the strongest, meanest, most talented or toughest. He certainly wasn't the "winningest," but he was our son and that was all that mattered. He was good. He hung in there with one of the toughest programs and most successful schools in the nation and made his mark. He was a champion.

Over the past few days, we had continued to rerun video tapes of John as he wrestled and played football. During those days, every now and then Ben would sneak in one of his tapes and liven up the setting. As a rule though, after I watched with emptiness, I struggled with how we'd never be able to look at those videos the same again. Or worse, he would never be taped again as an athlete. I knew even if he was alive, he'd never compete again, but this was a stark reminder that now there wasn't a choice. It would never happen.

Never videotaping his wedding, or college graduation, or opening Christmas gifts or going fishing. Never having Beth take photographs of John at birthday parties, or playing with the dogs, or barbecuing or fooling around in the back yard. Wow, things could change so sudden, and the change would change our lives forever.

It wasn't simply the pain we going through now. It would be there to some extent always. That was hard to imagine. It was hard to imagine that tomorrow everyone would be back east and we'd be experiencing deeper emptiness. My emotions vacillated between what I was feeling, sitting with everyone around us, to next Christmas not having John around, to the radio tribute, to the next day. I had no rhyme or reason to my thoughts or emotions, and I had no release from them, either. Grief filled me with further confusion, my emotions were mixed with pain, with uncertainty and no thought-control.

I walked down the steps from the wrestling room saddened at my drifting thoughts but proud that my family got to see a part of John after so many years of just hearing about what he had done.

Morning turned to noon as we arrived at the Minneapolis-St. Paul airport. We spent some moments, waiting for the call to board. In idle conversation, I felt the emptiness and loneliness creep in again. We said our good-byes with tears and hugs and the unspoken depths of our love. We had experienced as a family a first, having a child die and we had held together remarkably well. The Holy Spirit had brought us together and comforted us with each other, as families are supposed to do, but so often don't. I quietly thanked God for how He was at work in everyone's hearts and minds and providing the wisdom and discernment needed at a time like this.

We stood and watched as the last of the Chaya's disappeared through the jet way. We stood in silence, knowing they had accomplished a mission, and now we were on our own. As we walked back to the car, the inevitable was sinking in. We were going to be alone in our grief for the first time. The throng of mourners were gone, all getting on with their lives. The attention we received would dwindle and we would become a distant thought and prayer in the minds and hearts of our friends and family. No one would know of the loneliness, the emptiness, the sadness and the pain we'd experience because they wouldn't be there to experience it now. Only parents who lost a child could understand.

We returned to the house, enduring a quiet, somber car ride. The house was quiet now and empty. Our three children were out and would be out for the evening. The dogs seemed to be mourning as well. No more attention, treats, playing and pets on the head.

As the afternoon passed to dinnertime and then to evening, Beth and I replayed the previous Friday night's chronology. The anguish mounted as it turned 5:30 p.m. and we started reliving the events of that Friday night with John, now exactly one week ago. (I realized at that time, I needed to begin journaling again since I couldn't remember the facts.) By 6:30 p.m. we conceded defeat. I walked into the kitchen, looked at the floor where John died, looked at the kitchen chair he sat in, and relived the difficult breathing pattern. I thought of the popsicle he ate, the blanket

Beth put on his shoulders, the paramedics and police. The thought of the cold night with the flashing lights in the driveway just became too much. As the critical time in our mental enactment of the final two hours of John's life approached, it became unbearable.

"Jake, let's go out somewhere. It is too hard to stay here. It feels weird," Beth said to me. We sat in our individual discomfort and we didn't know what to say or what to do. Eventually I responded. "Let's go for a ride, or down to the lake, or just walk around the Burnsville Center."

It was now nearly 7:30 p.m. and we drove to the lake where I had spent so many hours with God. At the lake we sat in the dark car in the parking lot looking out at the ice fish houses. Dark and cold, we scanned the frozen waters. That summed up our evening, cold, dark, frozen, no life. We prayed and talked as we were warm in the car, but the emptiness was complete. There was nothing left.

We looked at the distant lakeshore with it's sparkling lights, mostly from the nestled homes and street lights. Some homes with their Christmas decorations still lit, illuminated the night. I felt all alone. None of those people even knew what we were experiencing, let alone know we were there. I started up the engine and slowly drove out of the lot, tires crunching snow in the deep January night. *Where do we go now? What do we do? How should we live our lives now?* It became evident that as we proceeded to our house, that we should make an intermediate stop at the church.

Fulfilled and comforted so many times at our church, we sought comfort once again. The janitor had the lights on in the sanctuary as we walked in. I glanced to the left at the area where John's final viewing was held and remembered the flowers, the jersey, the helmet, the Penn State gorilla. To the right at the reception area in the church commons were two small bouquets from the funeral. They looked fresh and well cared for. We entered the sanctuary, slowly walked to where we sat during the funeral and looked at the large bouquet resting on the cover of the baptismal. It, too, looked fresh.

We sat in the sanctuary in the same places as during the funeral. We re-lived the sermons, the jersey-draped casket, the flowers and the people. (We cried and prayed for nearly an hour.) We remembered the radio tribute, the newspaper article, and looked forward to the wrestling tribute tomorrow. We studied the sanctuary. The remaining flower arrangements in the sanctuary and commons area from the funeral touched our hearts. Yes, it really happened, it wasn't our imaginations; evidence proved we hadn't been dreaming.

We tried to comfort each other, as the minutes ticked by. It was the actual hour we dreaded. Although the coroner's report pronounced John dead at 9:05 p.m., we knew that it was between 8:00 p.m. and 8:30 that he died and as the hour approached, we anticipated it without knowing how to act or what to think.

Alone, we strived to find answers to new questions. *Was it morbid to relive the one week anniversary of the death of your son? Was it unrealistic for us to try to feel God, or the comfort of each other at this moment? What should we be doing, instead of sitting here reliving the toughest moment we faced as a couple?*

Beth and I said nothing as we stared at where the casket had been, only a few feet from us. Slowly we both felt the comforting peace and grace of God fill us. It was like warm syrup flowing over us. We started commenting on the choir, the pastors, messages, all the flowers, the music, the packed church, the expressions of the pall bearers, and the banner still hanging on the wall.

The spirit of God was ministering to us in His sanctuary. There was life, there was comfort, and the joy filled us as we prayed again. We weren't alone. He was with us. We wished John would have been there with us this Friday, but somehow we knew. Someone far greater, Jesus, was there and maybe John peeked in as well, to let us know he was fine and for us to show him how much we loved him and missed him.

How can you articulate standing on Holy Ground? How can you articulate the presence of God to someone unless they were experiencing it with you? At that moment, all that mattered was we had a Savior and a Comforter who revealed Himself and we were blessed. As we departed from the church back into the cold night, we carried the warmth of the Holy Spirit. We had made it.

Climbing back up the foyer staircase, we made our way into our house. It was after nine o'clock and we had endured the critical moments of life and death. Now were became filled with God's love and comfort. The house was quiet and empty and dark, the dogs didn't stir as we stood and looked around. A new chapter was beginning, having a family of five to care for instead of six. We knew we had to rely on God in the upcoming months and years to help us live on and hold John's memory near and dear.

REFLECTION

Time stands still with death. One week feels like one hour, sometimes a day , and sometimes it feels like one minute. I realized walking in the wilderness has no time. As the tribes wandered for 40 years in the wilderness, they probably didn't have a good perspective on time. It looked and felt all the same. I reflected at how often my mundane life while John was still alive had no appreciation of time. One more day, one more year, one more week. That is all I wanted. I would have done things differently. If you knew your most beloved had one week, would you treat them differently? If you had one day or one week, or a year to live, what would you do differently?

CHAPTER NINE

Messages sent in the wilderness -- Saturday, January 28, 2000

Saturday was an empty, lonely day. *Eight days and it seems like last night. Will I ever smile again or laugh?* Other than the mail, a few phone calls and short visits by friends, the day was a lingering after-effect. Saturday's dawn repeated another sunny cold display. I left the house early and went to my sanctuary, the lake. It was cold with a bitter wind-chill as I trudged through the snow. I stepped in my previously made footsteps and made my way to the little tree, my memorial site. It was my "sanctuary of the broken notes."

I stood there and prayed and meditated. My mind swirled again as it had every day I had come there. (Tears and groans came, what little noise I could make.) I slowly turned around and looked behind me at Buck Hill. No skiers on the slope yet, for it was too early. I looked to see if the ice fishermen had awakened. Only a slight whish of the winds through the trees and an occasional land vehicle traveling by broke the stillness.

"Lord, tomorrow I will face my Sunday School class. What do I say to them, Lord? I'm the leader of these adults and yet I feel like I can't lead. I don't know what to say or do. We are changing sheep into war horses and I don't feel worthy of teaching the class."

My mind stumbled over dampening thoughts. Then, deep in my soul I heard the words Roger Thompson had spoken to me. *Be authentic. Be genuine. People need to see real Christians and how they act in difficult times. You have clean grief. Don't be afraid to be weak and vulnerable.* I felt a peace move over me. I was still deeply saddened, but the sense of God being there and knowing that John was in heaven and had met Jesus, was so exhilarating. Words I had heard in my sanctuary over the past week echoed in my brain. *Be at peace, he is in heaven. Remember it is not what you do, or what John did, it is who you are and who John is, children of Christ. Go into your class tomorrow and don't tell them about yourself, or about John, tell them about Me. Tell them what Jesus has done these past days and how God has been with you.*

I was growing accustomed to hearing God so clearly at my sanctuary. His voice was so real, so sincere, it was so miraculous for me to be able to stand on a frozen lake and hear God's voice deep in my soul. Maybe this was how it was supposed to be, the Comforter comforting at the dreariest time. I felt a divine nudge. "Don't think about how you feel. Help Beth, help your children. Comfort them. That is why I put you on earth. Take care of those who love you," the Voice spoke again. I smiled, as a peace settled over me.

I returned home and checked my e-mail and fooled around with the dogs. Minutes later, Beth returned from her doctor appointment and declared that the tests had gone very well. (We prayed in thanksgiving and compared notes about each for our next appointments.)

We talked for a while without interruption, a relief in itself. We spoke about how we needed to keep supporting the kids, now that it appeared both of us were on the mend, but still very sick. Beth and I often talked about the tough emotional week and how it appeared that the kids weren't too negatively impacted by it. At this moment I wasn't feeling good about myself. Beth seemed to be handling the entire situation much better than I was and I admired her. She didn't take herself as seriously or overanalyze things as much as I did. I realized then and there, during grieving, I needed to just grieve, not try to figure things out, and to ride with the waves of grief.

We conducted our usual Saturday morning chores, as a force of habit with sadness and tears. Then, as the morning waned, we prepared for the phone call in the afternoon. The Apple Valley Wrestling Club would call us to come to the gym for the dedication. Phone calls broke up the afternoon and a stream of people stopped by.

Beth checked the mail and we received a letter from one of John's high school buddies who was a co-captain on the team. Mike was a great athlete and student and we were honored to have him as a pall bearer. He was the first person to respond to our funeral invitation to stop by or write a note sharing about how John impacted his life. The letter read:

Dear Chaya Family,   1/27/00

I just want to thank you for asking me to be a pallbearer in John's funeral. It was an honor for me. I must say that it was one of the hardest things I've ever done. It's not every day that you put a buddy of yours in a hearse.

I thought that I would write to you and tell you all the memories that I have of John. I guess I'll start when I met him. It was the summer following 3rd grade if I remember correctly. It was a summer school class and me, John and Dan Kersten buddied up almost instantly. From then on we were all friends.

I also remember playing baseball with John when he was younger. We played on a VAA baseball team together. John was our catcher.

Then came middle school. And football. What a great time we had. I remember in seventh grade our football team went undefeated. That was our glory year. That year me and John would talk about how we thought the team would be in the future. We were so excited.

I remember one play that sticks out like no other. John was on the kick off team. (They never took him off the field.) The kick didn't go deep and John caught it. He ran straight ahead and barreled through everybody. Touchdown!

Then came high school. Me and John were making memories together on the varsity team my sophomore year. We had a great team, not as good as the year before. I remember our first football letter sent to us by the Army football team. It was a thrill for us both. We would always check each others mail that we received that year. It was basically a competition. If I recall, I think John beat me. That year on defense, I was behind John all year. We worked together as lineman and linebacker. Neither of us would succeed without the other. I still remember me and him joking around in practice, giving each other a hard time. Those were good times.

Through high school I got to know John fairly well. Everyday we would ride to school together. It was fun. When you ride with someone in a car for a long period of time, you definitely have some interesting conversations.

Our senior year football was great. We were the kings. I remember before some of the games, John would put on black face paint to help him get revved up before the game. Those were the days I remember. Fritze would walk into the locker room, give his speech, then it was our turn to talk. Me and Mike Cubbage would have a word or two, but John would always take the floor last. May be it was right that way?

To tell you the truth I have many more memories that don't come to mind at the moment, but I thought that I would share the ones that do. To this day I can still hear his voice in my head talking to me. I'll always have those great memories. Thank you.

Love,

Mike Henrickson

We both read the letter in silence. (After a few minutes, filled with pride and sadness, I simply folded the letter and cried.) I was so thankful that Mike had written us. It was good to hear from one of John's close friends. It warmed me and transported my head and heart back to those high school days and the sports. The letter was a prelude for the rest of the afternoon as we physically stepped into the future to honor the past.

A member of the booster club had stopped by earlier in the week to pick up John's picture, medals and letter jacket for a display at the wrestling meet. Now, he called us and let us know it was time to go to the tournament for the tribute.

We walked to the doors and there to the left of the trophy case that we viewed the day before, was the picture of John in his senior wrestling team picture. His region and state individual and team medals hung alongside his letter jacket. I stood and looked in humility. People respected his feats and remembered him. I was weak as I entered the gymnasium. It was the first time in my life where I thought people were watching my every move. I knew I was wrong, but I couldn't stop feeling self-conscious.

We entered the arena and tried to act normally and find a seat in the bleachers. We read the loving dedication in the program and talked with a number of parents whose sons knew of, or wrestled with John. They expressed their condolences and as the eight teams lined up for the start of the finals, we were directed to the floor to stand by the Apple Valley team.

The school athletic director quieted the crowd and we were ushered to the floor and stood mat-side near the Apple Valley wrestling team. Eight teams stood in silence as well as the large crowd. I looked around, remembering the high schools John competed against as we listened to the dedication. His feats as a three-sport athlete were mentioned as well as his role as football captain, two-time all-state wrestler, all conference football player and being on five state championship teams. I held the program with the insert paying tribute to John. We all stood for a few minutes of silence, then each wrestler from Apple Valley and their coaches expressed their sympathy one by one. I think the crowd gave a polite respectful ovation in respect. The coach of one of the teams came to me and shook my hand and commented. "I remember your son wrestling against us. He took us apart. I'm sorry for your loss. He was a great athlete and I'm sure, a greater son."

I could only squint and nod as I shook his hand, too overwhelmed by this man's respect. We took a few more minutes of condolences then ascended to our places in the bleachers and watched the competition. We had met every Apple Valley wrestler and coach. We headed back up to our seats, knowing the whole arena was watching us, and probably wondering how it must feel and what we must be experiencing. Peace and joy was what I was experiencing, while also feeling overwhelming sadness. *This can't be really happening. This is where athletes competed, not grieved death.* John would have been proud of the team this afternoon. The Eagles won it all. The fellow wrestling heavyweight who was a close friend of Ben's, was Chad Redmann. Chad wore John's wrestling shoes for his match. I doubt if they had anything to do with the outcome, but the result was the same, the opponent was pinned.

John's shoes won again, so we congratulated Chad Redmann on his victory. We also told him how much it meant to us as a tribute. We sat in the bleachers, feeling the same eeriness of remembering watching John wrestle so many times before, and his graduation, and the night that he, a freshman, sat at the pep rally after the football team won the state championship. Now it would be no more new memories that would be created, but one to behold as a tribute.

We slowly moved out of the gym after the tournament, met a few lingering well-wishers and took a few minutes at John's memorial. One of the coaches had mentioned that the wrestling club was going to name an annual award, "The Match" in tribute to John for his sophomore achievement of winning the heavyweight match which clinched the team state championship. *What a tribute! To remember that match now was like watching a movie, like Hoosiers, or Rudy, where the underdog came up big. It was like David against Goliath and David won.*

To think that people did not forget that match and named an award in honor of John was deeply touching. Again, I sensed God was working in His people. The wrestling tournament was special. It hit me that John's death was continuing to impact other people. Yet life would go on. *It had to go on.* It would snow and it would rain. It would turn from winter to summer and winter again and each season would slip away, but there would forever be the event which caused time to appear to stand still.

I brought my head back to the present darkness of the deep night. It was very quiet. Eventually I made my way to bed after roaming around in the stillness. I would sit in the lounge chair and remember John's last hours there. I would sit at his place at the table where he said his last words. I would stand in the kitchen remembering the final traumatic moments, the paramedics, doing CPR, and then my memories would be numbed by the fragrances of the flowers and bouquets. (It smelled like a funeral home.)

I slid alongside Beth under the sheets and held her sleeping shoulder and arm. The memories were still so fresh, so vivid, so terrifying, yet so peaceful, so joyful knowing John was with God. *I wonder how much of heaven John has seen and if he met Dad yet?* I thought. What must it be

like in heaven? *Is there night time? Do they sleep in heaven?*
What do I teach tomorrow in Sunday School? I am unprepared. It's not
fair to them. I can't focus. My thoughts bounced back and forth about
heaven and earth, about John and about me. I drifted in and out of sleep,
but woke Sunday morning, feeling no refreshment. I was tired and
worried. *What was I supposed to teach in my Sunday school class this*
morning? I was formulating in my mind what God had been revealing to me,
but I wasn't sure I could articulate it. I knew God was directing me to handle
grief with pain and suffering, by focusing first on the facts, then my thoughts
and then my feelings. But I wasn't sure if that was just the way I wanted to
cope with this suffering. I had, for too many years always responded with
emotions first, then my self-concocted wisdom by my analytical thinking and
eventually looked at the facts. What was I really doing now? How would other
people respond?
God speaks through other people, including strangers and past friends
when you wander in the wilderness. You never know the impact a person had
during their lifetime. Do you have any idea of the amount of people you have
impacted in your life? When they write letters about you, what will they say?
Will anyone think it special to pay you a tribute? We don't live for those glory
moments or try to perform for accolades, but in our everyday lives, do people
take notice? Do your loved ones know who you are and who you aspire to be?
When would be a good time to tell or show them just who you really are?

CHAPTER TEN

Sunday morning brought the anguish of having to face my friends in the adult bible fellowship group I had been leading. Only two weeks earlier, I had started the class titled, "Changing Sheep into Warhorses." The title came from Zechariah 10:3, a prophecy about how God was angered by His leaders and shepherds and in end times would change His flock into majestic horses of battle, the Warhorses.

I learned in Job 39:21-25 what the characteristics of a warhorse were. Then in Rev. 19:11 the scriptures pointed out why the horse was a warhorse: his loyalty to the rider, Jesus Christ. Since I had heard this prophecy a year ago in Singapore, the words had become light before my feet for all these months. My goal in the class was to prepare these adults to mobilize for Christ. I didn't realize God would use John's death as part of my ministry. War horses now took on real life. It was as if my vision had taken a form, me.

Zechariah 10:2-12 *For the seraphim speak iniquity and the diviners see lying visions and tell false dreams. They comfort in vain. Therefore the people wander like sheep. They are afflicted because there is no shepherd. My anger is kindled against the shepherds, and I will punish the male goats; for the Lord of hosts has visited His flock, the house of Judah. <u>And will make them like His majestic horses in battle.</u>*

This powerful prophecy spoken thousands of years ago foretold God's anger during the end times. It spoke of the "re-gathering of God's people who have been scattered over all nations." His anger stems from his flock, Judah, for not having worthy shepherds. God states that He is angry at those who are His sheep, because they are wandering around. He is going to take some of His sheep and transform them into majestic horses of battle. The war horse. I looked through the scriptures to see what the attributes of a war horse were. Eventually they turned up. I didn't have to interpret any prophetic symbolism or define my own assumptions. God spoke directly to one of His own children in describing the attributes. God described the war horse to Job in the Book of Job.

Job 39:21-25: *"He paws fiercely, rejoicing in his strength and charges into the fray. He laughs at fear afraid of nothing; and he does not shy away from the sword. The quiver rattles against his side, along with the flashing spear and lance. In frenzied excitement he eats up the ground; he can not stand still when the trumpet sounds. At the blast of the trumpet he snorts, "Aha!" He catches the scent of battle from afar, the shout of the commanders and the battle cry.*

When I first heard of this description, I was intrigued. I wanted to know how to become a war horse. The term was dynamic, powerful, and majestic. I could envision the supernatural being, specifically created by God to rule, to conquer, to dominate, to intimidate, to overwhelm everything its path, to be the victor, to possess more power than all the nuclear bombs ever created. I wanted to experience that power. I prayed to God that I would be transformed by Him into a war horse.

In the spring and summer of 1999, I had been awarded a four month paid sabbatical. Being a short-term missionary with Steiger International for 11 years and also having started a non-profit humanitarian foundation, the White Dove Foundation, I anticipated four months of personal growth, rest and freedom to experience God in a new way. Plus I was frustrated with my career and was seeking God's direction.

I had been preparing to teach a Sunday School lesson to adults at my church when I came across scripture that deeply troubled me. Not only was I searching for purpose, I was now struggling with the characteristics of what people's attributes will be during the end times. I realized the scriptures were not only talking about non-believers, but believers. The scriptures were describing me and it didn't feel good.

2 Tim 3:1-5 *But realize this, that in the last days difficult times will come. For men will be lovers of self, lovers of money, boastful, arrogant, revilers, disobedient to parents, ungrateful, unholy, unloving, irreconcilable, malicious gossips, without self-control, brutal, haters of good, treacherous, reckless, conceited, lovers of pleasure rather than lovers of God; holding to a form of godliness, although they have denied its power;*

Verse five is what caused me the most trouble; "holding to a form of godliness, although they have denied its power;" shook me. *Was I being described in that passage? Was I an evangelical Christian who held a form of godliness, yet lived my life as if I was denying the power of God?*

I grew anxious. My devotions, prayer time, Bible study and meditation took on a sense of desperation. It wasn't intrigue or curiosity driving me, it was a renewal of my soul, my spirit, and a quest to know my identity. I looked forward to finding the truths. I concluded, "there must be truths hidden from me." I sensed God moving in me to discover what those truths were.

The first few weeks of my sabbatical were a time that I learned to relax. As I planned my four international trips, I felt balance. My family would be going on two of these trips and each of my children would get to experience what I had been doing in past years on short term missions trips. We were anticipating a great summer and I was anticipating new discoveries.

While visiting my first country, Singapore, I was with a missionary, Ken Green who shared the war horse prophecy with me and guided me to the account in Job 39. I was instantly convicted.

While on a trip to New Delhi to visit Ton Snellaert, a Steiger International missionary who was heading up the Delhi House, a rehab center nursing tuberculosis patients back to health and picking dying people up off the streets, I was overwhelmed by the heat, pollution, noise, filth, poverty and disease. I spent over a week with him and his team, combing the streets for the lame, the sick, the infectious, and the dead. We visited clinics and hospitals and the temples. Everywhere people lay dying and sick. It was overwhelming. The tuberculosis wards were nightmares. Dark, hopeless, and lonely. That was all I could think of. "Where was God in all this?" I asked myself.

We went to an emergency room and watched as sick, injured and weary patients sat around on the floor and benches waiting their turns for treatment. There had been one entire floor of a ward in that hospital that was relinquished to a pack of roving dogs, since the people with their religious beliefs put more value in the spirits of the animals than in the people needing medical attention.

I watched Ton. He was the closest thing to a war horse that I'd seen. His love and tenderness, his patience and care, and his spiritual gift of mercy were so Christ-like. One day our team went to the hospital, the multi-drug resistant tuberculosis ward. All morning we met with patients Ton had admitted from the streets. We washed them, brought clothes, gave them food and money. We talked with them and prayed with them. But I was struggling in a major way. My spirit was crushed. I cried out to God, *"Where are you? I can't even pray right. I feel so empty and inadequate and faithless. I don't know what to pray to You about, Lord.*

"I never thought people could suffer like this. I never imagined how empty and lonely and helpless these people were. I see their Hindu idols. I see their icons. This is so hopeless. They don't know about You. How, Lord? How can there be this much suffering with no hope?"

I stood crying and frustrated, ashamed at that moment that I didn't have the faith to believe God could do anything in that hospital. The team tended to one final young man and as we left the ward I looked around at all the dying faces. I was appalled. Going down the stairway in silence, Ton abruptly turned to me and his team and said, "Wait, we need to go back there. We did all the right things to help him, but we didn't pray for him. The most important thing we forgot to do."

We walked back up the steps and entered the ward and approached the man's bed. The crushing darkness filled my heart and mind instantly. I was devastated. The five of us circled the man's bed.

"Go ahead, Jake, you pray for him," Ton directed me as I put my hands on the sick man's head and arm. I began to pray with the translator. The patient burned with fever as I looked into his eyes. Slowly I spoke some words, but my faith was gone. I said words to God, but my belief was so devastated in seeing this man, I felt guilty that I didn't have any passion or compassion to really pray hard. In a few moments of desperation I finally came up with the only words I believed in. *Lord, help me in my unbelief.*

"Lord, I know this man can't understand me and he doesn't believe in you. But if there is some way you could comfort him and give him some peace and perhaps somehow let him feel Your presence, please help him."

We got up to leave and as I was walking away, feeling guilty and angry at myself, Aton, the missionary woman who was interpreting my prayer tugged my arm.

"Jake, he says he wants you to pray for him. He wants to accept Jesus as his Lord and Savior. Please pray for him."

Startled by her words, I turned again to him. I was confused emotionally and spiritually by what was happening. God was here, He was moving. My spirit stirred as I placed my hands on his arm and forehead again. I began to pray. I hoped he wouldn't die until I finished my prayer. The man, a patient in the multi-drug resistant ward in the largest tuberculosis hospital in New Delhi, India, lay in the dark, hopelessness, and loneliness of death. I prayed with Ton and Aton who translated and the man responded by inviting Jesus into his life. My eyes were pressed tightly together squeezing back tears of experiencing this miracle of God. Even in my unbelief, my faithlessness and my hopelessness, God was moving. God didn't need a perfect servant, he only needed a willing one.

Ton gave the man a Bible in Hindi and the weak man lifted the book up and whispered, "Christian, I'm a Christian." As I stood up, it looked like all the men of the ward were standing around us, seeking prayer. Death's darkness, loneliness and hopelessness melted as Christ's light shone brightly. It was like a revival hit that ward. It was bright now, there was hope and faith. Men didn't look so dead any more or empty or lonely. I looked around, completely drained and brokenhearted. I had been greatly humbled by God. As I stood looking into the eyes of the many men seeking prayer, I heard in the back of my mind, a still soft voice, "Warhorse."

I learned much that summer. I saw myself at times as the war horse, but more often than not, I was a sheep. The Holy Spirit wasn't done with me though, even when I thought I had learned enough. He was in the process of transformation, of instilling in me a passion to seek God to re-invent myself. It wasn't that war horses were better trained, or stronger, or smarter, or more powerful that made them war horses. The reason why a war horse became a war horse was because of his loyalty to his rider and master, Jesus Christ. God revealed the words in the Book of Revelation.

Rev 19:11 And I saw heaven opened; and behold, a white horse, and He who sat upon it is called Faithful and True; and in righteousness He judges and wages war. And His eyes are a flame of fire, and upon His head are many diadems; and He has a name written upon Him which no one knows except Himself. And He is clothed with a robe dipped in blood; and His name is called The Word of God.

Jesus Christ is the Rider, Faithful and True. His name is called "The Word of God." I am the servant, the war horse, looking into the rider's eyes and seeing the fire. All wisdom is in Him, He is truth, He is the Word of God, pure, holy, and righteous.

It became apparent that in order for any of us to be transformed, we first must be willing and available. Secondly, we must have a desire to fulfill all that God has created us for. And third, we must be willing to be transformed, to let go of our fears and comforts, lifestyles and careers and sacrifice.

I didn't realize God had been preparing me for His purpose and for the death of John that summer. I and my family certainly didn't feel like war horses as we grieved now, over our loss. I didn't feel like much of anything. But God uses suffering and pain as a time for intimacy with him. The hours, days and weeks that followed January 21st, were times God's voice was easily heard and His hands were equally as easily seen through the people around us. I was riding the currents of God's grace and as I would sink in the flow of the current of anguish, He constantly brought others to rescue me.

Ton Snellaert, the Dutch missionary who ran the New Delhi missions work whom I befriended gave me a book and much of the text was healing salve. One quote stood out that made my life and God's plan seem so uncomplicated.

"Had there been a better way, more profitable to the salvation of mankind than suffering, then Christ would have revealed it in his word and life." Thomas A Kempis.

But now, too wounded from John's death, I forced myself to prepare for the Sunday School lesson. I was empty. I looked at a good place to start. I had bottomed out. Emotionally, mentally and spiritually I was poured out. Proverbs 1:7 was a good place to start. It shed light on the beginning of knowledge. How would my best life look, if I surrendered completely to Jesus? I knew I had given it all to Him so many times before and taken it back. This time was different; I would seek His face.

My class was small, but mighty and they cared. The class was more of a testimony time of what God had been doing through our lives and John's death. I returned home from church that afternoon and savored a quiet time. The lesson had wiped me out. It was overwhelming to see my friends in mourning with us and still see God so visibly in them and in His words as I relived my missions trip to Asia a year earlier. God brought the past trip together with the present as I could see His hand and face in the year leading up to John's death.

This day had been a long day. The Sunday School lesson, the email, the day of sadness all were fruits of what God had taught me back in the summer of 1999. Never did I think I'd actually live out the lesson.

REFLECTION

God will prepare you and prompt you to apply what He has been teaching you, or has taught you in the past. Don't always look to the future for answers or reject the past. God's word is timeless. If you were near death, what lessons has God been teaching you that would be highly applicable?

Chapter Eleven

The changing wilderness -- ten days after

None of us were ready, but we decided to venture back into the schools and workplaces for that "first day back". My first day back to work was very trying. Previously talking with my vice president, Jeff Ramsey, he encouraged me to come to the daylong offsite. I walked into the large meeting room with all my colleagues, the first time I had seen them since the visitation and funeral. As I walked to my seat at the corner of the table, a few soft hellos came my way, but my cohorts seemed as reserved and self-conscious as I did and very little was said. My sickness was still a major obstacle and I felt like work was stealing my mind and heart from what was really important. I felt lonely and irritable. It was as if work never occurred before and this was my first day on the job.

Beth was working as a temp at the same company as me. I missed her and it was still early in the day. I came to the realization as I continued to replay the tragic moments and events following that Friday night, that this loss wasn't going to fade quickly, nor did I want it to. I didn't want to forget anything. The hurt brought refreshing cleansing and comfort. With each wave of grief, a deep love of Jesus flowed through me.

I grew more contemplative and meditative as I went deep into my soul. There wasn't much I understood, but I wasn't questioning, either. I would quiet my soul and listen for God. I was remembering my lesson from Sunday. The fear of the Lord is the beginning of knowledge. God's words always came. Not every word from Him was amazing or profound, but it was always wise. And it always was a still small voice, reassuring me I wasn't alone.

I attempted to get focused on what I had been doing prior to John's death. As I tried to recollect the happenings of two weeks ago, it was strenuous trying to catch up. I felt defeated as I sat in that "first day back" offsite. I mentally cried out to God for Him to help me see clearly what His will was and his timing. I prayed for the Steiger missionaries, my family and White Dove.

Though I sat in the work sessions, my mind was out of the room. I remembered a devotion I read.

1 Corinthians 1:17. For Christ sent me not to baptize, but to preach the gospel.

That devotion focused on how Paul welcomed heartbreaks,

disillusionment, trials and tribulations. All for one reason. All these things kept Paul in unwavering devotion for preaching the gospel. I prayed to God as I half-listened to the meeting.

"You are awesome, wonderful, loving and gracious. You have blessed us with an outpouring of love, peace, kindness, gentleness, joy, peace, mercy and truth. My greatest joy was experiencing truth when John died.

Strengthen, encourage and comfort us O Lord, so we can make it through this day as shining witnesses of what you have done in us."

The day was a reflection of my pain and sorrow and my attention span was weak and short. But I thanked God I had made it through the day. As we gathered that evening for dinner at our table, it was good to be back home. A member of our church family delivered a complete hot meal, and as we ate, it felt incomplete. One more table setting occupied by the big guy would have made it like old times. This meal was simply a reminder that the new times would never be like the old times.

Somehow, each day back brought pain and joy. The week turned out to be one of no regularity. We went to work and school intermittently. Teachers, students and fellow workers were supportive, comforting and encouraging, but each new day brought awkward moments.

I was amazed at how many people were suffering loss in their lives by death, illness, broken relationships or finances. I always knew there was pain and suffering in many lives, but now it seemed far greater. Perhaps it was always there. I had been too insensitive to the hurting around me. We attracted many like us. It was as if God was bringing us together as an informal grieving group. The amount of people was staggering. We never knew how many people cared for us, or even remembered us, yet as days wore on, God kept bringing His messengers.

As the days passed, we all had our moments when we had to escape. I tried to talk with the kids to make sure they were doing well, but they didn't open up and it appeared they were handling it as well as could be expected. Beth and I continued to be two united as one as we helped each other during difficult moments.

Scott and I had a few conversations in the late nights as he sought to better understand and to be comforted by God. He was excited as he shared how he struggled so much, yet when he prayed, God gave him comfort.

Two weeks after John's death, Scott and his band, "Anti-Sanity" played a benefit concert in memory of John. There was a modest crowd that attended, but what was important was that Scott was able in his own way, to handle the grieving process in a very mature manner and it was a loving tribute.

Another letter came from one of John's old high school buddies who were in the football and wrestling fraternity at Apple Valley. Dan had known John since third grade and they had been in nearly every class together and played football and wrestled. Dan was at the University of Michigan and was unable to attend the funeral. The letter was another glimpse of John we had not seen.

January 28, 2000

Dear Chaya Family,

I can't begin to explain how terrible I feel about your son's death. To be honest, it has taken me this long just to be able to compose my thoughts and actually begin to express them. I have to admit that when my father informed me of John's death last Saturday, I couldn't bring myself to understand what exactly it meant. I was in shock for the rest of the day and it wasn't until that evening that I realized what John really meant to me.

It makes me sick to think that I knew John for almost 12 years and never once explained how highly I thought of him. Now, the only way for me to do that is through my prayers and possibly by explaining to you, his family, how John affected my life so that you will always be able to remember him as a wonderful and truly unique person. I know that you already believe this, but I know it from a different point of view, one that may help you remember why such an amazing person.

The night I learned of John's death, I couldn't sleep. All I could think about was all the time John and I had spent together growing up. He was one of my first friends when I moved to Burnsville; we had about 50 classes together throughout all of elementary school, junior high, and high school; we were on the same football and wrestling teams since 8th grade; we ate lunch together almost everyday of high school; we sat on the back of the wrestling bus every trip since the 7th grade. Through all of this we shared so much.

I remember when John was in my 3rd grade class with Ms. Schmidt. One day in art class John drew a picture of a bike racer performing a stunt on his bike. I told John how I wished that I could draw like that and then complained about my messy drawing. John looked at his drawing, erased his name from the top of it, and then gave it to me, saying that I could turn it in under my name. John quickly drew another picture and hung it up on the wall. With my name on John's drawing, I took first place within our class. All the other students praised the drawing with my name on it and even though it was John's, he never said a word. The point of this story is that John, even as a 9-year old kid, took more pride in making other people feel better than he did in taking credit for his talents.

John's care for me did not end there. In high school, he revised (sometimes even wrote my papers for me; he taught me calculus when my math teacher couldn't get anything across to me; he briefed me on almost all of our English readings, because I was too slow of a reader and couldn't get my work done on time. It wasn't just in school that John helped me either.

During wrestling season when I was constantly dieting, John would wait to eat his lunch in the locker room, even though he was used to eating it with me in one of our classes. He knew that since I couldn't eat, it would starve me even more to see him eat. Moreover, John was always there for me. I constantly came to John with relationship, academic and basic life problems. I always knew that John was much more mature about everything and he could provide me with sound advice, which he always did. I would sit and complain to him about *my* problems for hours and he would just listen. Sometimes he wouldn't say anything and sometimes he would. Either way, I always felt better after talking to him. He was one of my best friends and I knew he would always be there for me.

Having said all this, you may be thinking that the only reason I liked John was because he helped *me*, but it wasn't just that, it was the unique, funny and intelligent sense of character John carried. I remember how incredibly smart John was. I would sit next to him in class taking notes constantly and he would be reading a book. When test time came, John would score a 100 and I would get a 75. Somehow he just knew it. He knew everything, whether it was math, history, English, you name it.

But John's intelligence was not limited to just academics. John, like no one else that I have ever known, could sense things about people. He could tell if someone was sad or was having a bad day and then would say something like "what's up man? Do you need to talk or something?" It was stuff like that that made John different than everyone else and it is the way I will always remember him.

As I said before, it makes me sick to think that I knew John for 12 years and never once told him all this. It makes me feel even worse that I rarely spoke to John over the past 2 years since we graduated from high school. Of course, it was difficult since we were so far away from each other, but I should have made the effort to continue contact, not John. John was the person who had taken care of me since we were little kids not just by giving me pictures, but also by being there for me when I needed him. However, when I left for college, I rarely made the effort to even e-mail him or call him when I came home for breaks. And now that John is gone, I can never make up for it. I can only pray he will forgive me.

As his family, I am sure that you have had many of these same thoughts; it is natural for everyone's family to do so when it has lost a loved one. You probably wish that you could have said something to John before he passed away or rectified a minor issue that was not settled amongst you. You must remember, however, it is not what you didn't do in just the past couple of weeks of his life, it was what you did throughout all of John's life. I personally know that you were a wonderful family to John and that he loved you all very much. I know this because he told me. He would always talk about how highly he thought of his Dad and the accomplishments he has made in life. He always talked about how his mom's cooking was the reason why he was such a big man. We also talked about what wonderful families we came from and how lucky we were to have parents that would always be there for us. I knew John very well and I know that he would never trade any of you for another family, not for anything.

As I said before, there are many things that I would have liked to tell John when he was alive. However, that is impossible for me to do now. My only sense of comfort is the fact that everything happens for a reason. Consequently, the only way for me to cope with John's death is to always remember the lesson I have taken from all this: You should never waive anything that you need to say to someone that you love. Although this is a difficult way to learn this lesson, it may have been the only way. For this reason, I will never again keep my feelings away from anyone that I love or that has helped me. I will do this because of John.

I will never forget John and how he affected my life. As his family, you must, as I know you are, be proud of John's accomplishments and the wonderful person he was. I know I will be proud just to be a friend of his.

Love,

Dan

This letter was brimming with so much sentiment. I had remembered Dan and his parents. They saw John as John, a unique individual and I could only admire Dan for who Dan was, an articulate fellow who was impacted by his friend. *I wonder if I have any friends who could say I had an impact on their lives. We all think we are good people, but when it comes right down to it, did I really impact anyone's life?* I quietly made a promise in my heart that I would try to make an impact.

I could not concentrate at work after that first week back. I took three days off over those next few weeks to grieve and regroup. I was tired and sick, although the bronchitis and sinus infection were lessening. I sometimes felt so fatigued I couldn't get a good start in the morning. I fought it, but didn't have the strength or self-discipline to force myself to overcome the pain.

During those days off, I would hurt. I would wander around the house. I would sit in church, or pray at the lake. I was constantly restless. Memories and mementos would trigger bizarre thoughts and emotions. I'd see his picture, pick up his watch, sit on his bed, look through his music, or look at his car. Sometimes there would be a memory, sometimes no recollection other than whatever it was, it was his. I replayed his death, moments we didn't see eye-to-eye, moments of great triumph, writings, past events, on and on the grief would come, wash over me and cleanse me.

It came in waves and washed ashore, then receded. Some waves would swamp me, others would create a lingering effect, some were dull, others intense, but I dreaded them as I felt them coming on. Yet I eagerly anticipated them as it was like a wave washing the shore clean. The grief was cleansing and refreshing and it proved I wasn't forgetting John. It hurt so much, yet felt so good.

I would ponder our relationship. I thought how things would be different if he was still here. Just having him around was always good, even if he was on the phone or reading.

His humor, sports knowledge, music, video games, playing with the dogs, reading, eating, travel, desire to have cool clothes and a car and jobs all made up who John was. I missed those things so much. I had taken much for granted and shown too little appreciation. While I felt bad at times, I also knew that we had a good relationship and related well and communicated. I cherished that last night over and over again. I watched the videotapes of him wrestling and playing football and viewed the tape of the mission's trip that he and Scott accompanied me on to Poland and Germany. Those two guys were in their glory as one night they got to sing back-up vocals for a rock band.

I felt God was changing areas of my life inside me and preparing me for the future. It felt as if God was using John's death to prepare me for the unknown. I caught myself throughout the day and night thanking

God for the blessings of having John with us for twenty-one years.

I had heard others tell me of the anger I would experience towards God and the "Why" questions, but none of that happened. I was so thankful John did die mercifully and quickly and without weeks or months or years of suffering. And the peace I received the moment John died, stayed vividly in my mind. He was with God in heaven.

It was such a privilege to experience God blessing John eternally. I was learning what a sovereign God really meant. Sovereignty is a great attribute to believe in, but very few people, I have learned, especially when it comes to death, truly believe God is sovereign. I either had to believe or not believe; there was no compromise. I believed without a doubt in God's sovereignty.

One morning during my devotions I sensed the revelation that one of the most amazing truths of God comes when we learn that God is in the common things and His deity is realized in the common things. I would look at the current day and then replay back the timeline of events to recapture the freshness of the sequence. God wasn't just in miracles or crises, He was in the common, every day details. Regularly, those details hurt, yet I was afraid I would forget what God had done, so I forced myself to think about them.

I found real emptiness in missing John so much. Every day I missed him more. I had traveled for business for years and had gone on mission's trips, and John had traveled and had been away at college, and lived on his own for a few months. Yet this missing was total. The simple reminders-popsicles, lasagna, his picture on the football button, his year book, his wrestling towel and his empty chair were constantly in my line of vision or memory.

I missed talking about sports and money and cars and the future and career and football. I missed him foraging through the refrigerator and cabinets, him barbecuing and cooking Mother's Day dinners.

God was at work teaching me lessons. I found there was no way I could anticipate a wave of grief coming, nor control the intensity of it. What was valuable early on was that I quickly learned when the wave struck, if I kept focused on God and prayed, the grieving was painfully refreshing. If I took my focus off God and put it on myself, feeling sorry or being a victim, I would spiral down deeply and feel a deep unrest, almost as if my emotions wanted to make me feel unworthy.

Pastor Roger's words on clean grief grew larger as the waves continued and being authentic took on a spiritual perspective. I knew people were watching and listening. I knew some people were avoiding us and others were seeking to help. I knew some didn't know what to do or say. I gained a deeper peace accepting that what I was experiencing was normal and real and that it was okay. I knew some people had questions and were struggling for answers and didn't understand God and were almost requiring an explanation as to why. I, in turn, simply lived hour-to-hour and day-to-day with a few minute-to-minute intervals, relying on God to help us through it.

Each day I would receive a portion of peace and joy and faith and comfort from God, just as the children of Israel received a daily portion of manna. And each day I was given enough manna to last for a day. In the grieving process, God blessed us with enough strength and faith and peace to last just enough for the day. Sometimes I was near panic thinking I couldn't go on, but He always provided enough blessings and faith to persevere.

I began calling my portion of daily coping strength as "Elijah's oil." In the scriptures, it told of a story where Elijah invited himself to stay at a widow's home. She had a son and was planning to make the final bread cake and she and her son would eat it and die. Elijah promised her as long as he lived at her house, the grain and oil would never run out. There would always be just the right amount. As my days wore on for my family and me, we realized that God was giving us just enough faith and perseverance to handle the grief. We received our daily portion of Elijah's oil and somehow we were making it through each day.

Oil of grace, gospel grace…God was revealing His grace more deeply and I was finally understanding. It was awkward relying on God during this time, because so many people offered us the opportunity to rely on them. Yet our faith grew in living through each day. No one can learn how to grieve by reading a book or discussing it. One has to experience grief and suffering to appreciate it and understand it. Words describing God such as omniscient, omnipresent, and omnipotent grew in stature and depth of meaning as I realized that only now did I comprehend the attributes of God.

I had thought I truly believed in God's character, but each day I realized how superficial it had been. Now my understanding grew deeper, higher and wider. My relationship with God grew more on who Christ was and who I was in Christ. I was also learning about the need for a balance between what I do and how God plans. Unconditional love was showing me God's position and John's position in God and it was so reassuring. Daily I grew more thankful that God was allowing me to learn His truths.

I saw a revival in Scott, a steadiness in Ben, a deep inner strength in Adrienne and a loving and supportive woman in Beth. I wasn't sure what they saw in me, but I saw who they were in Jesus. I concluded now, that with John, that nothing really mattered except his relationship with Christ and that was the same that mattered for me. The entanglements of each day became minor as I sought Elijah's Oil.

REFLECTION

Yet another lesson from the past. God's word never changes in the wilderness, even though the scenery does change. Whether it is work, family, school, letters, or relationships, death never is forgotten or minimized. There are times you want to get busy and forget or pretend everything is fine. But that is when other factors you hoped would be a substitute for grieving only compound the situation and create irritation, remorse, self-pity and desperation to simply get out of the forest. But you can't. You never really get out of it. How best would you cope with returning to life after a death, knowing the rest of the world is moving on and you are trapped in a wilderness?

CHAPTER TWELVE

Friends seek you out in the wilderness -- three weeks after

Two weeks after John's death, Dave and Lynette Treibwasser called us and invited us to accompany them to the Minnesota Gophers-Wisconsin Badgers basketball game. Dave and I had coached our boys in Stockade basketball for a few years. Dave had a great heart for young athletes and he had the opportunity to coach Ben and Scott. He and his wife were also attending my Sunday School class. I felt awkward getting out in public to do something fun. I wasn't in the mood to enjoy basketball, but it was a Saturday night and I knew it was best for us to start doing more than struggling with grief. Dave and Lynette made us feel comfortable and we had a very pleasant evening. I caught myself talking about the recent past as if I was mentoring or teaching someone as we conversed. I sank emotionally, realizing I was inadequate to simply articulate what was going on in my mind. The evening with Dave and Lynette was God's way of sending His love and encouragement.

Somehow I forced myself back to work on a more regular basis. The first week was a two day stint. The next week, three, and eventually I made it through a week. It was a major accomplishment when I made it through the whole week. Week two seemed to be a series of cruel coincidences. I would answer my phone calls and for some reason the people calling had no idea that John died. I had one individual who was extremely negative and personal because he felt our company had done him a great injustice and he was going to tell everyone in his path that it was their fault. After about forty minutes in which I listened without saying more than ten words, he lost interest and hung up the phone. And to be honest, I couldn't have cared less.

I remember sitting at my desk looking into space with the phone against my ear. *I really need this. I have no control over what has happened; he isn't interested in me helping or possibly knowing I can't help him. Plus, he couldn't care less about me. If he only knew. I wonder if it would even matter? Here's a professional earning half a million dollars a year and he's whining as if the world owed him something.*

Instantly as the thought of money hit me I sensed there was a deeper animosity. I recognized it within seconds. I was not only upset with his attitude and cutting words, it was the fact he was so arrogant about how much money he was earning. He treated me as second class. Because he had money, I should look at him as some favored species. After I hung up I dwelled on my attitude. It started to unfold. I had been asking God to show me the areas of my life where I was biased and conditional in my love. This was definitely an area. It wasn't as though I was jealous of wealthy people, or envious. I stiffened when I saw people use money as though it was more powerful than God, and I assumed if they had money and I didn't, then I was someone lesser in their eyes.

I half-attempted to confess my conditional love problem to God. I couldn't. I knew it was the right thing to do, but I was too insincere and my confession would only be an act and not a sign of repentance. The phone episode started a sequence of events where I knew God was testing me to see if I truly sought to repent from my conditional love, or if I was only blowing smoke.

A few weeks later, a brother in Christ, David Pierce, a missionary with whom I had shared ministry came from New Zealand and spent a few days with me. I marveled at how God brought the proper person into our lives at the proper moment. Friends, pastors, colleagues, and family somehow had this unique orchestration that was divinely appointed. When one arrived and fulfilled their purpose and departed, there was always someone else to step in. It felt like God had established a relay race team. Each person had a leg to run and a torch to carry. David was the next relay runner and torchbearer in our race.

Every morning and evening and at least four or five times each day, I found myself thanking God and telling him I loved Him. This always occurred after each torchbearer departed. God used the torchbearer, David, in some very profound ways.

David had a speaking engagement at Northwestern College - a Wednesday evening service. He invited me along, telling me I had to get out of the house. I reluctantly accepted. The first 20 minutes of the service were very difficult. My mind wandered. *Everyone was John's age, all worshipping, all fired up and cheerful. I'm so sad. John hadn't had a good college experience. He got injured and didn't make the football team. He started as the heavyweight wrestler for University Wisconsin-Eau Claire but was hurt and had a losing season. He was lonely, didn't like the party school, and academically he wasn't focused.* I cried in the chapel and spent the time hiding my grief from others. I doubt if anyone noticed. They were focusing on God. I was focusing on myself.

Then God spoke to me as we were in the midst of the worship time. *This is what John is doing in heaven. He is worshipping. There are no more* struggles, injuries, frustrations or worries. He was in heaven, worshipping. My peace and joy grew, thinking of what he was doing. The grief left me. God had spoken comforting words. I stood amazed through the remaining singing, staring at the worship band, humbled and comforted, basking in the afterglow of God's intimate wisdom.

David spoke to the thirsting crowd. His teaching always has a special anointing and this night was no exception. Except that his words paled in comparison to hearing God speak. John was worshiping in heaven. He is filled with joy and peace; he has made it. My attention left the room. *It is I who remains in this world, an alien as the scriptures say, but not an orphan. John was able to go to the place Jesus prepared for him and promised him. He just was blessed to go there earlier than me.* Spiritual fruits of love, joy and peace filled me to overflowing. I was learning what true worship was. I needed to learn it; I would be spending my eternal life doing it.

It was during David's visits that I experienced a new change in mourning. I had been grieving and struggling for days and people were always there. As the daily well-wishers dissipated, I was alone more each day with less interruptions. I prayed and meditated daily, sometimes hourly. I found the scriptures to be comforting but dry, and I was too easily distracted. But certain words and verses starting making a deeper impact. Two verses stuck out in my readings.

Romans 14:7-9 *For not one of us lives for himself, and not one dies for himself; for if we live, we live for the Lord, or if we die, we die for the Lord; therefore whether we live or die, we are the Lord's. For to this end Christ died and lived again, that He might be Lord both of the dead and of the living.*

Ps 57:1-5 *Be gracious to me, O God, be gracious to me, for my soul takes refuge in Thee; and in the shadow of Thy wings I will take refuge, until destruction passes by. I will cry to God Most High, to God who accomplishes all things for me. He will send from heaven and save me; He reproaches him who tramples upon me. Selah. God will send forth His lovingkindness and His truth. Be exalted above the heavens, O God; let Thy glory be above all the earth.*

David and I hung out for a few days, doing little but relaxing as friends. I had a brother in Christ, who cared. God spoke through him. He talked about how John's death impacted him, as he has two boys in their late teens. He had seen John grow up over the past 14 years. John had taken part in some of David's dramas and concerts. David hurt and he knew I hurt and he felt it was his job just to be there with me. And he was. It was humbling. God prompted a missionary from New Zealand to spend time with me during the dark season. God's sovereign hand was upon me. He had spoken good news to the poor.

David would come over for dinner and we'd spend time together and we'd go for coffee, or watch a video. He'd call me and we'd go for a ride. We'd go to radio interviews, meet people in restaurants or talk on the phone. I was slowly stepping back into the regular world, but I had to focus on readjusting to it. I had grown too accustomed to mourning on my own, withdrawing or talking one-on-one with people. I found crowds irritating, small groups too personal, and I grew self-conscious when I walked into settings where people knew. I still didn't know what to say and in most cases neither did they. Somehow, we melted into one group. Minutes, hours and days passed, and I was living in a shroud with the world flying by me.

What intensified as I returned to my normal daily activities was my loneliness. People who had been close to me and very supportive and helpful in the past backed away. I found myself perplexed by this behavior. I truly needed them to help me. I was confused when people who only a few weeks or days earlier had offered to do whatever we needed, now distanced themselves.

I felt sad for them as I could sense what was happening. Life had to go on. People had taken time out to offer sympathy and support and had stepped in when needed. Now there was more of a, "Let's give them time and space and not expect anything until they are ready" attitude. I wanted to move forward but they didn't.

Beth and I would speak often about how difficult it must feel to them. I felt like when I was in school and broke up with my girlfriend. Nobody was sure what to do or say. Everyone was hurting, not just my family, and I had to be patient and understanding. My friends and colleagues were dealing with something completely foreign to them.

I prayed for divine intervention. I prayed the Holy Spirit would bring conviction to me about those around me and take away the strain and tentativeness. I read in a devotion, "God does not give me overcoming life, He gives me life as I overcome." In Ephesians God says, "Arise from the dead." I have to get up. He does not always come and lift us up at our hurtful times. Sometimes He wants us to use His power to lift ourselves up.

On this day, grief hit me particularly hard early and I shut down and took the day off from work. I had mistakenly done some research on the internet on Acute Hemorraghic Pancreatitis. I slid into remorse as I realized I didn't know how painful and destructive the illness was. I also experienced relief and thankfulness that God was so merciful and took John home before too much suffering occurred. I read testimonies of Chronic Hemorraghic Pancreatitis patients and they were horrific. Lives were ruined, for some as many as twenty years. John could never have handled that well. Neither could we.

My daily devotions were very profound and the life source of my day. One devotion spoke of despair and how I needed to overcome apathy and lethargy, which was very deeply entrenched some days. I knew I had to trust God completely to rebuild my life and the lives of my family. Each day brought a new test as well.

The day the Death Claim Form arrived for my signature in order to receive John's insurance benefit was traumatic. Not having a large policy on John but making sure all expenses would be covered had been my primary goal each year with my benefits package. I believed in insurance and risk protection, but never thought I'd need to use it with a child. I did the obligatory duties, never believing it would be a prudent step of stewardship. I was both very glad and very sad that day.

REFLECTION

Would you be one of those friends who go into the wilderness to find a friend? Knowing the wilderness may be scary, sad, dismal and plain ugly, would you go in there and minister? Or will you wait for someone else to do it?

CHAPTER THIRTEEN

30 days in the wilderness -- one month after

I looked at my journal. It was February 21st, one month since John's death. As I prayed during my regular time in the darkness of the morn, my emotions were simmering. We were all struggling and every day each of us had to somehow manage to keep ourselves from unraveling and giving up. I found the old axiom true. If I kept my focus on God, I was able to overcome the grief. If I focused on myself, I would struggle deeply with hopelessness. The simmering episode was my own doing that morning. I was alone, hurting, worrying, confused and enshrouded with a harassing spirit.

I was feeling low, thinking about how hard it was to sign the death certificates, handling the death claim for John's life insurance and dealing with the medical bills. I focused on myself and started comparing all I was doing with how Beth had disengaged herself from these tasks.

In truth, I tried to shield her from the morbid tasks, but now I was feeling slighted. We weren't doing well taking care of the thank-you cards, memorials and follow ups. We rarely argued over the years of our marriage and never were angry at each other for more than a few minutes. We weren't arguing or angry now, but there was a tension between us.

On my own, I was beginning a new set of negative emotions. I was dwelling on why I had to do the difficult jobs. Plus, Beth seemed to have much more support from her friends than I did. It wasn't that people didn't try to support me. I often withdrew and grieved on my own with God, purposely not seeking intervention. Beth, on the other hand, was a part of choir and other ministries where the women stayed close. I was struggling with reality, with reason and with loneliness. Beth and I had weathered much, but I was looking at her as taking advantage of me. She truly wasn't, but I would distort the conditions and crawl into my cave of anguish.

As I fought to focus on God during this time, I felt the tears come. The futility, the anguish, the remorse, guilt, disbelief that the death occurred, and the loneliness felt like intense heart throbs every day. This morning it was more intense. *That's it, I'm staying home from work! Work doesn't matter, I don't matter, nothing matters. What difference does it make? I can fake it or succumb to it, but the facts are, I can't handle the truth today.*

Each day I prayed that the enemy strongholds would not attack. I knew the areas of my life where I struggled with sin. At times they would rise up as if a spiritual attack was occurring. For years I knew what could trigger an attack. It usually started with my pride and turned ugly. Sometimes I spiritually declared war and felt the presence of the Holy Spirit clothe me in armor and experienced victory. Sometimes I fought on my own and lost. Sometimes I gave in and lost the battle before it started.

Overly sensitive during grieving, I was far too vulnerable, so I knew when the grief came, the spiritual attack was right afterwards if I kept the focus on myself. Weaknesses of the flesh, temptation and insensitivity to the Spirit always doomed me. Anguish bred anger. I stayed as long as I could in prayer, living in my sanctuary of despair. Some days I conceded defeat and succumbed to the grief and stayed away from everyone except God.

I observed my wife and children over that first month. They were sad, sometimes angry, but they seemed to be handling their grief well. We all had our bad days and each of us grieved in our own ways and at our own times. I thought my children were handling it well, but in reality they hurt greatly and only afterwards did I know they struggled and lost focus in school. Grades and graduation suffered. But Beth and I knew none of us could simply go on as if John's death was just another event. So we decided to support our children by loving them and gently nudging them now and then but not pushing them. I knew how bad they felt, regardless or whether they showed it or shared it.

There were days at work when I'd leave my desk and wander through the Minneapolis skyways in tears, walking nowhere, unaware of my surroundings, too immersed in my broken-heartedness to care about anything. I knew my children had to sit in classrooms, study, learn, and take notes and tests. They couldn't get up and deal with their grief in openness or when they needed to. High school wasn't a good place to be in mourning. The workplace wasn't a good place to deal with mourning, but our children didn't have the freedom we had in our workplace. We hoped and prayed for our children.

Adrienne, the strongest committed Christian of our children, seemed to be handling it best. Scott was seeing God at work in his prayers and we talked about how he was doing. I was encouraged about Scott. Ben, though, was avoiding us and any conversation about John. He was angry and hurting. He had moved into John's room and wore some of John's clothes. That wasn't anything new. Ben always borrowed and tried to wear his brother's clothes. He left the room the way John had left it, clothes lying everywhere. Scott struggled with sleeping at night because when John was sick, he slept in the bunk in Scott's room. We tried to be supportive and understanding, but our children never showed much willingness to talk over things on an extended basis. We had to be there and support them when the opportunities arose.

David Pierce continued to call, and my brother Paul and my mother and younger brother Tom, stayed in touch. Those calls were a great help; reminders that we weren't alone. Beth had numerous friends calling her and we kept receiving cards, letters, treats and meals daily. I grew more dependent upon God as I saw how He was working every day, often differently from previous days.

I loved the relationship I was having with God. The scriptures took on a deeper, more profound meaning. I read the Bible voraciously. I found the scriptures would refresh me, and never completely leave my thinking throughout the day. It was as if the grieving made my mind sharper and more attuned to God's word and voice. Certain verses stayed with me for months after I read them.

Job 19:25-27 *"And as for me, I know that my Redeemer lives, and at the last He will take His stand on the earth. Even after my skin is destroyed, yet from my flesh I shall see God; Whom I myself shall behold, and whom my eyes shall see and not another. My heart faints within me.*

God was telling me the truth; comforting me with His scriptures. He wanted to inform me. He wanted me to know the truth, to know He hurt for me and that He cared. Another hour passed by as I studied. It was as if God was talking to me, teaching me as if I was sitting in the temple hearing His words. Before, when I read scripture, I would often lose focus or my thoughts would wander and I'd fight to keep focused. It was like having a conversation with someone and suddenly they get dull or overly analytical and you're looking at them but not really paying attention.

But this time was different. For hours it was if I was having a special meeting with the writers of the scriptures and God was there, not in person but in spirit. I may have been inattentive in the past, but now it was a joyous occasion, not a discipline. Nothing was forced. It didn't feel like studying. It didn't feel like I was reading. It was more like hearing speakers at a quorum on death and grief and hope and promise.

What a privilege it was to be an audience for God! I was being taught by the Master. I sensed my "standing on Holy Ground" phenomenon as I had the moment John died. It wasn't as intense, but it was as glowing in the revelation that God was present. This started a series of master classes over the ensuing weeks, where my devotions took on a transforming enlightenment.

Beth handled her time with God in her own way and was probably more at ease with the truth and the events that occurred. She accepted it all very well after that first night. I accepted it as well, but there was this burning desire to get to know God during suffering that made me pursue Him. I wasn't looking for answers, I was simply seeking the comfort that truth bears.

Adrienne, Ben and Scott came in and out of the suffering and I wondered aloud what it must feel like for them to have a brother die. It helped me understand that we all were experiencing death differently and the answers didn't matter, only the truth did. And the truth made us all move on to the next day. Elijah's oil still flowed.

I couldn't forget my children were going through life style changes as well as grieving. Ben was interested in playing college football and he was getting calls and letters to visit the schools and meet the coaches. The first school Ben wanted to visit was the University Wisconsin-Eau Claire, John's college. We made plans to visit the school with a teammate, Adam, and his father.

I dreaded the 90-minute drive, because I kept remembering the drives back and forth for John. A March thaw descended on the campus snows as we parked in the lot adjacent to the field house. We entered the field house. I felt the pain come, remembering that the last time I was in the field house was to watch John defeat his opponent in a wrestling match.

Now the main floor of the complex was empty and dark, mirroring my heart. We gathered in a room with a half dozen other recruits and we heard a variety of speeches and saw a highlight film. Then each parent and son had the opportunity to meet individually with the head coach. When it was our turn, we walked through the doorway into the coach's office and there in the corner was a mannequin dressed in the Blue and Gold of the Blugolds, the nickname of the team.

The gold helmet shook me deep into my memories thinking about the spring game John got in for a few plays. Beth and I had watched attentively as he went through warm-up drills with a hundred or so other Blugolds. Nursing an ankle injury, he hobbled and had limited range of motion. I felt sad for him, knowing he never missed a game in four years of high school and here in his first attempt at college ball, he wasn't one hundred percent.

My mind drew me back to the details of that day. The intra-squad game had started and immediately I could see the difference of size and speed in the athletes over the high school players I was accustomed to. "John is going to have his hands full in this game," I softly conceded to Beth. But it was a warm late summer afternoon and it was football, so I was completely entertained. *What's a Blugold?* That question popped into my head a few times, but this was college ball and I was seeing my son playing college ball, so I wasn't seriously looking for an answer. I was so proud of him.

John finally got in for a series of plays at defensive tackle. He hobbled but hustled and we were so thrilled. It didn't matter how he did, a Chaya was playing college ball! My dream had become reality.

We had talked over the two weeks he had been gone to college preseason camp and how he was hurt early in the first week and struggled to heal. We encouraged him and prayed for him, knowing it was his first time away from home and he was against heavy odds to succeed, and then being hurt made it more difficult. But he always hung tough.

As my mind returned to the coach's conversation, Ben and the coach interacted and the staff was very interested in Ben playing for them. I felt good and bad sitting there, not knowing what future lay ahead for Ben and acknowledging I'd never see John in a game again, something that I truly loved as his father.

The school would be checking Ben's grades and getting back to us the following week. Our meeting and interview ended and we cordially said our farewells. We departed from the office and met a couple of the ball players who took us to the dining hall for lunch and a tour of the school.

I felt happy for Ben. He seemed excited, but slowly as we made our way around the buildings the memories of John being there took my attention and I grew dismal. The dining hall was where John had his first college job. I looked around, thinking about how John spent his spare hours earning extra cash. We went by the dorm that John had resided in for a year. Instantly my sadness swelled, remembering the first day Beth and I had dropped him off at the school and helped him move in.

I flashed back to that late summer day in Eau Claire. As we got into the car to leave, John had looked at us as if he was being left behind in a new world and he didn't know what to do. We all hugged and said we loved each other and we slowly drove away as he turned and headed into his dorm. Beth and I drove in silence until we hit the interstate and she broke into tears. My eyes welled up as I missed him already and as we consoled each other, we conceded this was just one more step in growing up and "her baby was now in college."

Now, two years later, I looked at the same parking lot and felt the same emotions. Our baby was now in heaven. He was in a new world. I rode home in silence trying to make conversation, but I was devastated emotionally.

I fought to think rationally. I chastised myself. "Hey, get over it! Ben is opening a new chapter in our family and you have to close the chapter on John!" I said under my breath. But it was no use. Everything was still too fresh. I was defeated. This was one of those "first times since" and it caught me by surprise even though I knew it would be tough.

I found it easy to lose focus on a daily basis. Sometimes I would withdraw, too sad to talk over my feelings or my thoughts. I was comfortable being vulnerable and transparent. It didn't bother me to be seen crying or hurting. I felt ashamed being so open, but I was too humbled to do anything else.

I was experiencing a deeper passion and deeper understanding of life and God. Death had drawn me so near to God, and each devotion drew me nearer to understanding how God was working. I missed my son so much. I wanted to see him one more time. I had heard of people who lost loved ones. Some had visions, some dreams, some a sense of a presence. I didn't experience any of those phenomena. But through John's death I saw God more completely than ever before. Through John, I felt led by the Holy Spirit. I clearly understood my calling to feed the sheep and tend to the lambs and carry faithful people to their destiny. Two acts of being there for John solidified that calling. The first was when he accepted Christ and the second, when I held his lifeless body in my arms. I had fed and tended to this lamb and I had carried the faithful son to his destiny. But there was more. He was more than a lamb, he was a war horse.

REFLECTION

How can you compare thirty days to twenty-one years and feel so bad? Grieving makes days feel like years and plays tricks on your mind and heart. Everything in life becomes larger than reality. Death did that to me. It made life unbearable. No matter how strong one's faith is in God, or how strongly you believe in His plan, heartache makes logic seem irrelevant. Nothing seems to relate to each other. But God is always there. What would I do differently that first month of grieving? Nothing. It's something that you can't plan for or implement or change. Still, I would probably want to love my wife and children more if I could do it all over, because love overcomes all things.

Chapter Fourteen

Sixty days wandering and wondering -- two months after

It was early March and I had my first business trip planned for Orlando. It was a three day event in which four colleagues and myself would be meeting with some of the top financial advisors of our company to review the quality of advice from financial plans.

I arrived at the airport and was upgraded to first class. As I boarded, stowed my bags and buckled myself in my seat, the grief hit. Another "first time since" caught me by surprise as I buckled up and sat in 2D. It was the same seat number John had when we sat together on our return flight from Philadelphia last Christmas. I stared out the window thinking back to that flight. It had been a great vacation and as all of us got upgraded to first class, I felt like a father who had taken care of a providing a special treat for my family.

I kept my head turned to the window as if I was studying the gates and baggage handlers. I cried to myself and began thinking of the dread I would feel, being on my own for the next few days.

We took off. It was inspiring for me to see the vast horizon and expanse of the sky. Heaven. Heaven seems so big, so far away. *John is in heaven, so far away.* As I studied the sky, grief came. The sky took on a different dimension. God had created the waters and the earth and the expanse called heaven, but I didn't feel part of it all. John was somewhere I couldn't get to and the heavens looked so vast. That was the beginning of sadness that lasted a very long time every time I saw a sky, a sunset, sunrise, clouds or a starry night. John is somewhere far away. It is good he is there. I wish I was there, too.

As I took a shuttle to our hotel, I relived Typhoon Lagoon, Magic Kingdom and the Denny's restaurant where my brother Paul and I acted more like our children than their parents. Now I wanted to go home. The three-day trip brought a few new "first time since" and at times it was very unsettling. We were shuttled past a restaurant I remembered quite well from nearly ten years ago. It was a few months after my father had passed away, followed by the death of my grandfather only six weeks later. My mother decided we all needed to be together as a family and have some fun. So she arranged fifteen people to get together in Florida for two weeks, one week in Disney World, one near my younger brother Tom, near Bradenton.

As my bus parked at the hotel entrance, I departed sullenly and wanted to be alone. There had been so many good memories of Disney World and now it seemed unfair that I had to be there again, knowing it wouldn't be for wonderful new memories.

The next day was uneventful. We broke for lunch and had plenty of time to chat afterwards before the afternoon session started. I felt the waves of grief come as I walked away from my table and stood looking out over a lagoon.

There had been a recurring struggle for a few weeks, when I played out in my mind, if I was meeting a stranger and they asked, "How many children do you have?" I must have thought about that awkward question a couple of times each day. *He was, he is, he isn't. He was here for 21 years. He is in heaven. He isn't with us now. One day we will be together.* As the days wore on, I questioned myself. *Do I really believe that or am I saying it because that is what a Christian is supposed to say? God never let me down.* Every time that dilemma hit me in my doubts, God spoke in a whisper, reminding me what He did at the cross and what He did that night with John and with each moment after that for weeks. He would come at the right moment, before I had the chance to dwell too long on any doubts and He gently comforted me. In my mind I felt I had it all thought out. I found out how wrong I was.

That evening was a painful dinner as I encountered this question for the "first time since." The month of contemplating the question, "How many children do I have, how would I respond?" turned to reality. I had never came to a conclusion.

I was totally unprepared when a long time acquaintance, Nancy sat alongside me. She was very outgoing and likeable, so she was the energy of our group. I sat quietly listening and making small talk, but I remained fairly disengaged. Nancy picked up on this. She tried to get me included in the table chat and the inevitable occurred. "So Jake, how is that family of yours?"

Uncomfortably I responded, "They are fine."

"Fine? C'mon Jake, you have a bunch of kids, tell me how are they doing?"

Embarrassed and growing in discomfort, I mumbled. "They are okay."

"Okay," Nancy prodded, "tell me, how many children do you have?"

There it was. *What do I say? Do I have three or four? I don't have four now, do I? Yes, I will always have four. Do I say John died and make Nancy feel bad, or do I continue to act like an idiot?*

Somehow the look on my face was all Nancy needed to see. Realizing something was wrong, she put her hand on my forearm, nodded, and said, "it's okay". I finished dinner, opting out of desert, quietly thanked everyone for the evening, excused myself and returned to my room, totally distraught. I couldn't speak audibly. Finally, I prayed, *"Lord please help me. Be with Beth and the kids as they are alone now and we are separated. I need You, Lord. I love you and I know I can't go on without you."*

I felt sorry for Nancy as she didn't know, and I felt sorry for Beth being home without me and I felt devastated about myself. I wanted to go home. Was I pushing my business activity too soon? I argued with myself. I needed to come up with a way to respond to people who didn't know I was a grieving dad. I wrestled throughout the night trying to think of a way and replaying the dinner conversation over and over again.

I would have to approach Nancy the next morning and I knew I would have to keep myself together and not lose it. I called Beth and cried over the phone, feeling sad and sorry for myself and for her and for being unprepared (and for leaving her at home.) She was a great strength and her words were very comforting and refreshing. We prayed that we would have strength and courage.

As we gathered at the morning session, Nancy approached me and I could see she wasn't sure what to say. "Jake…."

"Nancy, I am sorry I wasn't able to talk to you last night, but I got caught off guard."

"I am very sorry, Jake, please accept my sympathy. I didn't know. Steve told me. I am so sorry."

She gave me a hug and we talked further about John and what had happened and how I needed to be able to answer those questions about my children. For the first time, I was able to tell a stranger what had happened and that the answer to the question was that I had four children, John, 21, Ben and Scott, 18 and Adrienne, 17. I then stated that we lost our oldest son a few months ago. It was hard to say at first, but it was also refreshing. The world had to know what heaven knew.

Later in the day, another long-time comrade, John Thomas, an advisor from Minneapolis who was one of the first people I met when I came to Minnesota, approached me during a break in the action.

Quietly as he stood over my shoulder, while I was sitting at a table, he asked. "Jake, is anything bothering you? You seem to be down, not yourself. Is something troubling you?"

"Thanks for asking, John. Yes, two months ago my twenty-one year old son died and this is the first trip I have gone on since his death. It has been difficult."

John stared at me, too stunned to speak. He just looked at me and I looked at him. "It's okay, I need time to adjust and not many people in the sales force know."

"I'm sorry, Jake," he said, as he put his hand on my shoulder. "Oh, that is terrible. What happened?"

I sat with my spellbound friend and explained the series of events. I could see he was very shaken and unnerved. I tried to stay light and give him an overview, but I knew anything I said would not soften the impact of death.

That night as we stood on the terrace of the Conservatory Hotel in the Magic Kingdom watching the fireworks, I withdrew from the crowd and observed them alone, remembering the nights I had stood with my family watching the fireworks.

I watched the pyro-tech finale and thought of the many things our family did and how much fun it was. Never again. Never will we be able to create a memory like that again. The last sparkler flashed and the sky went dark, matching my optimism for the future. *I would never have the chance to take John's children, my grandchildren, to Disney World.*

Back home, Beth had gone through some of John's old notebooks and put them on the table. Having returned home earlier that evening from my trip, I sifted through his doodling and graffiti. I ran across a short piece he wrote in a writing class in high school. I remember watching him compete in the wrestling tournament as a junior and talking to him about it, but seeing his words on paper captured more of his inner self and I was filled with deeper respect of what he had accomplished.

Going to State

It was Feb. 22, 1996, and I was sitting in the locker room at Richfield High school. It was 6 p.m., and I'd just returned from lunch and a quick nap at home after winning my semifinal match earlier in the day. I was to face Mike Stewart from Richfield in the finals. I felt pretty good about it as I was buttoned up my warm-ups and headed out of the locker room to the gym. He was 20-2 and I was 19-6, but I was rated sixth in the state.

I jogged a little in the hallway to warm up before I went out on the mat. I was a little nervous, but I always get nervous before I wrestle. My walkman was on full volume and my adrenaline was beginning to flow.

My coach came and brought me into the gym, and I took off my warm-ups and loosened up. My match was next.

We went out and went after each other right away. I scored the first takedown and then let him go. The period ended and I chose down. I got away to score another point, making the match 3-2. He took me down after thirty seconds, but I got away again, making the score 4 -4. The second period ended and he chose down. I couldn't keep him down for long and he scored another point to bring the score to 5 – 4. I took him down for another two giving myself a 6 – 5 lead. All I had to do was keep him on the mat and I was section champ and guaranteed to go to States.

He got away and we went into overtime with a 6 – 6 tie. I pushed him back and attacked his legs. But I missed and he scored a takedown to win the match. I put on my shorts and t-shirt and got out of the gym.

It turned out that I had one match left to qualify for States. I got all warmed up again, but I was more nervous. I was ranked in the state and still hadn't qualified for the tournament. I had to wrestle a kid from Wayzata who had sloppily made his way through the consolation tournament to get one last chance.

We got out on the mat and I realized two things. First, I had underestimated my opponent. Second, my finals match had completely drained me. The first period, which was very physical, but not very technical ended with a 0 – 0 tie. I chose down and got away to score the first point. After a minute we were both cautioned for stalling. Shortly thereafter, I was head-butted in the nose for the first time. I saw stars, but no big deal. I was cautioned for stalling and he was awarded a point. This happened due to the fact that I was so drained. After that, I was head-butted again. This time my nose broke. I saw lots of stars. Blood was everywhere. I was awarded a point and the match was stopped so I could get all the blood off me and get my nose plugged. My head was pounding and I just wanted to go home. But I had some business to take care of.

The second period ended without any more excitement. I was ahead 2 – 1. And I was furious. He chose down and I tried to keep him on the mat. He stood up, but I picked him up clear off the mat and brought him back down face first. His coaches went nuts, but after head-butting, the ref was on my side. He finally got away with a minute to go. I went after him, but I couldn't score. I was going into my second overtime of the night. The third period ended and we stepped back onto the lines for overtime. I was so tired. I felt like I was going to collapse. We started and I stepped into him and suddenly got a burst of energy. I threw his arm by, attacked his leg and took him down. Victory. I was going to States.

I got my hand raised and staggered off the mat. "I did it!" I yelled at my coach after sitting down in my chair. My head was spinning. I couldn't see straight and my nose was throbbing, but it didn't seem to matter. I made it to States.

I slowly folded the paper in half as I relived the match. I was so proud of John. He had made it to states as a junior. I knew he was tough, never a quitter. I knew he was a warrior with a champion's heart. He was a warrior poet.

We were so proud of all our children. Each one of them was an individual, God's unique creation. I had heard that term so many times, but at this moment it had a very deep meaning. No one on earth was like me, or any of my family, or John. God comforted me as I thought, *No one in heaven is like John.*

As Beth read the story I had handed her, the short message was almost a eulogy, a self-fulfilling prophecy. As in wrestling and now in his death, he had suffered, he had been hurt and he had underestimated his opponent. Yet he was a warrior with a champion's heart and he made it. It was a far greater achievement than making it to states. He had won the prize, heaven.

I had always admired his focus and commitment and loyalty to what he believed in. If a friend was in trouble or struggling, perhaps in the middle of the night, we'd hear John on the phone. Then we'd hear him going out, attempting to help who was in distress. John was John. The short story he wrote exemplified who he was. When he got focused, he was going to do what he had to do and very little ever stopped him. He knew how to take care of business.

It was March, and time for the 2000 state wrestling tournament. We struggled and then decided against going to it to root on the Eagles, who won the tournament for the second year in a row. Every time I thought about going, I hurt. Last year when John was home, we went to the tournament as a family and sat with the wrestlers and their parents and alumni. But now, it was all missing. We had a void and it couldn't be filled. We knew it would be awkward for us as well as the wrestlers and their parents, so we decided not to go.

Time marched on and I had to get on with life. I couldn't simply ponder disbelief, or withdraw, or pretend that all would be fine one day. Winter's cold would lead to spring's warmth and death would bring life in the seasons. But my walk with God and the question of how I was supposed to pray, or believe or worship seemed unsure, not because of doubt or unbelief, but simply because death was still so new to me. Nothing would ever be the same with God again and I was afraid I would lose my love and beliefs over time. Repeatedly I would think in three tenses: what life was like with John growing up, what was happening at the moment in present time and what was I to expect for the future?

We continued to talk with our children as we noticed they progressed through their hard times very differently and very unpredictably. Sometimes there was anger, sometimes, silence, sometimes good conversations. Often we talked about what happened, other times we relived the week, and other times we talked about God and how we were handling our emotions and getting on with life. I learned that for each of us, we rarely were able to articulate how we actually were feeling or what we were thinking. There are very few words one can articulate when going through suffering. Complaining brings no relief, crying is not comforting.

During this month, I explored the meaning of everything. I looked at people differently - my job, the meaning of life, purpose, death, vision, mission, missionaries, hope, and what I was supposed to be learning through this time. Grief was more an excruciating release of emotion and tension with great sadness, but it wasn't a trial or a test in my eyes. Life was patching moments together and trying to go through each day knowing it would be stretching and uncomfortable. Scripture that I had latched on to for years illuminated itself in my prayer and study. The Book of Isaiah filled my mind and my meditation.

Isaiah 61:1-3 *The Spirit of the Lord God is upon me, because the Lord has anointed me to bring good news to the afflicted. He sent me to bind up the broken hearted, to proclaim liberty to the captives and freedom to prisoners; to proclaim the favorable year of the Lord and the day of vengeance of our God; to comfort all who mourn and to grant those who mourn in Zion, giving them a garland instead of ashes, the oil of gladness instead of mourning, the mantle of praise instead of a spirit of fainting. So they will be called oaks of righteousness, the planting of the Lord, that He may be glorified.*

.........*giving them a garland instead of ashes.* I wrestled with my emotions and fought my thinking as my emotions mixed in. John was ashes. His ashes were at the funeral home and I was afraid to retrieve him. Every time the thought crossed my mind, I only followed up with the mental picture of the hearse slowly pulling away from the church. God hadn't given me a garland, a décor for praise. I was left with ashes. In the spiritual realm, I had no problem dealing with death and eternal life. It was faith, it was values, it was what I believed in. There were no doubts, no questions, no confusion. But in the physical, there were only ashes.

And the verses hurt more as they rolled on........the oil of gladness, instead of mourning. I was certainly glad John was in heaven. I couldn't image how I could live if I didn't know for sure that he was in heaven. But I certainly wasn't experiencing the oil of gladness. I didn't want to experience the oil of gladness. I was in mourning and didn't want to be anywhere else. Not once since John left us was I able to understand the oil of gladness instead of mourning. If I started out in mourning and tried to reason in gladness, it was forced and fake. I wasn't going to pretend. If I was having a good moment or hour, it wasn't the oil of gladness, it was a temporary reprieve from sadness and grief.

Somehow it seemed different from Elijah's oil of gospel grace. But just as there was oil for cooking, oil for making engines run smoothly, oil for producing skin softness and oil for manufacturing goods, there was Isaiah's oil and Elijah's oil. Oil for grace and oil for grieving.

But the verses didn't end, they proceeded further into my soul ....the mantle of praise, instead of the spirit of fainting. Okay, I thought, I can praise God. I am thankful and I sincerely do praise God for His plan of salvation. I had experienced it directly, but the mantle of praise only veiled the spirit of fainting. Moment by moment, I would feel spiritually, or physically or emotionally faint. I knew Satan was thwarted from attacking me and God's heavenly Host was protecting me, but fainting was always one step away. I can't go on, was my war cry for days, especially when I was alone.

I sought comfort in the truth, but the truth was too real. These scriptures didn't comfort me. They caused deep anguish. I was learning and re-learning the definition of anguish, my definition — utter helplessness and desperation with no words to explain the agony.

God was comforting me and teaching me and I kept asking him, "Lord, now that my son is gone, what is it I can learn from this? What is it you want me to learn?"

God was teaching me and each day the Book of Isaiah became more alluring in its truth and comfort. I would pray and meditate and study and recite verses throughout the Bible, but God kept bringing me back to Isaiah. I didn't understand it and some days it frustrated me greatly, but I kept searching. I knew that if I settled for less than God's truth, I'd make up my own truth and that would be the wrong route to healing.

One Saturday morning as I prepared for my Sunday lesson, I was attracted to Chapter 6 of Isaiah and God revealed to me a message. I had read this chapter many times and had heard many sermons and I think everyone knew the "Here am I send me!" response to missions invitations. But a new revelation came my way in the first few verses of the chapter.

What significance is it that the chapter starts talking about "the year that King Uzziah died?" I researched to see if it was simply a chronological benchmark or if there was some significance. I found the significance. Legends and some scholars stated that the prophet Isaiah was related to King Uzziah. Perhaps they were cousins. King Uzziah had favored Isaiah and appointed him as the courtyard preacher. And Isaiah was making a name for himself and his ministry. But as I studied on, the truth came. Perhaps God wanted this chapter starting out about the death of the king to point out something.

Perhaps Isaiah had been relying on Uzziah for his ministry credibility and authority. But with the king now dead, it appears God had removed the one obstacle from Isaiah that would change his ministry forever. Death brought Isaiah a vision. Death was not just a physical dying to self, but dying to that which stops us totally from fulfilling God's purpose. Isaiah became one of the most prolific prophets, the evangelism prophet, the forerunner carrying the news of the savior, all after Uzziah died. I cringed thinking the inevitable. *Did John die because God wanted me to look beyond my loves and desires to what God wanted me to do?*

Thoughts rumbled like distant thunder across my mind and the thunder grew closer with each passing thought. I was living moments of total contradiction. One minute I'd carry my line of thinking, then next challenge it. *What was God trying to teach me? Did John die because I loved him too much, even if I hadn't showed it?*

Was God telling me that sometimes a loved one has to pass on in order for God to take one to the next level? Had I been battling for so long with beginning ministries which were in favor of those around me, but I never had gone the distance and done what God truly wanted? Was there a new ministry coming? Was Isaiah released so his written words could release me? Was I making this up in my mind? Did I even have a clue what I was thinking? What was real?

Was this my ego talking, as if I was really somebody important? Or did God really have something for me that He was going to release me for? No, it wouldn't be an "Isaiah vision" but perhaps a liberating vision for me.

In the year of my son John's death, I saw the Lord sitting on a throne, ...
No , that wasn't correct!

It took me hours for the profound truth to reveal itself. The verses weren't about me having an "Isaiah moment," they were about dying to self and being crucified with Christ and not living for myself but Christ living in me. I had to surrender John. Deep within me I so cherished what John had been through the years that I tried too hard to make him successful. God proceeded to show me in detail how I tried to prepare all my children for success. They were my projects. I loved them and I poured everything I had emotionally and financially and socially into them. I wanted so much to be a good father that I actually stopped them from growing.

I shook with anger over my stupidity and willingness to compromise, thinking I was being the epitome of a good parent. I looked deep, I saw I had done ministry based upon acceptance of my children. I tried to be a role model, but everything was based upon my conditions. John's death changed all that.

Everything wasn't okay and I couldn't cover up anything. And God wanted me to be the person He created and not an illusion I created. Death wipes out illusions. Death wipes away the lies. Death wipes away the stupidity. All that is left after death is you and God. Isaiah 6 revealed that truth to me. It wasn't about great prophecy or great ministry, it was about death and freedom from the world and that which we create as idols in the world. Death was making me real. I was learning who I was, but more importantly, God showed me who John was and who John and I were, not on our conditions but His. I was learning who I was in Christ, not who I was in the world. I sat at my desk sobbing. For the first time I saw who John was in Christ and I was so guilt-ridden. *Why hadn't I seen who John was in Christ before he died?*

REFLECTION

This month was a crucial month in my grief. I was experiencing many "first times since," and it was much harder than I anticipated. Grief brings a whole knew dimension to loneliness and interacting with those who didn't know can be catastrophic emotionally. I wish I had been better prepared to meet people. I took my emotions for granted. It was becoming more evident though, that God was not allowing me to wander in the wilderness alone. Scriptures and the Holy Spirit were real and I was comforted greatly by them. One question I posed and continue to pose to God is this: Can a believer truly understand God's love and will without suffering?

CHAPTER FIFTEEN

There are too many trees in the wilderness -- three months after

I decided with the funeral director, to wait until April when the weather broke to retrieve John's ashes. It was now April, three months after, and I couldn't get up enough courage to retrieve John's ashes. We as a family had discussed what we wanted to do, but we couldn't make it happen. We had decided to place them at the Apple Valley High school football stadium under a memorial stone in the "Walk of Fame."

Ben thought we should spread the ashes over the playing field or at the spot John intercepted a pass in the Rosemount game at another stadium. We decided on the 'Walk of Fame" and also that some ashes would be placed under a willow tree and stone we would plant in our back yard, the "John tree, and the John rock."

The wilderness walk seemed to be overwhelming at times. I couldn't see the forest because of the trees. I couldn't experience life because of so much busyness. Too many trees to look at. I had emotionally recovered from the Orlando trip but was not looking forward to traveling. The pre-occupation of flying nearly 70,000 miles for the year blossomed with every phone call for business. I prayed for perseverance, "God, you comforted us and strengthened us each day. Now I need to plan my life for more than a day. I am more afraid of running out of "Elijah Oil" than I am about visiting my offices." God was faithful.

Beth, Adrienne, Ben and Scott were handling their daily schedule in their own way and they seemed to be progressing well. Receiving the death benefit from John's insurance allowed us to pay his medical bills and funeral expenses. Memorial monies continued to trickle in. The Apple Valley Coaches Fund received memorial gifts as well as the Steiger International Fund. Additional funds came to White Dove and they were disbursed for the work in New Delhi.

Scriptures continued to stream before my eyes almost every morning during devotions. God was gently transforming my desire to learn from His word. Regularly a simple verse would engulf me in a flurry of deeper cross-references and research. Occasionally a segment of a chapter would elicit a moment of comprehensive truth. Study and meditation continued to be special sessions with the Master. He was instructing me.

One of the significant truths revealed itself as somehow God had directed me to Isaiah 35. I had never heard of the "Highway of Holiness" and was intrigued and rewarded with a flow of living water as I read and contemplated that chapter. It leads us to hope. I was greatly edified and the words painted a picture of hope and peace. I treasured the words; they reassured me beyond what I had believed.

Isaiah 35:1-10 – Highway of holiness

The wilderness and the dry land shall be glad, the desert shall rejoice and blossom; like the crocus it shall blossom abundantly,and rejoice with joy and singing. The glory of Lebanon shall be given to it, the majesty of Carmel and Sharon.

They shall see the glory of the LORD, the majesty of our God. Strengthen the weak hands,and make firm the feeble knees. Say to those who are of a fearful heart,"Be strong, do not fear! Here is your God. He will come with vengeance, with terrible recompense. He will come and save you."

Then the eyes of the blind shall be opened, and the ears of the deaf unstopped; then the lame shall leap like a deer, and the tongue of the speechless sing for joy. For waters shall break forth in the wilderness, and streams in the desert; the burning sand shall become a pool, and the thirsty ground springs of water; the haunt of jackals shall become a swamp, the grass shall become reeds and rushes.

A highway shall be there, and it shall be called the Holy Way; the unclean shall not travel on it,but it shall be for God's people; no traveler, not even fools, shall go astray. No lion shall be there, nor shall any ravenous beast come up on it;they shall not be found there, but the redeemed shall walk there. And the ransomed of the LORD shall return, and come to Zion with singing; everlasting joy shall be upon their heads; hey shall obtain joy and gladness, and sorrow and sighing shall flee away.

I read in verse 8, "a highway shall be there, and it shall be called the Holy Way; the unclean shall not tread on it, but it shall be for God's people." God selected the words for me at that moment. I was grieving, yet I was smiling through my tears. God knew what I needed most, His comforting word. I didn't have to try to understand the theology, or pick up a commentary or concordance. It wasn't the words as much as the relationship.

It was a chilly spring morning in April as I closed my Bible, got up from my desk and wandered out onto the back porch. The dawn sun to the east pierced the purple, orange and white clouds, a stark contrast to the dark blue-gray skies of the west. (Filled with God's love, I stood motionless and senseless.) My heart had a fire growing as I surveyed the back yard and selected where we'd plant the "John tree" and lay a remnant of John at its roots. It was a fine moment to be a Christ-one. "Thank you Lord for being so merciful with John. Thank you for blessing us with him for 21 years.

I returned home from a trip and contemplated my mother's birthday and Beth's birthday, only three days apart. This was a "first time since," celebrating birthdays without John. John was usually the guy who got his siblings to at least get a card, or cook out or make sure everyone's schedule coincided for the birthday dinner at a restaurant. But now what? It would be painful for Beth as well as each of us. But it was Beth's special day.

We celebrated her birthday but it wasn't the same. It hurt. I could see at the table in our dining area, Beth was trying her best, but the empty chair immediately to her right would never be filled with her first born.

I sat across from her at our table with our children on both sides and thanked God in my birthday prayer, that His purpose for Beth was to glorify Him and one role was to be a mother. Her special purpose was to bring John into the world and now that his time was over, she would keep her purpose alive.

My next trip was to Boston. I have had a special love for the Boston area and the people that work for us there. My colleagues, nearly all fifteen, had supported my work and more recently sent flowers, memorials, notes, fruit, plants and cards during John's funeral. I struggled with seeing these friends because of my hurt in responding to all the questions.

My job was to help financial advisors document their advice to a set of quality standards. For most advisors, their clients didn't expect outstanding documentation. The frustrated cry of the advisor usually was, "Why spend much time on the documentation? Clients never read it anyway." This time I was ready for that remark.

"Many of us are corporate employees, correct?"

"Yes", they acknowledged.

"Well, you know our benefits package that we make choices on for our retirement plans, health and dental care — you know, the cafeteria plan? Well, every year we make choices. But corporate makes it easy. If we have no new choices or changes, we can call them in, fax or e-mail them in, or if we have no changes, we don't even have to respond. I had maxed out my benefit plans and have not had any changes for the past four years. This occurs in November and usually by December we get our documentation of benefits for the following year.

To be honest, I haven't read my documentation for years. I knew what was in them and had read company communications on features and changes, but no changes were needed. When I received the packet, I rarely opened it. I simply put it in my files. I only got the medical cards opened each year and ignored the rest."

I had the attention of the room, but only because it was a story. I hadn't said anything compelling and I wasn't sure how it was being perceived, but I continued.

"I was just like your clients, I didn't read any documentation, and so, I do agree, it was a waste of time and paper. For four years it was, until this past January when my son died."

Instantly, the room froze. There was an intense stare, almost a sense of being overwhelmed. I continued. "My son died on a Friday night, Jan. 21. A day later, suffering from shock and grief, I also faced the shame of incompetence. I started wondering if his health insurance and life insurance benefits were current. I wondered if the beneficiary designation was updated. And to top it off, I couldn't remember where I had placed the benefits package. I started to worry as I searched for it. I was chastising myself for being so lax.

"Eventually I did find my packet and reviewed the benefits, eligibility and designations. I uttered a prayer of relief to God as I saw that even though I hadn't done my job, the company's HR department had done their job, and had done it well."

I stopped in my presentation as I saw the power of the point in their faces. Later, during a break, Bob and Tim approached me. They congratulated me for the good presentation and Tim said, "Jake, what a powerful illustration. It may actually have been too powerful. We were all feeling your pain and wondering how you could even talk about John's death so soon."

Others followed and I knew I had accomplished two things. The illustration set forth a valuable lesson and it also made me feel good, that I wasn't forgetting about my son, but honored him by making him a part of my presentation.

I returned to Minneapolis, relieved. I would have a long weekend with Good Friday starting the Easter vacation. The past two weeks were very draining. Now I looked forward to a few days of rest and contemplation.

Good Friday morning opened with deep depression. The burden was overwhelming. I knew I was going to have a rough day from the start. I escaped to my lake sanctuary and stood on the shore of despair. I watched the sunlight bounce off the lake ripples, a gentle breeze pushing the spring warmth. I stood in the sand and looked at the Canadian geese, the wild ducks and a few gulls who made it south from Lake Superior. Birds were symbolic to me. To me, the bird represented the Holy Spirit. If only an eagle would fly by. "Lord, send me an eagle," I prayed.

I sat on the bench and contemplated God's truth. A profound truth had been revealed, again through the scriptures that I had read. -I have been crucified with Christ. It is not I who lives, but Christ who lives in me.-

This was the day Jesus died. The Son of God died for my sins, for John's sins. I believed it but so often I would claim the new nature only to revert back to the old nature. I struggled with that failure of the old nature. But now it took on a deeper meaning. John would never fall back into the old nature. He would live in peace and comfort and purity. He was the ultimate new creation. The old nature for him actually did pass away forever.

I thought about how brokenhearted God must have been on Good Friday. It was His plan for His Son, to die a horrible, painful death. At least John suffered less. I praised God for Good Friday. Jesus died so John could be in heaven. And John believed Jesus died for his sins so John was experiencing heaven, part of God's plan. I cried again as I walked the shoreline gently hearing the waves lap up against the beach. My heart was crushed and overjoyed at the same time. The crucifixion was so real to me. The cross was so real. The sacrifice was so real. Eternal life was so real. I loved the Easter scriptures. I clung to them, hoping that I would never forget the significance of God's plan. I returned home, peaceful over the episode I had experienced at the lake. I took the remainder of the day to soak in the magnitude of Christ's death.

That evening we went to our church service and the consequences of a day in solitude surfaced as I prayed before the service. My heart was overflowing with grief. I was experiencing death. Death in Jesus, death in John. Death in me. Everything had changed in these past few months.

I could only stare at the cross in our church sanctuary and cry. The worship service was obliterated by my grief and wonderment at dying, losing the old nature and being born again. For me it was supernatural. For John, it was physical and spiritual. The worship service ended and I couldn't move. I sat there crying, feeling foolish as people walked by. I was unable to control my emotions. Suddenly, there were others who I cannot remember sitting around me. I couldn't talk. I don't remember many people saying anything, but the spirit of God was there in His church.

Pastor Scott, Darrell and a few others prayed. I became more aware of the scene taking place. A small flock of God's children were ministering to us. My soul heaved with the groanings of the Spirit. I had no words. I had no comprehension. I couldn't speak. I could only hold on and experience God. He loved me. I actually felt God love me and His people didn't realize how dynamically linked they were. I was feeling God's love, directly in them and directly from Him.

Beth and I returned to the darkness of our home. Faint lamplight emanated from the living room. Pictures, plants and cards perched on desks and sills as gentle reminders. As Beth took the dogs out, I stood in the living room gazing at the emptiness. Still recovering from the happenings at church, I felt so alone, a dramatic contrast to only 30 minutes ago.

Easter Sunday was another "first time since." I anticipated a great worship time after having the profound Good Friday. Our worship service was held at a large Mall near our church because of the large crowds and our lack of space at the church. Beth sang in the choir, so I found a seat in the second tier, up front against the rail. To arrive there I had to pass many well wishers and I was polite, but pre-occupied. I wanted to find a seat and listen to the service. I wanted to hear from God. It was Easter. What would I learn today?

Pastor Roger had a very good message on hope and I sensed he was alluding to the deaths of John and a girl, John's age, who had died in a car accident, a short time after his death. The Holy Spirit was working in His words and they brought comfort.

As I drifted mentally from the Easter message, bathed in the Word, and music and the significance of resurrection, John kept filling my mind. Because Jesus died and rose from the dead, I knew John had died (but rose from the dead body) and met the resurrected Christ face to face. I had no idea how that meeting went, but I thought about how my meeting with Jesus would be. I looked forward to it and feared it at the same time. The glory of God filled me again as I realized John wasn't mourning this day. He was rejoicing!

I wondered what Easter Sunday celebrations were like in heaven. The spring sunlight poked through the mall skylight and flooded the area I was sitting in. I leaned forward against the rail and felt a hand on my left shoulder. It was Darrell. I knew he knew what I was thinking. I turned, reached up with my right hand and grasped his hand. The grasp told us all we needed to know. Our sons were in heaven because Jesus rose from the dead.

We gathered for our traditional Polish Easter dinner after church. It was another first time. We prayed over the food and the Easter baskets Beth had filled for each family member. One basket was made for John and his chair sat empty at the table. It was a good dinner and again the feast brought us together as we shared memories of past Easters. The Easter lilies we had purchased for John and placed at the worship service were now at our house, a reminder that we would never forget him.

We had a custom on Easter to "knock eggs" a Polish tradition of holding an egg firmly in your fingers with the pointed end outward and knocking another egg as we went around the table. One year one of our boys added a feature of knocking the egg against his forehead, which then became an ongoing ritual. It was recollections of these rituals that only a family can share and every time I lived through one of those rituals I could clearly see the purpose of why God created this family as He did. There was something about sitting around a dinner table that was cohesive. It wasn't about the food, it was about the individual presence of each family member, that only that family can identify with.

A flurry of phone calls came throughout the afternoon and evening. The glory of the day waned to the sadness of Easter without John. Every Easter evening since I could remember was a time I would reflect on the story of Jesus meeting the two men on the road to Emmaus. They didn't recognize who He was until after He was invited into the house for dinner and blessed the bread. I love the part about after He departed and how the men's hearts burned. So many times in the past three months I didn't recognize when Jesus was in my presence. I didn't understand until afterwards. But I did feel my heart burning, just like the men on that road.

A week later, Beth had the opportunity with our church choir to perform Brahms' Requiem together with the Bethlehem Baptist Church choir. The performance was held at Bethel College. I looked forward to going and it was one of the few times I'd get the chance to return to Bethel, as a graduate. The Requiem concert was performed in the Great Hall. As I took my seat I was impressed by its size as well as the crowd. I sat by myself, not wanting to be near anyone. As I read the program, I was drawn to the lyrics to the masterpiece. Primarily scripture, the words were deep.

The concert was excellent and one segment stood out for me. I was barely able to keep it together. It dealt with Death. I watched and listened. Beth was strong and so was Darrell. Their passion in singing was an outward expression of their following Christ. Their servant's hearts to my family reflected that passion.

REFLECTION

If you think your life is too busy and cramped with details, wait until death comes and preoccupies the busyness and details. It feels like a wet blanket smothering you. God is there, always. We simply lose focus. The unimportant things of life take too much of our time and effort to enjoy God's blessings. I realized that these months were the worst of my life, yet God was showing Himself in ways that I never experienced before. He was so real, so alive, so loving. Death was teaching me to look beyond life and see what God really has for us. Are you able to look beyond your day and see God? Do you hear Him standing at the door, knocking?

CHAPTER SIXTEEN

Surrender -- four months after

It was May and the moments of divine intervention and waves of grief seemed to be at the same intensity as the previous months. I was traveling regularly again. Isaiah's Oil and Elijah's Oil continued and I was constantly aware of them and how God was at work. My calls to Beth were better and we would console each other, she usually doing more of the consoling

A new fear started to emerge from a few seeds planted during the week of the funeral. I was becoming fearful that one of us was going to die. I fought through those times, but they seemed to surface more frequently. In some situations, when the kids weren't handling life very well, I'd think of the struggles John had and thought perhaps God would take them early. For my memories of John's death, John's last look and the presence of God actually seemed like something I was looking forward to. I was saddened, thinking how the rest of the family would feel if I died, but for myself, it was a good thing to look forward to.

The fears grew. I couldn't understand why I was so fearful. One day in a hotel room as I was locked into a prayer time, the agony of death threw itself full fury into my fears. I wept for over an hour. I leafed through scripture and through my tears read Isaiah 42:13. God was the ultimate life force with the absolute truths, and all I had to do was to see and hear.

Isaiah 42:13 *The LORD goes forth like a soldier, like a warrior He stirs up His fury; He cries out, He shouts aloud, He shows Himself mighty against His foes.*

In my spirit, God rose up. In my fears, God rose up. In death, God rose up. I read of His strength, His sovereignty and His power. I reread the scriptures. *How could anyone ever be a Christian and not believe totally in the Bible?* My fear was stopping me from understanding God's will. It was through the Bible that I came to an understanding. If God were to take Beth, Scott, Adrienne and Ben or me, all at once or one at a time, it was His sovereign will and I shouldn't fear. The intensity of the hour crescendoed in an emotional outburst. I was Jacob wrestling with God and was losing and hurting. All of a sudden the fear exploded. "Okay God. I concede. If it be your will to take my wife or my children, I accept that and believe it is best for me and those who remain here. I surrender. Your will is best. If their deaths make me the man of God you want me to be, then I will surrender them and surrender my fear. I trust You with everything, even the ones I love the most."

Peace came. I sat on my hotel room bed staring at the wall. "Have no fear, I will never leave you nor forsake you." My ears heard those words as if God had spoken audibly. All fear left me. It didn't return. I praised God. This huge burden had left me. Nothing mattered except that I knew God was faithful, and that I was His child and neither life nor death could keep me from Jesus. I continued to pray for well over two hours, mostly listening as God rebuilt me. I looked back over the years and realized consciously or subconsciously, that I had always feared the death of my family. I was afraid it would happen again, but now the fear left me.

For years, probably decades, I had done everything to avoid suffering and pain. That is only natural; it's human nature. I wasn't afraid to suffer; I simply calculated the amount of suffering and chose not to. But as I began my Christian walk 18 years ago, most of my new birth was filled with suffering. The Lymes Disease, the surgeries, the worry of paying bills, the inability to be a good father and husband, the missionary work, and my ministry at work were struggles. The deaths of friends and relatives caused pain. The conflicts learning to be a Christian, discovering and using my spiritual gifts, and the immaturity as I tried to serve and help were often difficult. I had lived the inner battle of spiritual warfare and the outer conflicts of that spiritual warfare.

For most of my life, though cowardly, I still led with my chin. It was the only way I knew how. Yet when I compared my situation to the suffering and oppression in India and Vietnam, I felt greatly blessed. It wasn't about finding comfort, but serving others, regardless of the consequences, the pain, the suffering. Would I pay the ultimate cost?

It was time to quit holding back. I was either going to totally believe or I wasn't, but there would be no compromise. It was time. I knew my calling, and my life purpose.

I knew the visions God had given me. Would I do something about them more than have them written down? I had feared not being accepted, being rejected by people and I was seeing the trap I had set for myself. I was too conditional. I had manufactured a little god. I was hung up on performance. I so wanted to be recognized, accepted and applauded for what I did and how I did it. That monumental morning's devotion changed all that. It was time to get out of my comfort zone and live and die for Christ.

Nothing mattered but knowing and following Jesus and obeying and believing. I knew then, that God took John from me so I would no longer dwell on the pleasures of watching him play ball or wrestle. I had incorporated into my lifestyle the expectations of perfect children, great accomplishments, success and the comfort and pleasures of them. I had done ministry, half-committed, because I wanted the joys of my children. I had set their lives up to succeed, but now I realized I was wrong. I lost John, the primary giver of that accomplishment and pleasure.

I hated the feeling of being a hypocrite and conditional lover. But that was me. I had to repent. But I couldn't. I had lost the passion to repent. With John gone, my comfort, my pleasure, and my conditional love were gone. It was time to take John's death and learn from it. I had to become something bigger and better tomorrow because God was something much bigger and better today. It would be difficult, but I knew there was no turning back. "God, bless me with wisdom and discernment to grow in You."

God used this time, as I began looking at new career opportunities. I believed God was going to give me a purpose and a cause to take my interests and passion beyond what I had been doing. He put this opportunity to me as a way to get my head back into the game and not obsess about John.

During this time, Beth had posted for a position as a full time administrative assistant in my department. I felt encouraged as she received an offer and accepted the job.

As a family we would be spending the middle of June on a mini-vacation at my brother's home in Florida. I thanked God for His hand being upon us. We knew the only hurtful upcoming event would be John's 22nd birthday on June 16. It would be a "first time since" and only a few days before Father's Day, another "first time since." In between Beth and I would have our 26th wedding anniversary on June 8th. The upcoming month looked like a great month. We anticipated the blessings and I felt God would richly bless us after having gone through a rough winter and spring.

We celebrated a quiet Memorial Day, a day of rest and reflection. As we thought of both of our fathers who fought in WWII and the many relatives who had gone on, we struggled with a newer meaning of a memorial. John.

I drove over to his high school and walked on the practice football fields and the shot put and discus areas freshly marked for the track and field competitions. He wasn't a memory to the students that now competed, but my memories were vivid. I trampled over the grass, contemplating how things could have been so much better, so different, so much more complete. I looked around at the pond, the baseball diamond, the stadium bleachers, the goal posts and the track. My life had been so blessed with sports. Never much of a competitor or a coach, I had just enough talent to be part of teams.

I quit thinking about all the what-ifs. It didn't matter. Would he have lived longer if he had received an athletic scholarship? If he had studied harder and had better grades, would he be remembered more? If he were everything I expected him to be, would I feel better or worse after his death?

Four months were gone now. Four months of deep grieving. Four months of life, with very little meaning in one sense and tremendous revelation in another sense. Life in this world meant very little to me. After the shadow of God's hand fell over me in that New England hotel room, the terror and the agony of giving my wife and children to God, even if it meant death, had scoured me. If I had no fear, no keepsakes, no desire other than following God, the pressure was off. There was freedom, complete trust and no purpose for me other than living my life for Christ.

God kept leading me back into the Book of Isaiah for His truths. The Isaiah Oil continued to be poured out. My thirst for the word remained steady and frequent. The moments I battled with doubt and confusion about death and heaven were infrequent but here again, I received the Oil of Isaiah. In Isaiah 43, there was redemption by name,

But now thus says the LORD, he who created you, O Jacob, he who formed you, O Israel: Do not fear, for I have redeemed you; I have called you by name, you are mine. When you pass through the waters, I will be with you; and through the rivers, they shall not overwhelm you; when you walk through fire you shall not be burned, and the flame shall not consume you. For I am the LORD your God, the Holy One of Israel, your Savior.

Then there were the times of deep thirst for some reality and some love. Those moments of weakness were drowned out with Isaiah 55.

Ho, everyone who thirsts, come to the waters; and you that have no money, come, buy and eat! Come, buy wine and milk without money and without price.

The times I fought to stay positive, to find purpose, to be an encouragement to others and to not give up on myself or God and especially those times I condemned myself and was angry at myself in my weakness, I heard the comfort of Isaiah 57:14-16.

It shall be said, "Build up, build up, prepare the way, remove every obstruction from my people's way." For thus says the high and lofty one who inhabits eternity, whose name is Holy: I dwell in the high and holy place, and also with those who are contrite and humble in spirit, to revive the spirit of the humble, and to revive the heart of the contrite. For I will not continually accuse, nor will I always be angry; for then the spirits would grow faint before me, even the souls that I have made.

God continued to use John's death to nurture the deep passion and compassion I had for those who were lost, destitute and oppressed. I was experiencing their suffering in my own way and when I was losing the battle of my will and my intellect, God brought Isaiah 58:6-12 to me to refocus me.

Is not this the fast that I choose: to loose the bonds of injustice, to undo the thongs of the yoke, to let the oppressed go free, and to break every yoke?

Is it not to share your bread with the hungry, and bring the homeless poor into your house; when you see the naked, to cover them, and not to hide yourself from your own kin? Then your light shall break forth like the dawn, and your healing shall spring up quickly; your vindicator shall go before you, the glory of the LORD shall be your rear guard. Then you shall call, and the LORD will answer; you shall cry for help, and he will say, Here I am.

There were so many times of darkness during these days. I felt helpless and empty, tired and spent and when the world around me was too busy, or too self-centered, I would feel sorry for myself, yet God revealed Isaiah 60:1-2 for new oil.

Arise, shine; for your light has come, and the glory of the LORD has risen upon you. For darkness shall cover the earth, and thick darkness the peoples; but the LORD will arise upon you, and his glory will appear over you.

REFLECTION

I never believed that I would come to a point in my life where I would willingly surrender everything to God, literally. I made peace with God and He removed my greatest fear, having my wife or another child die. It was a tremendous mental, emotional and spiritual battle. But afterwards, I lost all fear. I was at peace. I came to understand Jesus is Lord and savior. How about you? Do you have the faith to surrender it all to Jesus and not hold anything back from him?

CHAPTER SEVENTEEN

A wilderness destiny -- 5 months after

I continued teaching a Sunday class, Changing Sheep to Warhorses. We were using the prophecy of Zechariah as a starting point to mobilize Christians to step out and go where they have never gone before as believers. Job 39:21-25 was a reference of the power and strength and attributes of a warhorse. I had envisioned the warhorse many times and asked God to make me a warhorse for Him almost a year ago. A warhorse is a warhorse because of his passion and loyalty to his rider, the master. I had stated it so many times, the message was growing old.

One day as I was studying for the class, I read that in ancient times, warhorses were used to carry their dead soldiers back to the camp after battle. I was dumbfounded and emotionally scalded. God gave me a different perspective. I had told God I wanted to be a warhorse, but now He was showing me the other side of the warhorse job. God's warhorses carry the faithful until death. They carry the warrior to their final destiny. II Kings 14:20 was a simple verse that packed so much power and truth.

"They brought him back to Jerusalem on a horse, and he was buried with his ancestors in the City of David."

I reflected upon John's death; I was a warhorse. I had carried the dead, my dead son, to his destiny. I had carried a faithful one to his destiny in heaven. I was sitting at my bedroom desk when I learned of the new warhorse role. I couldn't move because of the grief. There I was, a broken note once again. But deep in my soul, there was a soft peacefulness, almost a feeling of fulfillment, of achieving something magnificent, far beyond any success I ever had experienced.

I remembered Beth telling me that Sunday morning after John's death that we had coached John to his ultimate championship, his heavenly reward. Now it came back as a complete prophecy. Now I understood her words more deeply. The brightest light of truth, the spiritual truth, the gospel truth flashed through my being. I was blinded by it. It was as if I was on the road to Damascus and Jesus confronted me. I couldn't move. Jesus had revealed His truth to me...to me....

I didn't deserve this privilege. It was so humbling to realize that for the first time in my life, God had shown me the fulfillment of my life purpose. I was to carry the faithful to their destiny. Previously I had come up with purpose statements, life mission statements, vision

147

announcements and life goals. They were statements I truly believed in, "being a stepping stone for others, being as Joseph – glorifying God wherever I am at, being as John the Baptist, a lone voice, crying in the wilderness, preparing the way of the Lord."

I still believe in those statements for my life, but Jesus leading me through John's death, with my wife by my side now, went deeper. *I was to carry the faithful to their destiny.* I was to carry, not to stand out in front and direct, not to command, not pave the way and rid the pathway of obstacles. I wasn't supposed to lead or delegate or coerce others to carry the faithful. I was to get underneath the burden, lift them up and carry them to their destination. I was to carry the faithful to their destiny.

Who were the faithful? How would I know which one? How would I know what their destiny was? My spirit was willing, but my flesh was weak. I didn't understand the future; I didn't understand what it all meant. I started to think deeply on this significant word from God.

All my questions of a few moments earlier disappeared. I knew I hadn't been prepared at that moment to carry John to his destiny and it was now revealed to me that I would never be prepared to carry a faithful one to their destiny in the future. God would do the carrying. I only had to be available and willing to be the warhorse, to want to carry, to go the distance for one of His. How does one articulate the message God has spoken? It would take me months to truly understand what this warhorse role really meant. It was very evident that it would come through personal transformation and only by the Holy Spirit.

Perplexed, I sat in silence, listening for God. Deep in my heart I knew this warhorse was not a glorious role. It was not an ego-building, highly visible, earth-shattering role. It would be difficult, challenging and at times seem impossible. A tidbit of truth God revealed to me soon after was that I would always need Elijah's oil. It would be my life source.

Days elapsed as I wrestled with the purpose of carrying the faithful to their destiny. The truth was contrasting. In Job, the warhorse was incredibly prepared, fearsome and had the attributes of a winner. In 2 Kings, the warhorse was required to do the most grievous of work. No joy would be found, only fulfillment; no mercy, no life, no victory, just the long road ending in death. I tossed the two scriptures back and forth; trying to understand how the warhorse would handle both. Wouldn't it be too much to understand? It would be a rollercoaster ride. The rest of my life would be one of not holding back. There would be highs and lows, rapid ascents, rapid descents, warp speed, crawl pace.

I had to carry the faithful to their destiny. What a noble role! In Job 39 and in Revelation 19, my role would be to go into battle, forge ahead, carry the master, be fearless in battle, be alert for the commands, never turn back from the sword, be swift and fierce, carry the weaponry and mock the enemy.

In Revelation 19 my role was to see heaven open up, and look into the eyes of Christ, burning with fire. The rider is victorious and I am to be loyal to the rider, one called the King of Kings and the Lord of Lords.

Then my heart would quicken in 2 Kings 14:19, the horse bringing the dead to be buried in Jerusalem. Every which way I read and prayed those verses, God's glory shined though. The battle, the burial, the rider, the New Jerusalem, the ultimate destiny all led to Jesus. I was finished with pretending, finished pretending how I was supposed to act and think and speak as a believer. It didn't matter any more. I didn't totally understand the theology of those scriptures, but I did understand the Voice that inspired them to be written.

Moments melted into hours, hours into days and days into weeks. John's death remained painfully fresh. Every wave of grief consumed Elijah's oil, but somehow the warhorse, the eagle and the dove penetrated the grief and replenished the oil.

Life's events mounted. There was our wedding anniversary, Ben's prom, graduation and open house. There was John's 22nd birthday and our family's mini-vacation to my brother's place in Florida.

One evening I found myself crying at the supper table over Ben. He was upset at his teacher, at us, himself, the world, probably at John as well. I was deeply hurt in my love for Ben. I wanted to help him. I wanted him to know I cared and I loved him and that it was okay. But my words and intentions misfired and now I cried in my sadness for him.

The same happened to Scott and Adrienne. Grades, work habits, commitment and school were always sore points over the years and with this season of suffering, flashpoints became more frequent. I knew I had to be unconditional in my love, yet be a parent and hold them accountable. It didn't happen. Our children were in denial and Beth's and my efforts were constantly misinterpreted. It was a daily lose-lose situation.

We attended Ben's graduation ceremony, thinking he had met his requirements only to find that he needed a three- week session over the summer. He had chosen not to go to a four-year school to play ball and now I understood why. Still, we were proud of him as he attended the ceremony and afterward we chaperoned at his graduation party.

Attending other graduation open houses as well as the one we had for Ben brought back the wounds of the most recent memories, the funeral. Many of these hosts were the same parents who came to us in tears, mourning John's loss with us.

Scott, on the other hand, was not graduating. He had chosen an alternate education venue and was doing well, but his uncompromising position and temper set him apart, so the conventional approach to parenting was ineffective. His heavy metal gothic scene was a sharp rejection to his twin's look and Adrienne sided with Scott's look.

Beth and I had our hands full. They were all good kids and we loved them, yet they had set out on their own paths and we struggled to maintain some structure and accountability. I obviously passed my pride to the next generation, yet the balance I had and priorities of character - God, education and stewardship stopped at their rebellious years.

Now as each was progressing to the next level of life, we saw the cracks in the foundation. John's death only widened those cracks. Beth and I read and reread the parable of the prodigal son, knowing we had to love, be patient and look for opportunities to accept unconditionally. Fortunately, Adrienne had time to catch up and she appeared as the most steadfast of the three as the grieving progressed. We'd make it, but it would have been difficult even if John was still alive.

The month continued to flow with a negative undercurrent. Every wave of grief seemed to possess a strong undertow; every event of joy seemed to be neutralized. We marched on. We looked forward to the Florida vacation to get away, but we'd be gone on John's birthday and Father's Day. We combined a business trip with a vacation and we were hopeful the blend would be productive and joyful. We needed a change of scenery. I prayed I could be the warhorse, but I felt too weak and unwilling to run the race to win.

June 16th, John's birthday, dawned warm and sunny. I dawned sad and moody. Twenty-two years ago, it was a sunny warm Pennsylvania sunrise. I was driving home from the hospital, after pulling an all-nighter with Beth. John Edward Chaya was born. I was flushed with pride and dreams. A big boy, healthy, a sure "Penn State All American." I couldn't get over holding him in my arms those first minutes in the delivery room. I cried with joy, proud of John, very proud of Beth and proud to be a dad. I watched the sun come up, praising and thanking God. I couldn't wait to get home and start calling people, even if it was 5:30 in the morning.

Twenty-two years later, standing on the hotel balcony, my eyes burned with tears looking at the sunrise, as the memory of John's arrival mixed with thoughts of those morbid phone calls, informing the family of his death. I labored on that balcony, unable to comprehend the life and death of a child. In my arms. I held him in my arms at birth and death. There was a bittersweet injustice about that scenario, but also a sense of honor and nobility. I was the Job 39 warhorse and the 2 Kings 14 warhorse.

We were set apart from the majority of American parents and somehow we didn't want that authority or parental acumen. We were helpless and shameless in our plight. *O God, comfort us. Help me this day to get it together. I have no desire to perform in my meetings today. I want to stay here and mourn. I can't go out there. I want to hole up with my family. I don't have the warhorse spirit, or Elijah's oil. I don't have the peace of the voice of God at this moment. I feel I am in the Garden of Gethsemane. What to do?*

I squinted through tear-filled eyes at the horizon. God's gentle whisper came. The silent thunder rumbled through my soul. God spoke, "John, I was with you in the delivery room long ago and I am the same God who was with you beside your son's kitchen chair. You have been blessed. You have seen your son's three births. Remember that I was also with you in John's bedroom when he was five as he prayed and invited Me into his heart. Very few parents ever experience three deaths of their children. Death passing from the womb to earthly life, death from the old nature to the new as a Christian and physical bodily death passing to eternal life in My kingdom."

God had spoken so gently, yet deeply. The magnitude of three births and deaths were beyond my understanding. I confessed I couldn't totally grasp this revelation so I read Revelation 19 about the New Jerusalem.

Later that day we picked up Ben at the Tampa airport and arrived on Anna Maria Island. We joined my brother and sister-in-law, Tom and Lynn, for grilled seafood on their deck.

The adults tried to converse and we did accomplish some laughs and redefined moments. We relaxed as we talked about John. None of us were much good at articulating feelings, but we were able to be there for each other and God knew it was exactly what we needed. The Florida vacation was sad and happy. I learned that almost every day was a day of contrasts, and the vacation taught me to appreciate the contrasts. Sadness was doing the great fun things like fishing and swimming without John and happiness was knowing we had a fine family and a great brother and sister-in-law with whom to enjoy the Florida sunshine.

My children's disengagement and restlessness in their life flow appeared to be constant. They were lacking in motivation. They were struggling, and I hopelessly stood on the sidelines as they denied me access. The travel, events around graduation, John's birthday, our vacation, anniversary and Father's Day, introduced with excitement and anticipation developed into a parade of events which sailed in and out with very few lasting memories. I was sad. I felt life had cheated us out of special times individually and as a family.

The grieving process and life were getting more difficult and complex. I wanted to run away, get all the answers, then come back and fix everything. My acceptance by, and interaction with, my children was dry and barren. We gave each other space but our lives revolved around more questions than answers. Beth's words were always the same.

"We have to keep loving them." That is all we could do. I confessed that God must have said those same words millions of times over me when I acted like my children. I was no different from my children. Except for one child; he was different. He was in eternity, living with God.

REFLECTION

Destiny. An interesting word. Life and death, both are part of one's destiny. A birthday is always special because it is a benchmark towards the final destination. It is symbolic of an earthly walk and one can measure success and failure, maturity and significance, events and experiences and memories. Remembering the moment of birth with the moment of death is both cleansing and excruciating. How will you remember the birthdays of loved ones once they are gone? Will you accept their destiny? Will you be at peace with your destiny? Will you be a warhorse and carry a faithful one to their destiny?

CHAPTER EIGHTEEN

No mercies in the wilderness -- 6 months after

Thinking perhaps that at six months the grieving process would magically evaporate and I could reverse the downward spiral of negativity, I rudely learned that life has no mercies apart from God. Most people had disassociated me with death and I felt the season for them was over and everything should be business as usual. I wasn't able to step up to the plate. Ben did finish his requirements and all three kids were working, so at least there was some engagement for them beyond what I could offer them. Beth had begun a full-time position working in my department and we were getting our house fixed up, so there was progress. Yet my wounds continued to run deep. I felt worthless and removed.

My sanctuary time continued to be rich. I eagerly walked by the lake every chance I got. My time with God continued to be my anchor. I continued to process the truths of the warhorse, my life purpose and reveled in them, knowing one day I'd be able to articulate them and apply them. For now, they sat on the shelf, but I was at peace. Their time would come.

I sought God earnestly and prayed for comfort, wisdom and discernment and hope. I knew the waves of grief would cover me and recede, and then I could move on, yet I found myself swamped in negative thoughts, pain and suffering over the loss. God moved in revealing His truth to me.

I looked back at what He had been teaching me and that became the major breakthrough. Reflection...not about my past, but reflecting upon God and how He had worked in my past and John's past. Then He guided me to look to the present. The additional wisdom He imparted was for me to look at the facts of where I was in the past before John died and where I was now...and how I got to where I was now.

He had taught me to look at the facts, the truth of this Creator and who He was and who I was and who I am and realize God doesn't change. Just as He was with Beth and me the night John died, He was with us before that time and since that moment. But He didn't stop there. He put a passion in my heart, a renewed spirit, a desire to look into the future and take my companionship with Him and my time and events and experiences and filter them all through the scriptures. He showed me that He had planned my life and John's life, and mine wasn't done yet. He showed me that He had planned my future and I needed to get on with it and that He would always be there.

I spoke with many people and prayed and sought counsel in every area of my life and it unfolded, only as God could unfold my future. David Pierce said that I had authority in three areas of ministry: stewardship of time and money, having faith to step out of my comfort zone, and understanding pain and suffering.

As the moments of grief blackened my horizon, I forced myself to look at the grief through an openness of how God was going to use it to help others. I found I could recognize the anguish beginning to occur, so instead of falling down, devastated emotionally by the death, I started to study it as if God was teaching me how to use it to comfort others.

Jeremiah 31:13 Then maidens will dance and be glad, young men and old as well. I will turn their mourning into gladness; I will give them comfort and joy instead of sorrow.

2 Corinthians 1:3-7 *Praise be to the God and Father of our Lord Jesus Christ, the Father of compassion and the God of all comfort, who comforts us in all our troubles, so that we can comfort those in any trouble with the comfort we ourselves have received from God. For just as the sufferings of Christ flow over into our lives, so also through Christ our comfort overflows. If we are distressed, it is for your comfort and salvation; if we are comforted, it is for your comfort, which produces in you patient endurance of the same sufferings we suffer. And our hope for you is firm, because we know that just as you share in our sufferings, so also you share in our comfort.*

I had been trapped in my own thoughts and feelings until I read those words in 2 Corinthians. Satan had duped me into believing no one else ever felt despair or grief. He deceived me, causing me to believe I was worthless and death and despair was the way I was going to live forever.

I pushed myself to focus on God and others, not on myself, and I began to minister and Beth followed. All along it had been happening, since the viewing and funeral, yet it was from a brokenheartedness to comfort others who knew not what to do. Now our brokenheartedness was for those who were going to confront the loss of a job, a loved one, their own identity, a spouse, finances and spiritual fruitfulness.

The Book of Isaiah continued to draw me back to it daily. My dilemma was in my sullen outward attitude and inward attitude. One morning by the lake, God helped me refocus and renew myself. Isaiah 57:14-16 convicted me of the need for a contrite and humble spirit.

It shall be said, "Build up, build up, prepare the way, remove every obstruction from my people's way."

For thus says the high and lofty one who inhabits eternity, whose name is Holy: I dwell in the high and holy place, and also with those who are contrite and humble in spirit, to revive the spirit of the humble, and to revive the heart of the contrite.

For I will not continually accuse, nor will I always be angry; for then the spirits would grow faint before me, even the souls that I have made.

I wasn't angry with God or death or any profound object or occurrence, but I was sensing anger about something. Having learned the difference between anguish and anger, I knew anger was growing in me. I was angry at life. Isaiah 57:16 was a "solar plexus shot" at my personality and attitude. If I continued my ways, I knew everyone around me would lose their spirit and grow faint. I couldn't expect to change others when I couldn't change myself.

God broke our hearts for His work through John's death. What did that brokenheartedness look like? For me, it was a passion to share the gospel and make disciples. It was to focus on my own spiritual fruitfulness while focusing on my marriage and children, my business, my ministry, my friends and colleagues, my community and my church.

God took it the next step and created a fire within and He gave me a mission. I was able to see what my passion would be if I fulfilled God's purpose for me. As I prayed on the passion and the purpose, God caused me to look back and look at the present and then look into the future. It took time, but it became clear: my purpose in life was to make disciples and destroy Satan's domain in the marketplace. The marketplace was business, media, church, government, education, and philanthropy. I looked around and the marketplace was dark and Christians and non-Christians were in pain and suffering. They were losing, and for many believers, they had given up on sharing their faith and hope in the workplace. But the marketplace became my purpose, my mission in life.

There was a purpose in John's death and it was now being revealed. God gave me a passion, then a mission and the specific vision. I had an identity, I was to be a warhorse, carrying people to their destiny.

Beth and I were invited to friend's, for a cookout with the leaders of our Stockade program from church. Beth and I were to be honored. Our church's basketball team went undefeated and won the championship. Dave Triebwasser and the other leaders had dedicated the season to John. We were humbled by the tribute. The team gave us a team picture that they had signed. They also gave us the medal from the championship. I felt contrite and humble; renewed in the flesh, mind and spirit. It's funny how love does that. Putting others first always brought love.

Darrell and Marge Sanborn also attended and brought the video of their son, Jeremy, coaching John's sixth grade team. That team also went undefeated but lost the championship by a point. The video stunned me. I fought to stay in the living room to watch it. There was a young John, at least a head taller than every kid on both teams. My anguish grew. It was John, alive and well, doing what he had fun doing. My heart was pierced, my grief overwhelming. I had to turn away from watching it, as I feared I'd lose it completely. There was laughing and joking and candid observations by the two dozen or so leaders, yet I could only listen. I couldn't speak. After the video, Dave and Ron presented us with the team plaque dedicated to John. I still was unable to speak.

John died, not of his own choosing, but as Darrell said on the day after John's death, "If you asked John and Jeremy if they wanted to come back, they'd say no." I saw something bright in the future. I could learn from John. I could learn more about God if I was sensitive to His prompting, obedient and truly believed in the power of Christ. Still, I couldn't comprehend what could actually happen.

If I only knew what John knew! I was restless, but not enough to take the next step and truly experience the broken bread and poured out wine of the Savior. Throughout the summer I argued with myself in my sanctuary. When would I actually step out and do something?

God observed my self- talk but never intervened. This was not supposed to be easy. Enduring was a character builder. Obviously I would have done it a different way, more to my comfort and pleasure. But then I would have had John's plan more to my comfort and pleasure.

No matter how much time I spent at my sanctuary, I wasn't hearing what I needed to do. God was with me. He spoke to me on the subject of being renewed and not simply conforming. I wasn't renewing or conforming. I was in a state of limbo without direction.

Isaiah 58:6-12 glowed one morning during devotions.

Is not this the fast that I choose: to loose the bonds of injustice, to undo the thongs of the yoke, to let the oppressed go free, and to break every yoke?

Is it not to share your bread with the hungry, and bring the homeless poor into your house; when you see the naked, to cover them, and not to hide yourself from your own kin?

Then your light shall break forth like the dawn, and your healing shall spring up quickly; your vindicator shall go before you, the glory of the LORD shall be your rear guard.

Then you shall call, and the LORD will answer; you shall cry for help, and he will say, Here I am. If you remove the yoke from among you, the pointing of the finger, the speaking of evil, if you offer your food to the hungry and satisfy the needs of the afflicted, then your light shall rise in the darkness and your gloom be like the noonday.

The LORD will guide you continually, and satisfy your needs in parched places, and make your bones strong; and you shall be like a watered garden, like a spring of water, whose waters never fail.

Your ancient ruins shall be rebuilt; you shall raise up the foundations of many generations; you shall be called the repairer of the breach, the restorer of streets to live in.

It was an "Oh, wow" moment. Having been mentored by Ton Snellaert, the Dutch missionary in New Delhi, on these scriptures, I knew exactly what these words meant. But now they had an added truth.

Not only was I to care for the hungry, the naked, the poor, oppressed and afflicted in third world countries, there were people with those physical and spiritual conditions all around me. How would God use me to break the yoke of oppression and loosen the bonds of injustice?

I felt envious of John. He would never have to deal with those elements ever again. Was I going to always be questioning God and asking for His will to be revealed, when deep in my heart I knew His will? I simply didn't want to pursue this argument further. Had I learned from John's death? For John there was no more turning back, no more repentance needed. Was I going to be a man of God, or not?

"Listen," was the answer from God. I wasn't supposed to have the logical answer. I was supposed to listen. That seemed to always be the answer, but I wanted more. I wanted to know the what, the why.

God and I went deep. I had no trouble believing in God and His Word fulfilled in the big life issues. John's death raised no doubts or questions for me. My questions came around the little details of the lesser events. Bottom line, I only wanted to listen to God according to my conditions.

"Incline your ear, and come to me, listen so that you may live." Say the scriptures. I believe John's final words and look on his face was physical evidence of performing those tasks, and God keeping His promise.

The inspired word of God was simply an exercise of listening to His voice. If I was going to pay back the many people who loved us during this difficult season, I would have to put them first. Not just talk or write about it, but actually do it. His voice was telling me, "Come and live". So simple, so pure, yet so complicated and difficult.

I could see how God wanted me to use my three ministry areas of stewardship, faith and suffering to make disciples. I listened to Him. I was to be a comfort to those people. God next instilled visions for me to accomplish my mission and fulfill the passion He had placed in my heart.

He gave me a vision for my marriage -- to encourage and support Beth to become the leader He wanted her to be. He impressed upon me to mentor her in her professional and spiritual life.

Next he gave me a vision for my children -- to love them unconditionally and be the "prodigal father for them so they would be enabled to grew nearer to God and fulfill His purpose for them.

He gave me a vision for ministry at Steiger International, to mentor guys who were searching for their purpose. The vision was expanded for David Pierce and the organization, that I was to earn money and make a profit in my business so I could provide for missionaries all over the world. God impressed upon me to speak and teach and disciple other missionaries as well.

He wasn't finished. He next gave me a vision for my church. For years I saw the church as God's instrument of peace and hope and deliverance in sharing the good news and acting on unconditional love. But the religious institutions seemed more interested in running their church instead of following God's commands. Now I saw God move my heart and mind into fulfilling His purpose for the church and I was to be a servant, standing in the gap and helping wherever and whenever he prompted me.

His next vision was the humanitarian foundation that Beth and I had started as a result of Beth's mother's death a few years earlier. Everything seemed to be fitting together as we saw the White Dove Foundation providing humanitarian and financial support to those who were without literacy and education.

And the vision for my job was to mentor business owners and organizations so others would be clear on their passion, mission and vision.

God had moved and He had moved in the darkest months of my life. I saw His spirit fill me and work in the lives of others and there was peace and joy. I started using the term, "joy in the journey" every time my grief hit and it changed my thinking and feelings completely.

But now that I had the passion, mission and visions, what should I do with them? How do I make them reality? God was faithful. He continued through my wilderness journey to impress upon me the process. His next steps were to show me all the obstacles that may stop me from fulfilling my mission and achieving my visions. He imparted a new fire in my soul for me to make a commitment, to dedicate my life to making those visions happen through His power in the Holy Spirit. He wanted me focused. Eventually I made a dedication to Him of each of those visions.

Still, everything seemed esoteric. It was all talk. It fascinated people and entertained others and everyone thought it was compelling but I don't believe anyone thought for a moment it was a reality check. God stressed my need to break down the obstacles with goals to overcome the obstacles, so I could measure if I was succeeding or not.

God wasn't done and I knew this season of grieving was orchestrated by God in answer to my prayers . The fourth of July introduced us to a new experience. We went to see the movie, *The Patriot* starring Mel Gibson. It was a story about a motherless family during the Revolutionary War. In the great movie, Mel Gibson's character lost two sons who were killed by soldiers. The movie's emotional impact in those death scenes was huge as Gibson was superb, capturing the multitude of the emotions of death compounded by the anger of war.

My emotions were stirred deeply as Mel Gibson captured the essence of my own pain as he responded to his son's deaths. The movie built in tension and as I sat in the theatre, my emotions built at the same speed. I was like two people sitting at the movie. One person was focused on the movie and the second person was responding to the movie by living out John's memories.

I learned a valuable lesson about the people who lived and fought during the American Revolution. They paid a price. They lived and died with a passion for freedom. They fought against the greatest of odds and they won. Their sacrifice was so great and to look at a movie depicting these settlers and American leaders as common folk put together by God to overthrow a world power, deepened my emotional stirrings. Was I ever going to believe in something deeply enough to die for? I knew that I believed in what John died for.

REFLECTION

What would I do if I didn't have the word of God and the Holy Spirit working in my life through John's death? I don't know. I have observed people who don't believe in God deal with death and I am not sure how they find comfort or hope. I think it is much more difficult for them to bring closure and they must be experiencing some incredible inner struggles and doubts as well as fears and agony. I don't think it is any less or any more painful dealing with death if you believe in God or don't; I do think knowing a loved one is in heaven allows recovery and rebirth of your own soul to journey further.

CHAPTER NINETEEN

A memorial in the wilderness -- seven months after

The summer was passing quickly but the memories remained and the grieving didn't subside. I wasn't sure if I was normal anymore. Was I supposed to be healing? Was this causing a state of depression for me? I didn't know. I had thought through much and understood little about dying.

In early August, I went to Rosemount stadium. It was the last place I had returned as John and I had shared so many memories of him as a four-year warrior of the gridiron. It hurt as the warrior memories filled my heart. I walked where John used to warm up as a defensive lineman, where he went out to mid- field as a captain for the coin toss, and to where he recovered a fumble as a freshman on the 2-yard line against Rochester. I walked where he intercepted a pass against Rosemount, where he sat on the bench during breaks in action and where he stood on the sideline. Football had been so much a part of his life and a part of my life.

I stood where he used to come over to us after every game, win or lose. He would hug Beth, shake my hand and share the performance, wanting to know how he did, but more importantly, letting us in on his world. And now the chapter was over. But I wanted to cling to the memories of who he was on the playing field.

The following week I had to take another step in the process. I finally got the courage to go to the funeral home and pick up John's ashes. I called on a Friday and spoke with John White. "How about I stop by Sunday evening - will you be around?"

"Yes, I have some work to do," he said. "No one will be there. What time works for you?"

Our plan was to meet on a Sunday evening; yet throughout the day it felt like a cloud on the horizon. I got up enough nerve and drove to the funeral home. John led me into the foyer, then to his office. I stood and waited as he retrieved the container. I felt a cold numbness in my emotions. *This is morbid. I was picking up the remains of my dead son. I'm going to hold him once again. I haven't touched him since I kissed his forehead at the funeral. I hadn't held him since January 21 when I hugged his body in the hospital room.*

John White emerged with a small white cardboard container. I had to sign a final paper and he handed me the box. It was heavier than I thought but still small. I guessed it weighed about 12 lbs. I thanked John again and climbed into my car. I placed the box in the passenger seat and slowly drove away, feeling very weird. *I was taking John home one last time.*

I pulled into our driveway and parked the car. But I didn't get out. I sat there for a moment; then opened the lid of the box. In it was a plastic bag with a twist cord and a small medal with the crematorium ID. I read the medal.

Southern Minn
Cremation SVC Echo, MN
2124

I stared at it. *John Edward Chaya had a new ID, 2124. He had an identity in life and death. Thank God he is more than a number in heaven.* My mind swirled as emotion swept in. I untied the twist cord and opened the bag. It was small particles of bone. Various shades of gray. Obviously, all his remains were there, his clothes, his body, my tie. I felt empty. *Twenty-one years of life is reduced to a small container. This is all I have of a son? All the memories, all the fun, all the struggles...All the achievements, the disappointments, the laughter, the tears, the good and the bad times... John's birth and his death, now all of him was reduced to this small remnant. He was a big boy. Sometimes when I watched him on the gridiron or mat, he was bigger than life. And now...ashes. It didn't seem fair. But death is never fair.*

For some weird reason I wanted to touch my son again. I reached into the plastic bag with my index finger and thumb and daintily picked up some granules. Emptiness filled me as I held the particles. *This is it. This is all that is left. It didn't seem right. He was so much of my life. He was conceived by Beth and me. We were part of God's plan to create John. And we created a big son. But this brought all the closure I feared. There would only be artifacts and memories. There would be memorials, but there would never again be a John.*

I closed the bag and the box and proceeded into the house. I handed the container to Beth, but couldn't say anything. I felt like I did the day I stood on the frozen lake, "a broken note." I couldn't speak and felt ashamed that I couldn't console and comfort Beth. I walked out onto the back porch and looked at the sunset and "John tree." I sat in a swing hammock and stared. There were no words. I was a sad father whose son had come home. There was no consolation in it. Just dread.

August 19th, Pastor Roger, Ben, Scott, Adrienne, Beth and I stood at the football stadium. It was a quiet warm morning. At 9:00 a.m. we gathered around a tile and a square hole prepared for the ceremony. It was sad and I wasn't sure what to do. Thankfully, Roger knew. He explained why we were there and that he would pray and read some scripture, give each of us an opportunity to say a few last words, and then we would put John's ashes in the square hole and place the memorial tile over it.

I looked at our rugged family and knew this step was important. Roger read the words from Isaiah 61:1-3. Roger spoke about the significance of this memorial and Beth and I said a few words, as our children remained silent. I asked if any of them wanted to say anything, but I knew they wouldn't. They were in their own worlds at this time. We all were. I knelt down and poured about half of the contents into the gravesite. I covered the site with topsoil and sand and then laid the memorial tile in its place. I read the letters again on the tile again.

John Edward Chaya
Our Champion
In Christ
6/16/78-01/21/00.

We stood and looked at the memorial. It was quiet. Tears flowed and we hugged each other. I remembered Roger's last comment to Beth and me. "You are both 'oaks of righteous' " which I knew came from Isaiah 61:1-3. As we concluded, I turned and walked away by myself, onto the football field.

The stadium was empty. I strode out to the hash mark on about the 20 yard line. I cried as I looked over the field. This used to be a practice field and junior varsity game field only. Memories flashed through my mind as I remembered John as a sophomore playing on the field. I thought of the times I came by to watch him practice, or the many times I picked him up after practice.

My head and throat hurt as I grimaced at the thought of Beth and I watching Ben play his final year as a senior on this field that was opened for the 2000 season. The stadium would be packed and we'd see John coming in, looking for us as he'd come to see his brother. He usually lasted a quarter or so sitting with us, then found a few buddies. At the end of the game, he'd come down to the field, say a few words to his brother, and to the coaches and players as they lingered. He was an Eagle and always would be one. He knew it was important to support Ben, and didn't miss any of his games. It was fun to have John around.

A fleeting sadness came with the realization that after seven years, we had no more boys playing football for Apple Valley. Our careers as sports parents had ended and it left a void. Now as I stood looking up at the bleachers where I used to sit and thinking about how proud I was watching all three of my boys play football, John's death brought a deeper hurt.

We slowly made our way to the car. Mike Garrison reappeared as he said he would, to take care of the final seating of the memorial stone. We thanked Roger and drove home for one last piece of business. Standing in our backyard, I dug a hole next to the weeping willow tree which was a few months old. I poured the rest of the ashes into the hole, covered them with topsoil and sod, then placed over it the stone that John had rolled into our yard when he was about 8 years old. We said a prayer and hugged then we silently walked up the steps to our porch. God gave us a peace at that moment. John would always be a part of our household, in the physical sense. I smiled as I thought of the times we played baseball and football or horseshoes, and had grilled in our backyard. We had many great times out there.

Later that August, Beth and I invited Roger and Joanne to a cookout at our house one Saturday. As we sat around the table after the meal, Roger asked me a rather intriguing question. "How do you hear the voice of God?" He and I had talked much over the years and since John's death, we shared many of those "God moments" when we couldn't exactly say what happened, but we knew it was from God. I felt quite honored that he'd ask me such a question, pre-empting it with the fact he was preaching on hearing God's voice. I was further honored and humbled when he asked if I would like to preach one Sunday on how God had been faithful to us during our loss.

One evening, I took John's former girlfriend, Katie, to dinner. John had been like a big brother to her. He had been a big brother to many girls and it frustrated him. But John seemed always frustrated with girls and romance, money, career and college. I asked her if she felt there was something missing in his life with love. I asked if she thought that we as Chaya's had not shown him enough love.

God spoke through Katie to me. "I think it was the other way around. John saw your marriage and your love and he set that as a standard, and no relationship he had measured up."

What she said blew me away. We received so many notes and letters and chats from people whom he had impacted, but Katie's words added an intimate dimension, his love for us. I had not often seen that side of him. But God knew it was important for me to meet with Katie. God was bringing closure.

REFLECTION

Bringing closure means something to me now. It isn't the same as bringing closure to a church service, or a business deal, or the completion of a book. Closure is one step nearer to realizing destiny. How have you brought closure to issues surrounding death and suffering? Have you had the opportunity and missed out? Do you still have events in your life that need closure?

CHAPTER TWENTY

Fields in the wilderness -- eight months after

Fall, my favorite season arrived, signifying football season. The thought of not having any boys playing football struck me almost daily with strokes of sadness. So many years, so much fun, so many ways to forget the rest of the world and spend time being proud and having fun watching competition. I had warriors for sons. Sure, they weren't warriors as King David or Joshua, but in my own little world, they were warriors of the gridiron. Something I always loved, but something I wasn't.

I had spent 30 years playing, coaching, and watching football with more at stake than just being a fan. I was there as a player, a coach, a loyal supporter and a parent of players. Beth and I would escape to our sports world with our attention solely on the contest, knowing they had heart, and that was all that mattered.

So much of me died on the athletic fields after John died. I would walk them every now and then, reminiscing, replaying games, reliving the experience, laughing through tears, remembering antics, words or the sheer joy of the game. Emptiness filled my world this September. Too much had changed.

Watching college football was a passion. To have the whole family yelling at the television, dogs barking, and snacks everywhere was my dream come true as a parent. For years it was a simple tradition, but constant. A few times when Penn State would come to play at the Metrodome in Minneapolis against the Minnesota Gophers, we'd go as a family and totally immerse ourselves in the event. We were all loyal and rabid Nittany Lion fans.

Now I sat in the empty living room on a Saturday afternoon and fought to concentrate on the game. My mind dwelled on what used to be. Those memories created melancholic depression. Never would it be like that again. Tears would come as I relived the crowded living room, the banter and bravado, the whining and complaining over referee calls, or poor plays. We acted like it all mattered so much.

This September was different, every day of the week. The simple joys, the energy release, and the family, just weren't there. So much was missing. It was John's death, it was the death of relationships, of experiences, of tradition. That hurt greatly. The collateral damage was a surprise. It wasn't just a new season of life and we move on. It was a changed season that could never be recaptured the same again. I stopped watching as many games on television. I occasionally attended an Apple Valley game, but the vacuum was immense.

One day I was so distraught, I cried out to God as I stood on John's memorial stone at the stadium, "Did I make football such a god, that you are taking all the joy of the past from me?" I squinted through tears as I stood looking out over the early morning dew-soaked field. The smell of the crisp air, a gentle breeze, the fresh grass clippings pasted to my moist shoes, and the sun glistening, made this my sanctuary once again. God's peace came. I inaudibly heard, "No, I am not taking away anything. I am making you see it differently."

I cried as I walked beyond the stone onto the field, thinking back at last month's dedication and placing John's ashes there. "You're right, God. You are making me see it all differently. It hurts so much looking at it this way."

"I hear you, John."

"Father, I can't go on. Everything makes me think of John. And fall was so much a part of our lives with football. Now I have only memories. I thought grieving would diminish with time. It feels like it is getting worse."

"This is another 'first time since' episode for you and I know it hurts."

Then the stillness set in again. It was a very quiet day. It was a beautiful day, one I always loved to cherish. It was like God had given me this moment and this day, just to share it with Him. John was gone. The fall would never be the same. The family would never be the same, but God would never change. He was always there and always faithful.

I wanted to do something to make everything better. For some weird notion, I thought that as a Christian, I could do something and my grieving would get better. What could I do at church? What could I do for my family? What could I do for my colleagues, and my board members? What ministry held the secret? I turned down the street and headed to the lake. I needed time at my other sanctuary. I was getting restless again.

I sat on the lakeside bench seeing the first colored leaves of fall and the truth surfaced. My spirit life is a hidden, obscure thing. I spoke out loud to myself. "These leaves are beautiful. Green with tints of yellow, red and oranges. Is that my Christianity, attractive leaves on a tree so others can admire it? Where is the fruit? There can be no fruit without the power of God. The activities are only leaves. It is my personal relationship that produces power."

I must get rid of the plague of the spirit of this religious age in which I live. The kingdom of Jesus Christ is a personal relationship with Him, not public usefulness to others. It's about the sap of the tree and the fruit of the tree, not the colored leaves of the tree.

I remembered a point in a book I read that stated we all hide out in our past. We forget God is in the transformation business. We are being called to be more than we've ever been before. God can reach us at our lowest and loneliest.

Transformation business...that is so true. Where was I living? And was I allowing God to transform me? I didn't know where I was living or why I wasn't being transformed, but I knew this to be true, I was in the midst of change and everything centered on my relationship with Jesus. It wasn't about the football games, or the memories, or the past. I confessed that God can't transform the past, nor should I expect Him to. Nor should I resist transformation. My job was to love God with all my heart and soul and mind and strength.

September was a difficult month. God was teaching and I soon learned that it wasn't easy to give up the past and quit longing for it. Not much was happening. I fought to believe all events are under the sovereignty of God; consequently all the trials of my life are connected at once to the life purpose that God designed for me. All providences are doors to trials and tribulation. Even a merciful God allows events by His sovereignty and too often I thought I had some control to pick and choose my trials and tribulations

I was learning that I could never have possessed the precious faith that now I cling to if the trial of my faith had not been like unto fire in my past. God had been preparing me for years, building my faith, so at this deep tragedy, I could endure it. I learned I was beyond the fall leaves, that I was a tree that never would have rooted so well if the wind had not rocked me in missions, or in my career, or ministry. The autumn leaves never fall until the sap is stopped. And God is in control of it all.

Peace was a covering for me. Every time I visited the lake and walked the trails that fall, the leaves thickened in color, then shriveled and blew away. What remained was hope. New leaves would come, but only in time. God's time. Until then there may be barren trails, bitterly cold winds, snow and ice, but God had orchestrated His timing and I was warmed by the deep inner voice letting me know John was with Him, that it was His time, my trials, my tribulation and my loss, but His sovereignty that makes each life a life worth living.

I knew that there is a dark and stormy valley called "Death." John crossed it and one day I would cross it, and God was promising to be with me as He was with John. What did John experience, what awesome world opened to him and will open to me? How astonished will I be? What scene of glory was revealed to John and what will be unfolded to my view? No heavenly pilgrim has ever returned to tell. John won't come back and tell me, though one more visit would be great. But I know enough of the heavenly land to make me welcome John's call and welcome my call with joy and gladness. The journey of death may be dark, but I will go forth on it fearlessly, knowing that God is with me as we walk through the gloomy valley, and therefore we need fear no evil.

Charles Spurgeon said it best, "The vale of tears is but the pathway to the better country: this world of woe is but the stepping-stone to a world of bliss."

REFLECTION

You really can't compartmentalize life when there is death. My son was not just an athlete, or a son or a special creation from God. He was many things just as we all are many things. So often in the prime of our busy lives, we think a certain aspect of living is so important that we sacrifice our time and effort gleefully. But after death, you can only look back at memories and realize what was once so important is part of something much bigger. If the closest person to you died, how would you handle the memories of that person's favorite activities? Would you feel you were relevant in their lives, or did you go your own way and live for yourself and not for others? What do you need to change today to see that God has a much bigger plan for you? What will you be remembered for?

CHAPTER TWENTY ONE

A lone voice in the wilderness -- nine months after

Roger Thompson had begun his series of sermons on "Hearing God" and he was interested in having me preach on a Sunday to share our experiences of how God spoke during the death and now grieving process.

I had spoken a few times at Berean. Once I had preached at a Saturday evening service, but never before had I preached in all three services. I was humbled, yet honored. Rarely had anyone with a gift of preaching ask me to speak.

I went to the lake repeatedly to come up with a message. What do I say? I cried out to God. Roger had been a good friend, but I didn't want to hurt his reputation by saying the wrong things. He and his wife prayed for me and sent me notes of encouragement. The night before I was to speak, the throng of men at the men's retreat prayed earnestly for me. I sensed many people had the same doubts as I did. Where would I get the strength to stand in front of a large body three times and tell them how God spoke to me in the darkest moments of my life?

I had enough material for ten sermons. I had sent Roger some of my journal that I had been writing since the funeral. He told me to simply tell the story of what God did during those times.

Early Saturday evening, I wandered around the lake paths. And God spoke. *Don't tell them about you. Tell them about Me. I will touch hearts and minister to them. It's not about you, or John, or life or death. It's about Me, the risen Savior, and what I have promised.*

This was too easy. I was only in the woods a short time when God comforted me with those words. I had a complete peace about me. There it was. I was supposed to speak about hearing God's voice in suffering, and He just spoke as I was suffering.

I slept well that night and in the morning went back down to the lake to speak with God again. There was no anxiety, fear or tension. I felt like a warhorse, ready for battle. All I needed to do was look into the eyes of the rider.

The service began and as I listened to the music, I experienced the building excitement and fear of forgetting what was important for me to emphasize. *I scanned my notes and then the feeling of total inadequacy swamped me. Who do I think I am? I don't belong up here. I'm not a preacher, a pastor, or an evangelist. I shouldn't be up here.*

The offering was taken and I looked at the program to see that I was next. Pastor Paul Siewart would introduce me. I checked my lapel microphone and as Paul started to introduce me, my only thoughts were, *Paul, you need to take it from here. I can't do this. I'm not the right person.*

I don't remember his final words but I shook his hand and felt something I never felt before as I peered across the congregation. People knew who I was. They all knew. They seemed just as unprepared to hear me as I was to speak to them. I could see the compassion in their faces, as well as the attentiveness. It looked to me like they really wanted to listen to me. I looked at my notes and began my topic, "Suffering Brings Intimacy With God."

There was an outpouring of love and mercy as I invited the people to come forward. I stood and waited. I felt the power of the Holy Spirit. I wanted to walk out of the church as the director Greg, and the soloist finished the closing music. But I couldn't. Slowly one, then two more, walked forward. Others rose from their seats. I looked across the different aisles. About 30 people came forward, some crying, some staring, some uncertain what to do. I hugged some, prayed with most of them, shook hands with others. My heart broke for those who had lost loved ones. God had anointed the message and the fruit stood before us in His sanctuary.

The second and third services followed the same pattern. Although I changed parts of my message, I felt so close to God and felt my words were exactly what He wanted me to say. Rarely had that happened before. The third service was an evening service and as we gathered to pray before the service, word came that Greg's father had died earlier that afternoon. I stayed there in the church pew remembering Greg's comment. "Jake, I love doing ministry with you."

We had been sitting on the steps leading up to the dais, relaxing after praying with the last people in the morning service. Now, I was thinking how God may have used that message to prepare Greg for the loss of his father. Knowing Greg was much stronger than me, I wasn't sure if I had had any impact, but as God constantly reminded me, it isn't me that produces fruit, it is Him.

REFLECTION

The distinct authority you gain through experiencing God in a way others rarely do, is a very ordained attribute. Fellow believers in America are void of the many hardships and suffering that the rest of the world experiences. Most fear discomfort and suffering and everyone avoids it. That's human nature. But authority needs to be accompanied by pure motives. Humility comes with authority, if your motives are pure. God is at work then. The Holy Spirit is able to work through a suffering servant if the focus of the servant is on ministering to others. Do you find yourself using discomfort as a prideful "martyrdom" so your ego is built up? Death removes all pride. Humility is all that is left after death comes, both for the living and for the dead.

CHAPTER TWENTY TWO

The deep drink in the wilderness -- ten months after

God has been working for the past nine months on what I should be doing to bear fruit, fulfill His calling and be a steward of His blessings. Thursday night as I flew home from Washington DC, it became clear. A construction collapse of a new tunnel at Dulles Airport, which trapped a worker underground, was now going into its second day. As the plane was diverted in taxiing around the terminal and site, I looked out the window and saw the rescue trucks, lights, ambulances and desperate rescue team, worn out, yet hoping. They knew where they were and they knew where they wanted to be; they just didn't know how to get there.

These past two weeks of struggle were used by God to prepare the way of the Lord in my heart, mind, emotions and attitude. When I was finally poor enough in spirit, broken and humbled and just listening and not asking, God spoke.

I want you to create a learning center in the Twin Cities. A "train the trainer center", training willing servants to teach English as a Second Language, provide medical relief and mentor business skills. I knew that for over a year, but now it was becoming very clear. It was where I wanted to be but I didn't know how to get there.

I heard in my mind, "*there are many frustrated Christians who know where they are and realize there is more to their Christianity than where they are now. They know the scriptures and have felt the prompting of the Holy Spirit and deep inside they want to serve Me, they know they want to die to self, to sacrifice, to take up their cross daily and follow Me. They know they are to make disciples and bring glory to Me and advance My kingdom, but they don't know how to get there.*

"Use the believer and the unbeliever to fulfill your calling. You are an apostle. You go where no one else goes. Now take people to where they never have been before, spiritually, financially, emotionally, vocationally and relationally. Start your program with churches and businesses and professionals and youth groups and college professors. Bring them together and I will bless the learning center and prepare the servants to go beyond what they see, and give them a faith and an obedience to go and do the acts of truth, love and grace. Then they will be blessed for who they are and who I am and My kingdom will advance. Look for the people in the throes of their woes first. And remember, I will be with you always."

Did I know where I was and where I wanted to be? Did I know how to get there? I tried to plan my work, focusing not on the will of God, but on what I thought was the will of God. I knew I had to be honest with God and with myself as I assessed where I was and where I wanted to be. So many months had gone by, but at times I couldn't honestly assess my grief, my emotions, my thoughts, my actions or my reactions. I knew I had to be honest, and once I recognized the truth, I couldn't compromise it.

Having read Oswald Chambers devotions for a few years, I saw the integrity of his writing and his wisdom and discernment from God. I settled in one evening to read a devotional and once again, God used His creation to teach me my next step.

In Genesis, it states a passage concerning God speaking to Abraham about taking his son and sacrificing him.

"He said, *'Take now your son* …Genesis 22:2.

As I read the passage and then read Oswald Chambers devotion, it prompted me to look deeper at who I was and what it was God wanted me to do. In Genesis 22, God's command is, "Take *now*," I was caught by the urgency and the immediacy. God didn't tell Abram to talk it over with his wife, or his pastor, his family or a professional counselor. The command was direct and simply. Move out…get going…don't think, simply obey…Don't analyze the situation and get all the facts and the latest opinion polls. Take action now.

This message hurt. I wasn't sure what to do, but I knew that where I was, was not where I wanted to be going. For months I had enough self-talk going on to neutralize me completely, and I was growing restless. I had great arguments with myself. I was so good at it that I could argue both sides and completely foil any activity. My passion was more of a wish. I knew what was right and when to do it; I just wanted to rationalize until I no longer wanted to do it.

I was finding more excuses every day. I simply wanted to be by myself, withdraw, and control my destiny, on my time schedule and at my convenience. What I now battled with was how God worked during those days surrounding John's death. It wasn't a series of contemplations and committee meetings. God took my son and I had to get on with life. We stood on holy ground together; He stood in the midst of my family at the hospital, the funeral home, the church, our house, my workplace, the kid's schools. He set forth His proposition and we carried it out.

I fought my argument, of, "Just when would I have thought John should have died? Would I have picked age 3, 30, 55, 70, 90, or anytime after I died?" God didn't give me the choice, but I had to rely on Him, not blame Him. His timing is always right. But what about my timing - is it always wrong? Once again, I learned, it is never about me. It is about God. If I am to climb to the height of God's will, I can never wait until later—it must be done now. And the sacrifice must be worked through my human will before I can actually perform it.

"So Abraham rose early in the morning ... and went to the place of which God had told him" Genesis 22:3. How easy is that? It is not so easy. But it is simple. God spoke to Abraham, just as He spoke to me.

Abraham did not choose what the sacrifice would be. God told him the sacrifice was his son. I realized now that this story was a prelude to God's plan for His own Son. God was making Abraham do something as an impersonal legalistic God. God was using Abraham to tell the world about what was to come and how serious God was about sacrifice. All too often I want to be in control. I want to be able to choose what I do to serve God, and have contingencies, even if it gets too hot.

Oswald stated, *"Always guard against self-chosen service for God. Self-sacrifice may be a disease that impairs your service. If God has made your cup sweet, drink it with grace; or even if He has made it bitter, drink it in communion with Him. If the providential will of God means a hard and difficult time for you, go through it. But never decide the place of your own martyrdom, as if to say, "I will only go to there, but no farther." God chose the test for Abraham, and Abraham neither delayed nor protested, but steadily obeyed. If you are not living in touch with God, it is easy to blame Him or pass judgment on Him. You must go through the trial before you have any right to pronounce a verdict, because by going through the trial you learn to know God better. God is working in us to reach His highest goals until His purpose and our purpose become one.*

That profound truth pierced my self-centeredness. "Okay God, it's not about me, it's about you. You have given me a sweet cup at times and you have given me a bitter cup."

I was inclined to only drink of the sweet cup, as if I deserved it. This had been a hard time and a difficult time, but as Oswald Chambers instructed - "go through it." I knew I didn't have a choice; it just happened. But I knew I had an attitude to be shielded from. That attitude hadn't made itself a fixture, but every now and then, I would compare myself with others, compare my life when things went well up to now, when things weren't going so well; and I knew that so many others had grown bitter over the death of a child, or their "unfair impersonal, legalistic God" thinking.

Too many people always blamed God for loss and suffering. Too many people got into judging God and I didn't want to fall into that attitude. Sure it was difficult, but when I looked at what could have been and how God's grace had been with me, my family and John for so many years, I couldn't question the difficult time. I had been blessed far beyond what the rest of the world was receiving and I was unworthy and undeserving.

God had shown me the theology of pain and suffering. Because of sin and the fall of mankind in the garden, natural and moral sin would ruin our standing with God. Pain and suffering did not come from God, but from mankind's sin. God did not create pain and suffering or create sin. Satan did because of his free will and mankind has suffered at the hands of sinners ever since.

God also showed me how deserving of His wrath I was, for I was a sinner, separated from God and I deserved only His wrath. God also showed me that through His grace and what Jesus did on the cross, I was saved from eternal wrath. So I realized that although I had been suffering and there was a lot of pain in our lives, we actually deserved more and by the grace of God we only experienced little. I saw the truth plainly. I was thankful that God kept me from more pain and suffering, because deep down, I knew I deserved it.

I rose early in the morning and went to God's sanctuary to meet with Him. I rejoiced that although the pain was intense and sometimes unbearable, I was always in communion with Him. I was thinking beyond John, to Beth's death, and to Ben, Scott, or Adrienne's death, to my brothers' deaths and ultimately to my death. Would I be willing to drink from the cup? I thought I had made peace with God in that hotel room months ago, but I knew God was prompting me again. He was keeping me alive to understand completely what His will for me was and I would live it out obediently before my time ended on earth. I had to fulfill my purpose. That may not be the purpose I wanted to fulfill, but I didn't know. All that I did know was that I was to be obedient and move, not ponder the command.

REFLECTION

I was realizing it all comes down to prayer and scripture. The Holy Spirit communicates through prayer and the written word. There is nothing else that can reveal, comfort, quench, or challenge, like the word of God. It is timeless. The prayer the Holy Spirit prays for us in our spirit is beyond our comprehension, but we need to use the Bible and take time to hear. Do you lack in the Word and prayer? Are you about God's business without a communication plan? Is it time to return to the basics and allow God to speak to you through the scriptures and voice of the Holy Spirit?

CHAPTER TWENTY THREE

A new season in the wilderness -- eleven months after

As each month passed, I found my pattern true. I'd look over a calendar and see how many "first time since" events were to occur. This December, held my birthday, Christmas, our family pilgrimage to Pennsylvania, New Years Eve, and winter. Little things loomed as emotional events, like putting decorations on the house, buying Christmas presents, and my missions trip to India, Thailand and Vietnam. I would be gone nearly three weeks. Christmas time would also touch on years of memories and Beth's sister's death. I was struggling with the emotional heaviness of the month before it started. My last mission trip had been with John and Scott.

I had waited over a year (17 months) to get back on track. My heart was always broken in these lands for the people. I'd fly to Bangkok, then to Ho Chi Minh City, spend four days there working with our ESL school and underground church leaders on expanding our work as well as do ministry. Then I'd go to New Delhi with Ton for five days and see his mission with the medical rehab, the street kids center and emergency care shelter. From Delhi, I'd go to Nagpur, India as we were planning a series of new projects with a cyber-café, computer lab, and ESL school and agriculture programs. We would then return to Thailand and visit a village on the Thai-Myanmar border. I'd fly home December 19.

My element of ministry is listening to God on mission trips. Over the past 13 years of short-term mission work, God had transformed me most through these trips. The past eleven months had been a major learning and revelation period so I expected some amazing revelations as I packed for Asia. I was apprehensive as well. I had been very tired from business travel for over a year. I looked forward to long sleeps on the flights. God blessed me with some on the flight to Vietnam as I slept 17 of the 23 hours.

We made our way to the Bong Sen Hotel in Ho Chi Minh City and met with a woman named Noeline. She and Anthony had worked some miracles to keep our fledgling school afloat. As we met and heard the personal struggles of a missionary working with people who were oppressed, we knew God was at work, yet the enemy was not at rest. Acts 12 talks about persecution and the power in prayer. Prayer and believing in prayer are the primary paths to victory. These past months confirmed that and I had learned that praying in the Word was something the gates of hell couldn't stand against. I had treasures from God.

My treasure was John, Beth, Scott, Ben and Adrienne. My treasure was in the people in Vietnam. My heart was with them. Then the truth came. "Don't look at people for what they are doing, look at who they are. And don't look just at what they are doing now, or who they are now, but look at who they will become in the future as they fulfill God's planned destiny."

It was becoming clearer. God was using this trip to help me understand my purpose. Matthew 10:6-10 shed its light. One verse stood out. "Go rather to the lost sheep of Israel. As you go, preach this message: The kingdom of heaven is near. Heal the sick, raise the dead, and cleanse those who have leprosy, drive out demons. Freely you have received, freely give."

God moved in those three days in Vietnam. It was humbling. We saw our school, the New Vision Learning Center. It was well equipped, well staffed, profitable and a vibrant learning environment. It had been a tough year but I was excited. There was visible evidence that what we were doing was ordained.

I met Tony and Ton at the airport in New Delhi late at night. I had flown from Vietnam to Hong Kong then to New Delhi. Ton was his usual "Jesus looking" mystic and Tony, a New Zealander, had the fiery eyes of a compassionate servant. It was great to be with them. I was taken to their home, and felt that was an act of divine intervention in itself. Ton and I had a great chat in the van as he had made arrangements to stay in the Mongolian colony area of Delhi. It was safe, Spartan, and cheap.

I slept well that night but I felt a fear coming. In the morning during my devotions, my fear grew and I couldn't define it. I had read a great devotional on the four things that bring peace:

1. Prioritize the will of others before my own. (Matt. 26:39)
2. Determine to possess less stuff rather than to acquire more stuff (Matt. 10:10
3. Always take the humblest position and don't take yourself so seriously. (Luke 14:10)
4. Seek fulfillment of God's will before everything else. (Matt. 6:10)

God was moving in Ton and his team, but beneath the work, hearts were heavy in this hard core ministry. Their work was significant, but in the total equation, small in a country where death, suffering, sickness, poverty and oppression ruled. I admired him, a suffering servant, pushing on regardless of the odds. He truly was denying himself, taking up the cross and following Jesus. I saw his Elijah's Oil; it was a tanker compared to my little jar.

Ton was reading *The Imitation of Christ*, by Thomas A Kempis, an early Catholic monk and mystic. It caught my spirit immediately as I glanced through the pages. I was being prepared to go deep, for my own growth and to better minister to Ton. Ton was a cultural contrast wherever he went. He was fiery and compassionate, pushing the limits, supple to God, forceful against process and institutions, obedient to God. It was refreshing to be around this fellow. His vision and mission was huge. It scanned the horizons of the forgotten, the wounded, the forsaken and abandoned. I would have self-destructed living in this setting. Ton blossomed in it.

My own pre-occupation with death and suffering moved to the extreme. While I had tried to be a witness before God and persevere through my season of grief, Ton had had a five-year season of grieving as he ministered to the lost and abandoned in New Delhi. It was hard core as far as humanitarian and evangelical works go, but here was a man "ruined for Christ".

Now as I sat with Ton, I felt the love in his heart come through. (He knew I was hurting.) He knew his friend was suffering and nothing he said or did would change the conditions but he also knew Jesus was Lord and Savior and deliverer. We quickly got into a conversation on God and unconditional love.

My brother taught me much that morning over Mongolian pancakes with honey. His words echoed Isaiah 35:3-10. As he spoke I was thanking God for bringing His words to flesh. The joy of the redeemed rang out in the scriptures and in Ton's life. "…eyes of the blind opened, feeble hands strengthened, knees steadied, deaf ears unstopped, leaping lame, mute tongues shouting and gushing water and streams in the wilderness and desert." Ton was preparing the way, the highway of holiness.

Thomas A Kempis articulated my life best. *"Many love His kingdom in heaven, but few will bear His cross, many desire His comfort, but few desire His suffering; many want to share in the feast, but few in His fasting. Many follow Jesus to the breaking of the bread, but few to the drinking of the Cup of His passion, many admire His miracles, but few will follow Him to the humiliation of the cross. Many love Him as long as they experience no hardship."*

Contemplatively I asked myself the ultimate question. Do I love Jesus for who He is or for my comfort?

I spent an afternoon with the kids and staff at the Street Kids' House. Twenty-five abandoned children age four through adolescence live there. A year earlier, they had only procured the building, but now it was alive. Ton came back in the early evening. As we sat around the table during a power blackout, candles were lit. Gaby paraded into the room with a large birthday cake. It was my birthday and somehow they knew and presented me with a great cake and a huge homemade card. It was a collage of cut outs that all the children had worked on. They had all signed it.

After they sang, Ton led us in a time of prayer for me. Again I was humbled. I felt the all-too familiar throat and face tightening as I listened to passionate prayers in the native tongues of the children. One little girl was deep in her prayer; I was amazed by her voice. I opened my eyes and saw a spirit-led intercessor. No adults have ever prayed like that in my company. My prayer life paled before her's. But there I was again, comparing performance, as if it mattered to anyone but me.

The distant fear grew each day in my soul. I couldn't identify it or cast it out. It was deep and search as I did, it evaded my grasp until the last morning as I woke. All of a sudden I was whisked into a weird scene in my mind. My hotel room surroundings grew gray and blurred as I saw in the depths of my mind - John. But something new happened; it was as if I became John and was experiencing death from his final moments. The terror was excruciating. I felt the coldness and fear. I saw the destruction of the mind and body from the inside and I was dying. As I was dying, the terror grew unbearable. I screamed in agony, totally abandoned to the enemy and to the last moment of life.

I had never experienced such terror. I had been in dangerous situations and felt those terrorizing tremors many times, quivering as if ghosts were real and murderers were lurking and unknown monsters lived around me in dark places. The fear was incredible and I couldn't make it stop. I called to God but He didn't answer. I saw John's face and felt his dying.

I had almost drowned in the ocean one summer and felt that terror. I had been in traffic accidents and detained by the police in Vietnam for a short time for bringing Christian literature into the country, but those moments were a "two" on a scale of ten to what I was experiencing now.

I shook, I quivered, and I felt John dying. Somehow I opened my eyes in my terror and saw a more terrifying sight. The door to my bathroom was open and the mirror was in full view. The reflection was terror. I saw my face as I had never seen it before. My eyes were bulging, my neck was thick and red with flushed cheeks and sweat on my forehead. My mouth was gaping wider than I ever had opened it. I felt as if my jaws had been extended by a vice, but no sound could be heard. I looked like an evil spirit. I rocked forward and backward. I seemed suspended in time, experiencing the moment of death, feeling my spirit pass through death and hell to life, as if John was experiencing it again. Finally I was released to cry out and the terrorized scream tore through my lungs. Ultimate anguish. My body shook, rolled, twisted and shrieked in pain. I wasn't in a seizure but it felt as intense. *This is death. This is how terrorizing and spiritually painful death is.*

In the few minutes it lasted, I watched my face as my head throbbed and tears poured out. I saw the horror, the nightmare of the lost and the broken; the futility, mockery and failure left me delirious. I had seen too many dying and lost in the hospitals, on the streets and in the houses. My polluted dreams, visions and imaginations rapidly destroyed any self-worth and feeling of strength.

It was beyond humility. It was unmerciful humiliation. There was no physical pain, but spiritually I was terrorized and annihilated as if I had been crucified. It was my son's death that had triggered this episode and I was deeply broken. The emotional and psychological pain churned away any sense of reality and self-worth now.

This is what John experienced! No, God! Please, I didn't see it that way. I saw his struggles turn to peace. I saw him relax. I saw his face of contentment; I heard his last words. He wasn't in fear or terror! Where is this coming from?

Suddenly I was found myself laying on my side in my bed drenched in sweat, my head and body still throbbing. The terror left. Then the pain left and I fell asleep.

I awoke in a daze. I was uncertain what had happened. The prevailing fear had departed, but I wasn't sure if I had dreamed the entire episode. Thankfully, the terror and horror were gone. I knew something had happened, but I wasn't sure what. I wasn't even sure if it was from Satan or God. I knew I had a mind-blowing experience and would probably never tell anyone. Who would believe me? Who could realize from my words what had really taken place? Peace returned to my being. Nothing had ever been that intense. I pondered the episode, but told no one.

There had to have been a reason for that event in the hotel room, and I knew God would reveal it to me. I pressed hard to remember this wilderness journey to see if God had given me a glimpse of why this would take place in India. And true to His nature, it became clear.

My mind went back to the six month anniversary. I remembered the brokenheartedness and the resulting passion to share the gospel and make disciples. I remembered how I was to focus on my own spiritual fruitfulness while focusing on my marriage and children, my business, my ministry, my friends and colleagues, my community and my church.

God had created a fire within and He gave me a mission. I was able to see what my passion would be if I fulfilled God's purpose for me. I now understood the passion and the purpose. God caused me to look back and look at the present and then look into the future. In that Indian hotel room, I saw my death of the old nature and the birth of the new creation. My purpose in life was to make disciples and destroy Satan's domain in the marketplace.

There was a purpose in John's death and it had been revealed. God gave me a passion, then a mission and the specific vision. I had an identity, I was to be a warhorse, carrying people to their destiny.

I grew content and joyful. I had passion, mission and a specific vision. But late that night, I prayed and God revealed more than one specific vision. He gave me multiple visions so that I could see in them, how to fulfill my mission.

Along with the vision to bring the love of Christ into the marketplace, He gave me a vision for my marriage, for my ministry with Steiger International, for the White Dove Foundation, for Ben, Scott and Adrienne, for Beth, for my church and for my business. Every vision aligned with my purpose of making A-level disciples. With each vision, God also revealed that I was to take people to where they had never gone before and to transform the "haves" to transform the "have-nots."

I was flushed with excitement. Never had I seen my purpose so clearly defined. Transforming the "haves" meant that through the power of the Holy Spirit, I was to transform those in society who "have" money, talent, skill, time, and blessings from God, to not keep it for themselves. They were to be transformed, given a new mindset, to go out and give to others, so those who "have-not" opportunities, or money, or talent, or skills would have hope, first in God and second, in those who were willing to give. The vision of transforming lives grew. I was to help people who never had a chance, or had blown their chance, to be given a chance to impact the world.

I let my cynical mind start to talk me out of this newly found mission and set of visions. *Get real!* I thought. *You're a dreamer! Forget it. Do what*

you have always done, it is good enough! Get serious, who do you think you are?
Then God got serious. He started to reveal the entrance strategy and the tactics and the tools of actually getting it done. He revealed a design like Nehemiah had, to rebuild the walls of Jerusalem. There was an entrance strategy, followed by a growth strategy, followed by an exit strategy, culminating in a maintenance strategy (which was living a life based upon spiritual maturity and bearing the fruits of the spirit in practical ways.)

God had placed upon my heart the realization that I was ordained for a season in history, and He had all the ministries, business opportunities, colleagues, partners and resources provided for me to fulfill that purpose and vision. I didn't have to do any of it myself, just like I didn't have to mourn by myself or try to get my life back together after John died, by myself. He was lovingly nudging me to turn it over to God and allow the Holy Spirit to precede me, prepare me and make it all happen. Out of death and deep grief came hope. The test of faith was in believing what the scriptures said, "I am with you always."

What did that brokenheartedness look like? For me, it was a passion to share the gospel and make disciples. It was to focus on my own spiritual fruitfulness while focusing on my marriage and children, my business, my ministry, my friends and colleagues, my community and my church.

I reflected on what God was doing that dark night in India. He had taken the sixth month glimpse of brokenheartedness and expanded it. He had taken the next step and He had created a fire within me and He gave me a mission. I was able to see what my passion would be if I fulfilled God's purpose for me. As I prayed on the passion and the purpose, God caused me to look back and look at the present and then look into the future. It took time, but it became clear, my purpose in life was to make disciples and destroy Satan's domain in the marketplace. The marketplace was business, media, church, government, education, and philanthropy. I looked around and the marketplace was dark and Christians and non-Christians were in pain and suffering. They were losing and for many believers, they had given up on sharing their faith and hope in the workplace. But the marketplace became my purpose, my mission in life.

There was a purpose in John's death and it was now being revealed. God gave me a passion, then a mission and the specific vision. I had an identity, I was to be a warhorse, carrying people to their destiny. The night brought light and eventually I fell asleep, knowing there was hope. John's legacy would carry on through me.

As I boarded a plane for Nagpur, India the "city of snakes", I knew the most intense part of the trip was coming, or so I thought. I left Tony on a cool Delhi December morning, confessing that I had lost and found my passion, my purpose and my being since John's death. And I had vision now to go forward.

Nagpur proved to be a delight as Anthony and I met with Pradeep and Suneeta, a married couple ministering in a church and many villages. In two days God put together a plan for future project work and we were completely protected from the enemy.

We returned to Bangkok and traveled to a village where we conducted a worship service in the jungle, using a tarmac as a place to sit. Over a hundred villagers attended. Anthony and his church plant team had planted the beginnings of revival in this highland. I was filled with a great peace as Anthony asked me to share with the people. I felt God there among us. It was a great evening. As I rode back in the van, I compared it to the time when Ton asked me to share with all his people out at the site of the new ashram. God was allowing me to experience His work. I knew it was time for me to take a step in faith.

Returning home to Minnesota, I was drained. But it was a "good" drained. As I returned to America I knew I had only a few days until I'd be in a resting vacation with my family. It was Christmas time, my favorite time of the year. We'd all be together and celebrate. I also knew this "first time since" would be difficult for the family.

We opened our Christmas presents on Dec.21st, prior to departing for Philadelphia. Beth and I knew it would be emotionally draining, but getting back together with family would be a positive. The first day of winter was cold with plenty of snow on the ground. There was sadness in all of us. We tried to celebrate our early Christmas, but it was in vain.

Scott struggled, Ben pretended not to struggle, and Adrienne hid it well but after all the unwrapping and teasing, we were hurting. Scott didn't bother to hide his pain. He was upset and we all knew why. I sat in my chair, John's last place of suffering, and felt all of our suffering. Scott didn't want to go back to Pennsylvania. He said it was boring and last year if it wasn't for John and he spending a lot of time together he'd have been lost.

I knew what he was really saying. He missed his brother and this Christmas wasn't going to be fun without him. We let him vent. A bit later he came back up from his room, apologized to Beth and we mended our hurt feelings. The joy of this Christmas would never be the same as in the past. We didn't want to lose it but we had already lost it. At least we were aware of how painful this "first time since" was and it was good to know that we still thought much about John, but it was still too fresh to accept it.

The week in Philadelphia was a time of renewal. Beth and I had our moments as she was living with the pain of losing her sister six weeks before John died. But with our family we bowled, went to the movies, feasted, napped by the fireplace, played board games and shared the past. It was a quiet holiday. I had time to spend with my brothers and their families. God had blessed us with having all three brothers together for Christmas for the first time in years. My mother was in her glory and her house was the perfect setting to experience the past with the present.

Our year ended and none too soon. The year Two-Thousand had many "first time since" experiences and as I climbed into bed, way before the New Year's bells, I silently cried to myself. All I could think about was January 21, 2000. It had been a very difficult year and I thanked God for the Elijah's Oil, the broken note adoration and learning how loving and merciful He was in good times and the not so good times. It had been the season to die and be reborn, but as I nodded off in slumber, I felt so far away from John. I confessed that I'd need much longer to grieve before I could manage my inner feelings. I also was accepting that perhaps, it wouldn't be so bad if God allowed me to grieve until I met John again in the fulfillment of my destiny.

REFLECTION

Did you ever think that every experience and event in your life is preparation for the future experiences and events ordained for later in your life? As a new season was born, I didn't feel adequate or prepared. I didn't want to move into a new season. I wanted to stay put. But God wouldn't let me. He had been preparing me for months for this new season. It didn't make it any easier, but it did show me God is sovereign, omniscient, omnipotent and omnipresent. No matter where I went in the world, He was there and nothing was out of His control. The year 2000 was the most difficult time of my life. Somehow God had used my past life to prepare me for the year and somehow I knew the year 2000 would be a year of experiences that would prepare me for the upcoming years.

CHAPTER TWENTY FOUR

The first year anniversary -- one year later

January 21, 2001 was a day we very much dreaded, yet anticipated. The first anniversary. How was that supposed to feel? People had supported, encouraged and shared insights of their grieving process. They also had shared the list of "first times" and associated experiences, but how was I going to feel? It was a Sunday morning and I awoke and lay in bed staring at nothing. It didn't feel like any special day. It felt depressing but nothing new. I relived a few moments of the day a year ago, trying to piece the memories together.

I thought about the hotel in India and how God opened my spiritual eyes and ears to my passion, mission and vision, but nothing else had happened since then. Maybe none of it was real. Maybe Satan deceived me.

I arose, fired up my computer and reread my journal of the day that John died. I felt miserable but it felt good that I could still grieve so deeply. I wanted to remember everything and relive everything as a special tribute to let myself know that I hadn't forgotten him one bit.

I sat staring and crying at the words on the computer screen. *This still doesn't feel like it really happened.* I opened my Bible, paged through verses, closed the Bible and bowed, and with my head in my hands, and gently rocked back and forth. *How could this still seem so unbelievable, so unreal?*

We went to church and as I slid into the pew, I saw the bouquet of flowers we had ordered for a memorial. When I focused on the flowers my mind instantly popped open the memory of the funeral and all the many bouquets. My eyes filled with tears over how many people had paid tribute then and how we were continuing to pay tribute. The "clean grieving" was here to stay and it was a good grieving.

Beth and I struggled uncomfortably through the service and read the note in the church bulletin announcing the flowers and for whom they were in honor. People came to us individually and in groups, some quick in passing, some standing patiently and others hugging, crying and shaking hands. God was moving again. He was showing us He loved us greatly and was merciful, and through His people we had the evidence.

I walked down the hallway to where my class was held and there was a huddle of people who had just come out of the classroom. Hearing they had gotten together and devoted the normal class time to praying for us humbled me.

One year later. One year to the day our son died. The first anniversary of our son's death. John died a year ago. I restated the fact in a variety of ways, trying to believe what I was saying. The fact seemed false, like it actually didn't happen. I wanted to see John in church, in college, wrestling, playing football, cooking, reading, sitting with him at ball games, cheering with him and yelling at the television during Penn State games.

Together at family dinner, we said a prayer, ate and went around the table, each given a chance to reflect on what we learned from John's death. A theme rose up. John was cool. He had made a much bigger impact on people and each of us than we thought and that we all missed him greatly.

Ben, Scott and Adrienne left the table and Beth and I sat commiserating. It was a sad day indeed. From my chair, I sat looking at the stove and the John tree in the back yard. That was all that remained. I felt hollow. Twenty-one years, now twenty-two years and only the joy of the past remained. It had been a glorious past. Eyes filling with tears, I grieved. I may feel I'm in the darkness, but one day I, too, will be in heaven and never again be in darkness.

Revelation 2:17 comforted me further. "He who has an ear, let him hear what the Spirit says to the churches. To him who overcomes, I will give some of the hidden manna. I will also give him a white stone with a new name written on it, known only to him who receives it."

I wondered if John received the white stone with a new name written on it. Or perhaps this scripture meant John would be waiting until Jesus returned and all that believed would receive the white stone and new name at the same time.

Was I ready? What if God sent word that it was my time? Was I ready? Blessed is the servant who will be found ready!

A year later I could understand the truth. I am no holier when I am being praised and no worse for being accused of faults. I am who and what I am. None are counted greater or lesser than they are in the sight of God. No matter how many years separated us, no matter the sins and faults, good deeds and praises, one day John and I would stand before the Savior, equal in His eyes.

I wanted to get up from the table but I couldn't. Words came from Proverbs 31:8, "Speak up for those who cannot speak for themselves, for the rights of all who are destitute. Speak up and judge fairly; defend the rights of the poor and needy.

Where did that come from? God was revealing His word and it came at such an illogical, weird time- the anniversary of John's death, after a family dinner. While sharing our grief, I received another piece of God's purpose puzzle. Proverbs 31:8 gave me depth in my purpose. It was a reminder to me that my God is faithful and constantly on the move.

In July of 2000 a friend and colleague from Florida agreed to meet with me and discuss his financial planning practice. I hadn't seen Charlie for about ten years but I remembered him. As I sat with him over lunch, I could see that he was different, more focused. As we talked over lunch he told me about a fellow who had written a book called "The Wright Exit Strategy". Bruce Wright was the author and he was promoting a very compelling process of how to reach affluent clients and provide lifetime financial advice. He gave me a copy of the book and shared how he had contracted with Bruce to develop a personal business plan that focused on creating and living out a perfect calendar. I was intrigued to see a person that convicted, so I eagerly anticipated reading the book.

Now nearly six months later I had read the book three times and had started applying some of the book's principles. In a short period of time I was re-kindling a flame in my work. I had been growing more bored as each month passed by in my career. I had a good job but there was no challenge and with all the company's changes, I was seeing diminished value in my services.

A new career had brought me to a new understanding of who I was professionally and that I had value in my expertise. Feeling under-appreciated, under-valued, and under-performing, I was ripe for a new conquest. Bruce's material provided exactly that.

A new person surfaced as well. Liliana Nealon was an American Express employee from New York. She had attained the role of being the corporate senior sponsor of the Christian Employees Network, SALT. Beth had met her at a Christmas luncheon where Liliana was the guest speaker. They hit it off instantly and in the course of a month, I talked with her over the phone and found a very intriguing Christian woman who had lost her husband seven years ago. She had a fiery passion and compassion about her, and I had the opportunity to visit her on a business trip to New York. God was uncovering divine appointments and I wasn't even aware of them.

I had been clinging to certain scriptures for years but the past year expanded my repertoire and stretched my thinking, especially with the attractiveness of the Book of Isaiah. But I was growing concerned. I was studying and learning and my sanctuary time and devotions were the daily and weekly highlights. I realized God's puzzle pieces were coming together but what would I do with the big picture? My heart and mind contained many new learnings but I was struggling to articulate them in a meaningful way. I was feeling like John. (During his last year, he was growing frustrated. He knew where he was and where he aspired to be, but didn't know how to get there.) So much was trapped inside me. I wanted to release it, but I couldn't. I was also uncertain where it would go once I did release it.

A Kempis wrote, *"The world grieves over worldly loss; we labor and hustle to gain some small profit, forgetting the harm to our souls and seldom recalling it. We attend to matters of little or no value and neglect those of greater importance."* Those words gouged my soul. Did I labor and hustle to gain small profit, forgetting the harm to my family's souls and seldom recalling it? Did I blow so many opportunities over my lifetime that I was running out of time?

I had blown so many opportunities in my life fleeing reality, or making stuff up so I would cast a fabulous impression on others. God took me a step closer to the truth. I had earlier learned about "the person behind the person" but now it progressed to my having to allow the outer person to die so the person behind the person could live.

Tony Yacconelli's book **Dangerous Wonder** talks about taking opportunities with childlike faith. "There is the skill of not trying to understand everything, but to experience it." I can't and shouldn't try to understand everything about Jesus. I should experience Jesus. His thought-provoking writing challenged me. Had I abandoned myself to a new life in Christ, or was I just learning about it and talking about it and not experiencing it?

Yacconelli defined "holy moments" as being in the presence of God, frightened and amazed at the same time. I knew I had plenty of holy moments in the past 18 years and especially since John died. But now what? Were they only that, temporary moments in time, almost solely for spiritual entertainment?

Abide in Him. I was experiencing so much that at times I felt overwhelmed trying to keep up with my brain. My heart was filled with the new experiences as well, so the intellectual met the passion and I could hardly contain myself. I coped with John's death more successfully when I contemplated what God was teaching me. It was simple to live the Christian life, simple, but not easy. The scriptures caressed my emotions and logic, spun deeply into my psyche and pierced the core of my inner soul. I was learning about life, because I was learning about death.

As the waves of grief swept over me, I would look at them and feel God in them and admit that they were only feelings and that God had something greater for my future, a renewed life, based upon Christ's death, manifested through the death of John. Hope blossomed.

REFLECTION

Are you abiding in Him? When you look back over the past year, can you see how God was at work in your life? Have you experienced the eternal and present relationship with God that supercedes all other experiences? Have you relied on the Holy Spirit to lead you or are you walking on your own, only thinking God is in charge? Is the word of God, His scriptures, filling your moments of holiness? So much happens in your life over a year. For me, it was a moment in the wilderness. One day when I am in the "promised land", my entire life in the wilderness will have been a mere puff of smoke, a slight lingering of the wisp of a fragrance, then gone.

Chapter Twenty Five

Another tree in the wilderness -- sixteen months after

As the months rolled by, God was faithful. He continued to provide oil primarily by His messengers and through His word. A new struggle was being manifested in my grieving process. I knew I was in trial and tribulation for sixteen months, but now I was looking at the situation differently. Being a faithful reader of Oswald Chamber's devotional, **My Utmost for His Highest**, I found God provided me an author of God's writings to refresh and renew me. One such lesson was on adversity:

John 16:33. *In the world you will have tribulation; but be of good cheer, I have overcome the world*

God showed me that others knew about pain and suffering and death. He showed me how to "be of good cheer." I was learning I wasn't alone, and much greater minds and hearts had been wrestling with the same issues as I. I found great comfort in knowing these minds and hearts had deep insight from God and they were used to provide the oil. I was seeing how to be a war horse in the Job 39 sense as well as in the 2 Kings 14 sense. I was to change sheep into war horses, as a servant leader, fearing only God and being loyal only to the rider, Jesus Christ. I was also to carry the faithful to their destiny with unconditional love, godly wisdom, discernment and compassion.

A year and four months ago, John died. It seemed so long since it happened. My family and I experienced joy in times of trouble, the deep groanings of the Holy Spirit and the light of the gospel. I learned what being "ruined in Christ" meant and what Elijah's Oil was. In 1 Kings 19 God illuminated His word as a still small voice, His way of guiding me through John's death.

1 Kings 19:11-15

The Lord said, "Go out and stand on the mountain in the presence of the Lord, for the Lord is about to pass by." Then a great powerful wind tore the mountains apart and shattered the rocks before the Lord, but the Lord was not in the wind. After the wind there was an earthquake, but the Lord was not in the earthquake. After the earthquake came a fire, but the Lord was not in the fire. And after the fire came a gentle whisper. When Elijah heard it, he pulled his cloak over his face and went out and stood at the mouth of the cave. Then the voice said to him, "What are you doing here, Elijah?"

"I have been very zealous for the Lord God Almighty. The Israelites have

rejected your covenant, broken down your altars and put your prophets to death with a sword. I am the only one left and now they are trying to kill me too.

The Lord said to him, "Go back the way you came and go down to the Desert of Damascus. When you get there, anoint Hazael king over Aram. Also anoint Jehu, son of Nimshi king over Israel and anoint Elisha, son of Shaphat from Abel Mehola to succeed you as prophet."

For many years as a believer, I had been zealous. I had tried and both failed and succeeded to motivate people to go farther than they ever have gone before for the Kingdom of God. At times it had been like a powerful wind, at times like an earthquake and at times like a fire. There had been great manifestations of the Holy Spirit at work, mountaintop experiences, miracles and profound moments doing and observing God's work.

But since my son's death, God has not been in the wind, earthquakes or fire. He has been a whisper; a still, soft voice. The whisper of God comes to me, and I think to others, during times of humbleness, brokenness, loneliness and emptiness. The attributes of a zealous, loyal servant, a war horse for God has been the wind, earthquake and fire. But the obedient, abiding and believing attributes have come in the still, soft whisper of God.

I saw a patient, loving God, waiting for us to get over the excitement of the winds, earthquakes and fires and hear His whisper.

I understood that I must be more than zealous for the Lord. I must be waiting and listening. There can be no unity, no peace, no joy, no purity or simplicity without waiting and listening. I must be humble, softhearted, teachable, sensitive, loving and single-purposed. Only by listening to the still small voice can Jesus teach me to love unconditionally.

When I hear God's whisper, I must seek to listen more deeply, seek to offer myself to Him and to have a teachable heart. I believe God has asked me the same question He asked Elijah many times, "What are you doing here?"

And I have responded as Elijah, telling of my zealousness, my woes, or trying to save the lost, restore and plant churches, minister to the poor, sick, suffering, captives, and those imprisoned in darkness. And like Elijah, I have seen my works ineffective, destroyed, attacked, mocked and even worse, ignored. Does God value me, yet allow my work to be met with ineffectiveness?

I knew that I am to anoint others, to make them radical leaders, warhorses who are listeners first, then doers of the word. My call is to move people where they have never been with God, humble, meek, contrite and single- minded. Always giving glory to God and not to myself; always advancing Him and not me; and always thankful for His mercy and grace. All this, while learning to live with less, making others more important than myself, submitting to the will of others and taking the lowly position so others can move forward.

God did not punch my time card at the end of twelve months of grieving, declaring He had given me the season of clean grieving and now it was time to set me free. Others would be losing children this year, others would suffer, lose loved ones, and be racked with pain, desolation, illness, oppression and brokenness. On the contrary, God was faithful and would not forsake me. Grief brings joy if you abide in Christ and in obedience, God will continue to take you to higher levels of anointing, understanding and transcendence. I had been in a cycle of surrendering and taking back, surrendering and taking back, until I was so frustrated, I didn't want to take back. Then I realized where I was: at the altar, and living sacrifices don't escape from the altar, they surrender to it.

John had no choice. He had ultimately surrendered his life and he couldn't take it back. I was supposed to surrender my life and live as a sacrifice for Jesus. My place for this was earth, John's is heaven.

The Apostle Paul gave a simple directive in 1 Cor. 10:31"… *whatever you do, do all to the glory of God"*.

I outwardly made it look like all I was doing was to the glory of God, but John's death didn't allow me to pick and choose what I did. God had done it. I couldn't say one thing and do another. I understood my schizophrenia. I actually did things for my glory and said I was doing them for God's and once I got other people to believe that, then I could believe it. That scenario melted with death. I had to live with a new dimension, a new integrity of who I was. I had to quit living for myself and live for God and others.

I looked at the Bible and saw miracle after miracle and how so many people at that time didn't notice them or didn't believe they actually happened. The journal of Christ, born of a virgin slips into the tragedy of Herod killing all those children, the story of Moses receiving the ten commandments drifts into his people's idol worship of a golden calf. The truth of Jesus' resurrection descends into a fish over coals on the seashore with his best friends not knowing who this Stranger was.

Was I losing my faith? Were my beliefs faltering? The awesomeness of standing with God on Holy Ground was a fading memory. Did it really happen the way it happened, or was it now diluted by worldly cynical thinking? I felt my mind and heart betraying me. Was all this anticlimactic and my life was now sliding downhill? I wasn't sure. Then God spoke and brought me a great revelation.

Matthew 11:2-6 "When John heard in prison what the Messiah was doing, he sent word by his disciples and said to him, 'Are you the one who is to come, or are we to wait for another?'

Jesus answered them, 'Go and tell John what you hear and see: the blind receive their sight, the lame walk, the lepers are cleansed, the deaf hear, the dead are raised, and the poor have good news brought to them. And blessed is anyone who takes no offense at me."

I read the scriptures and felt the power of God surge through me as an electrical charge. *John the Baptist had doubts too. A man of his distinction, the voice of the forerunner was doubting.* The common events of everyday life can sap the life from anyone when we look at the events of life as central to our focus. Jesus had comforting and encouraging words for the messengers to take back to John. Jesus' answer was perfect. He instructed the messengers to show the fruit of Christ's ministry. It wasn't the intellectual nature of God, it was His spiritual nature and the spiritual fruitfulness. Jesus never tried to convince anyone about who He was. He simply spoke the truth, and gave simple directions.

"Go and tell John what you hear and see: the blind receive their sight, the lame walk, the lepers are cleansed, the deaf hear, the dead are raised, and the poor have good news brought to them.

If those words were good enough for John the Baptist, they were good enough for me. I confessed immediately that I had a tendency to look for the super-spiritual, the dramatic, mystique of God instead of the plain truth. I had mistaken, as John the Baptist did, that the "Jesus-experience" was about amazement and miracles and awesome power and when He didn't satisfy my sensory perceptions and intellectual curiosity, then perhaps He wasn't the true messiah. Perhaps I should look elsewhere.

This delusional behavior began to manifest itself more in my daily calendar. It got to the point that scriptures and prayer weren't enough. I couldn't simply meditate and think and pray and contemplate God. I found myself buying books about God. I was slowly pulling a John the Baptist. I was doubting the presence of God in my own life and substituting the relationship experience with what authors thought. I realized these authors were great men and women of God and talented writers, but I also realized I was looking for answers from them and not from God. I needed more from God and I thought reading books would give me more of God. Writings by people like Oswald Chambers brought great insight and comfort, but these writers were not Christ incarnated.

John the Baptist needed to refocus his beliefs. Jesus simply said, "refocus". Don't buy John a book, go tell John what you have seen and heard. I learned that it's one thing to go through a crisis glorifying God, yet quite another to go through every day glorifying God when there is no audience, no stage, and no one paying even the remotest attention to me.

I wanted to be able to say, "Oh, I have been sanctified and so blessed by God during the death of John; look how wonderful God is!" But to do even the most humbling tasks to the glory of God left me feeling inadequate. I was forgetting that it was the power of God I needed, not another mountaintop experience, to see God working in us. To go unnoticed requires the Holy Spirit in me making me absolutely humanly His.

Death taught me about the true test of a believer's life. It is not about success but faithfulness on the human level of life. I tended to set up success in Christian grieving as my purpose, but my purpose was to display the glory of God in my life, and to live a life "hidden with Christ in God" in my everyday walk as written in Colossians 3:3. God wanted my relationships with him, my family and cohorts to be the very conditions in which the ideal life of God could be manifested. "Go tell them what you see and hear." I was learning the same lesson once again. It's not about me. It's never about me. It's always about Him.

REFLECTION

Don't wait until death comes to get serious about your relationship with God. Don't rest your soul on a Savior, but also on a Lord. Is Jesus Lord of your life or only Savior? I believe one can't make Jesus Lord until they have a relationship that has created sacrifice. Death and suffering causes appreciation of what God has done in our lives. Death impacts people. The Savior impacts people. The Lord rules His people and those He rules graciously seek to be ruled. I am learning that making Him Lord is not a one-time event or even a series of events. It is a daily walk. And He knows some days we will fail. But He also knows we aren't perfect, yet.

CHAPTER TWENTY SIX

Known in heaven and hell -- eighteen months after

Over the months, God didn't abandon me, nor did His word go unfruitful. He honored His promises to me a sinner, undeserving and unrepentant and He was faithful. I learned a few lessons from His word and from His messengers.

Then came a new crisis, my own life crises. From 1997 through 2001, I had had a season of trial and tribulation. Beth and my children have, as well, been participants. I lost my job due to a political power play at my company. I had two knee replacements due to the ravages of Lymes Disease and increased neck and shoulder problems that had deteriorated my strength and muscle usage. I totaled my car on the way home from a Bible study when a driver "hydro-planed" across a highway. I visited the emergency room twice for kidney stones. Our house was hit by a tornado and two weeks later, a severe hail storm. Beth had lost her mother to cancer a few years before, and her sister six weeks prior to John's death. Then John died. Approximately a year later, our daughter Adrienne had kidney stones that caused multiple complications and surgeries. I wondered what was happening.

Was it spiritual warfare? Three of my five scheduled missions trips were cancelled due to death or illness as my daughter had a previous personal crisis in 1999. Then in July of 2001, I suffered a heart attack that caused about 30% heart damage. After an angioplasty and two stents, a changed diet and cardiac rehabilitation, I stood again before God, listening.

When John died, I felt the "Elijah experience." The earthquake, the fire and the wind and then the still small voice of God all occurred. My heart attack was more like Peter being released by the angel from prison. I was ready to meet Jesus. I didn't want to die, yet there was a sense of anticipation in meeting Jesus. I had seen John die and I saw his face at the last moment when he met Jesus. It was a look of joy and peace, comfort and love.

So I was ready. I prayed for forgiveness of my sins and asked for God's mercy. I didn't want to meet Him face to face knowing I struggled with sin. But I also knew I was going to heaven. No more Lymes Disease, no more death, no more heart attacks, no more pain and suffering. No more disappointments, or frustrations, or emptiness or fear. Freedom. I was ready.

But that would have been the easy way out of God's wilderness journey and I knew it. It was humbling, to have no control, no understanding of what was happening and no power to change anything. A few days after my heart attack, when I sat in the cardio rehab area with seven other men, I realized I was the youngest by thirteen years. Intently, I listened to these men talk about how their lives changed. They ate differently, they worked differently, they exercised differently and they lived and thought differently. And the reason for all this change in their lives was so they could live longer.

I was seeing men fear death. I understood the night before, as I lay in the emergency room waiting for the angioplasty, that I didn't fear death, including my family's deaths or my own death. Now in rehabilitation, I made up my mind that, I would not change my life to simply live longer if I didn't live my life totally for God.

I had better start living a life for Christ instead of just trying to live longer. To live an extra couple of years in my mind, wasn't worth it if I didn't live for Christ.

The heart attack never had me feeling as if I were actually going to die, but I wasn't sure how much of a normal life I'd have to live afterwards. I didn't realize all the stress I had endured in my life. Reflecting on these past months of my life, I often thought that the primary reason I had a heart attack was because I had a broken heart.

Acts 12: The night before Peter was to be placed on trial, he was asleep, chained between two soldiers, with others standing guard at the prison gate. Suddenly, there was a bright light in the cell, and an angel of the Lord stood before Peter. The angel tapped him on the side to awaken him and said, "Quick! Get up!" And the chains fell off his wrists. Then the angel told him, "Get dressed and put on your sandals." And he did. "Now put on your coat and follow me," the angel ordered.

So Peter left the cell, following the angel. But all the time he thought it was a vision. He didn't realize it was really happening. They passed the first and second guard posts and came to the iron gate to the street, and this opened to them all by itself. So they passed through and started walking down the street, and then the angel suddenly left him.

God rescued his people just at the right moment. Prayers were answered. Peter was in a dark cell. It was late at night. The bright light cut through the darkness. I thought about how many times I had been facing pitch-dark dilemmas. At times there seemed to be no solution. We grieved, we prayed, we worried, we sought counsel, and we strategized and analyzed, but to no avail. We needed a burst of light.

The angel tapped Peter in the darkness to awaken him. His church was praying for him, but Peter was not praying, he was sleeping. It was time to wake up and to awaken others. I thought I would never drift back to that dazed and confused state of spirituality after John died. I thought that I had learned much and I would never back slide into "spiritual lukewarm ness." But slowly I slid.

After Peter was awakened, he still had sentries guarding him, he still had the chains binding him, he still was in the inner dungeon, he still had two guard stations to elude and he still had to open the gate.

The angel told Peter to quickly get up, get dressed and put on his sandals. Then he had to put on his coat. Then he had to follow the angel. The angel gave him the direction and it wasn't a trial run; they were leaving. I wondered if Peter knew what was happening.

Somehow the sentries disbanded. Those guards, chained to Peter could have been symbolic of the social and cultural guards watching over me. To me the chains were faint-heartedness and hard-heartedness. When I was faint-hearted, I'd start many new things, have a zeal and a passion, but weaken, and the idea or ministry or passion would wither on the vine. My other guard was hard-heartedness. That came from an "unteachable spirit." Too often I had too much pride to listen and learn from others. With John's death and my total focus on God, I forgot how God was using others to teach and comfort. My pride got in the way. So faint-heartedness caused me to start things but never finish them and hard-heartedness caused me not to start anything.

Then there were the chains that fell from Peter's wrists. Those chains could have been disappointment, frustration, fears, ignorance, insensitivity, indifference or injustice in my life. I had been a new creation in Christ but I was chained up so tightly that I had no power, no authority and I lived a mediocre life. What chains did I need to have released so I could be free? I needed to release the chains of disappointment, emptiness and unfulfilled dreams. I feared my death, the death of my wife and children and I feared I'd run out of money before I died. Once John died I lost the fear of death to a family member. Now with my heart attack, I lost the fear of me dying. The third fear of money went away. It was an unfounded fear.

My thoughts went back to the hotel room in India. *What had I died to? What was I born into?*

Peter passed through the first and second guard posts. Again, on Peter's journey, he ran into more obstacles, the guard stations. But he continued in the power of the Holy Spirit by following the angel. There were no permanent obstacles when he followed God. What obstacles were keeping me from living the life God had promised me? What was stopping me from living a life free of fears and worries? I allowed those obstacles to have more power than God in my life. God had given me passion, a mission and specific visions to fulfill that mission over the past months of grieving. But the obstacles had stopped me from doing anything about my mission or visions.

Then Peter came to the final obstacle: the big iron gate. That gate was closed at night. It was the gate into the city. It took twenty-five men to move the gate, so it was not heavily guarded, since no man could move it on his own. Peter and the angel didn't need to find the right set of keys, or get a battering ram. It opened by itself. The last obstacle blocking Peter's freedom surrendered before the power of God. I kept thinking as I lay on the operating table, *Is there one last obstacle holding me prisoner?* Was I struggling to open doors and overcome obstacles with my own strength?

A month after my heart attack, by God's grace, I was with Steiger Ministries in Poland and had the opportunity to meet with over fifty missionaries and base leaders. Beth and Adrienne accompanied me. For many, it was the first time we'd be seeing each other since John's death.

I had my world rocked when I heard a missionary say that he wanted his name known in heaven and hell. My first reaction was negative. Then he read the following scripture and those verses convicted me. One statement said it all… "The spirit replied, "I know Jesus, and I know Paul. But who are you?"

Act 19:13-16

A team of Jews who were traveling from town to town casting out evil spirits tried to use the name of the Lord Jesus. The incantation they used was this: "I command you by Jesus, whom Paul preaches, to come out!" Seven sons of Sceva, a leading priest, were doing this. [15]But when they tried it on a man possessed by an evil spirit, the spirit replied, "I know Jesus, and I know Paul. But who are you?" And he leaped on them and attacked them with such violence that they fled from the house, naked and badly injured.

I had to ask myself, "If I was confronted by an evil spirit, would they have heard of me prior to the encounter, because of who I am in Christ? Or would they mock me and humiliate me and disregard who I was because they didn't know I had Christ living in me?"

If hell doesn't know who I am, I will probably end up fleeing, humiliated, defeated and injured from spiritual warfare and the evils of the world. Perhaps that is why our society has little respect for the Christian. I was hoping that through the grieving process, I had become a better witness for Christ, but how could I be sure?

As I heard those scriptures and contemplated the words about the leading priest who fled, beaten, naked and humiliated, I grew convicted in the Holy Spirit. So often, I wanted everyone to know that my name was in heaven. I wanted to cast out demons and do great things in Christ's name. But my efforts ended up as embarrassing attempts, oozing hypocrisy and feeble efforts where I was mocked and defeated.

My son John, was introduced to Jesus at age five. Had I been too pre-occupied over the years to introduce others to Jesus? Did the evil spirits know who I was? Did hell know who I was? If I was to live in the power and authority of Jesus Christ, he would be glorified by my obedience. Does anyone know I am a child of God? Does hell know that I am a "Christ-one?"

I heard the Holy Spirit comment, "Seek to have heaven, the world and hell know who you are. Remember, at Judgment Day, it will be better to have a testimony than a title. Heaven and hell respects no one for their accomplishments on earth, but they revere obedience since that is what impacts the power of heaven and hell."

I had to do an obedience check and learn that if heaven, the world and hell know who I am, it's because of the power of God residing in me now. I had seen God change my steps in the past six months, but until the heart attack and then the missions trip to Poland, I had not added up all those steps.

My bigger issue was conditional love. As I looked at my conditional and unconditional acts of love and words, I knew I had most people fooled. I was fairly unconditional in my deeds, although far from perfect. God had transformed me over the years to be tolerant, fair and accepting, especially with my loved ones. But I was still struggling with my inability to communicate with unconditionally loving words. As I stated earlier in the book, I set forth to repent from my words. But as I was transforming my words, I uncovered an attitude, which was my bias against wealthy people. I couldn't decipher what it was for years, but now it revealed itself. Envy, jealousy, lust, materialism or arrogance, I couldn't tell. I knew I had to repent from those feelings and attitudes. I was angry at wealth and wealthy people. I saw it spoil and destroy people and cause dysfunctional behavior. I saw runaway greed and little financial accountability.

I saw an arrogance in the lifestyle of wealthy people, and an "illusion of wealth lifestyle" for those that were not wealthy. But I had to overcome my prejudice and judgmental attitude. Could I love a wealthy person? I saw too many hypocrites and was watching money become the language the whole world spoke in.

So I set out to repent of my conditional ways. The experiences I had in Asia had grounded my prejudice years earlier. Wealth had caused an imbalance in the world. The process was fairly simple. Mankind thrived on injustice. Since Cain and Abel, the falleness of mankind bred injustice. Injustice then manifested itself in indulgence, leading to ignorance, leading to insensitivity and the ultimate, indifference.

Wealthy people just didn't care for anything they couldn't experience as comfort or pleasure, so the poor in India and the oppressed in Vietnam were only two of the lands of injustice. In the circles I walked in, most people were too self-indulgent, totally unaware, hard-hearted or uncaring. There were a few exceptions but I would come home from Asia, travel in America and see so many yachts harbored on lakes and bays, that it would sicken me after seeing so many people in need. I despised everyone's wealth but my own. My myopic view was indifferent to areas such as Africa and South America, which probably had worse conditions. So I conceded that I was angry and judgmental at myself as well. God had shown me a blind spot and I had to decide what I'd do about it.

So I committed to repenting of my conditional love towards wealthy folks and looked at how I could minister to them. I didn't know exactly how to do that sort of ministry but I had started working with advisors who were focusing on affluent clients and had been gathering learnings or what the affluent looked like.

My mission and visions were defined, but I didn't know how to take the next step. I had learned that I had many obstacles impeded any vision achievement. I looked to that divine appointment in my life, Bruce Wright to help me define a way to overcome the obstacles. I hired him to be my mentor and guide me into developing a macro strategic plan to align my mission, visions and goals by overcoming the obstacles. As we worked together, God revealed that I had to change my career. I was a mentor. I was a disciple maker. Period. I had always reverted back to a coach, teacher or mentor throughout my life and now I saw that in order to take John's legacy to the next level, I had to fulfill my purpose, thus fulfilling his purpose.

Bruce became a stepping stone as I saw where I needed to go. While Bruce helped me define the big picture plan, I needed a way to execute it. The plan I had helped me focus when memories, depression or grief hit me..

As the waves of grief swept over me, I would look at them and feel God in them and admit that they were only feelings and that God had something greater for my future, a renewed life, based upon Christ's death, manifested through the death of John. Hope blossomed.

I learned I needed an Entrance Strategy to be a mentor in a business and ministry vocation. The Holy Spirit, through answered prayer, directed me to the scriptures to develop an entrance strategy. A process evolved.

Pray and follow the promptings of the Holy Spirit

Act on your Passion and Mission -"Build a vertical bridge" acting on your beliefs.

Assemble a team of dedicated and exceptional people.-"Build a horizontal bridge"

Define your passion, purpose, vision, and/or identify your problems.

Create a brilliant game plan focusing on results.

Define expectations for the team, then get commitment.

Seek God to empower those people around you to help you succeed.

Execute AND Hold everyone accountable to their roles.

Communicate effectively

Stay focused on your God's promptings and don't settle for mediocrity

As the days turned into weeks and the sadness would come and go, I would cling to the steps God gave me and by being focused, I saw it all come together. Vision led to execution which resulted in results, if accountability was maintained. I sought others as well as myself and God, to hold me accountable to act on what I believed.

The journey continued and as I shared my steps and the new process with others, I found most people, about three in every four, weren't wired mentally or emotionally to think about the big picture first and then the details. They politely listened and would go where I was mentally, probably out of compassion. But the one in four that were wired the same way; who thought about the big picture first and then aligned all the details with it, became very encouraged in their own personal and business lives.

I was amazed that through the death of John, God had opened an entirely new world for me. I often included John in my mentoring as I could see that God had used John and John's death to teach me how to do my ministry.

What helped me most was realizing that I wasn't supposed to help everybody. I was only a messenger, not the messiah, so when seventy-five percent of prospects observed my work and weren't interested, I didn't take it personally. God didn't want me to try to work with everyone. Jesus talked about that in the scriptures.

Matthew 13:3 Then he told them many things in parables, saying: "A farmer went out to sow his seed. As he was scattering the seed, some fell along the path, and the birds came and ate it up. Some fell on rocky places, where it did not have much soil. It sprang up quickly, because the soil was shallow. But when the sun came up, the plants were scorched, and they withered because they had no root. Other seed fell among thorns, which grew up and choked the plants. Still other seed fell on good soil, where it produced a crop—a hundred, sixty or thirty times what was sown. He who has ears, let him hear."

Matthew 13:18 "Listen then to what the parable of the sower means: When anyone hears the message about the kingdom and does not understand it, the evil one comes and snatches away what was sown in his heart. This is the seed sown along the path. The one who received the seed that fell on rocky places is the man who hears the word and at once receives it with joy. But since he has no root, he lasts only a short time. When trouble or persecution comes because of the word, he quickly falls away. The one who received the seed that fell among the thorns is the man who hears the word, but the worries of this life and the deceitfulness of wealth choke it, making it unfruitful. But the one who received the seed that fell on good soil is the man who hears the word and understands it. He produces a crop, yielding a hundred, sixty or thirty times what was sown."

I saw frustration in the eyes of many of my colleagues and clients, friends and loved ones. They wondered where I was going with this and why they didn't think like I did about their future. One day a business owner, in his frustration, blurted out. "Jake, I'd love to think about my future. I'd love to have hope and move forward in my faith. But I have so many problems I have to solve today. I have to worry about taking care of them first!"

The following weeks, his words rang out, over and over again. "I have so many problems I have to solve today. I have to worry about taking care of them first!"

I asked God for wisdom and understanding. "How could I help the people that were looking to take are of problems today and not think about the future?"

It took a couple of additional weeks, but God revealed another process to me for problem resolution. Again, I began with the time frame and context of the problem. I prayed for wisdom and discernment, reflecting on how God worked in our problem-solving during the darkest grieving days.

I needed to know when solutions needed to happen as well as how long people were dealing with the problem. Then I had to motivate people to look at the problem or the perception of the problem. Through discussion, we would come to a conclusion, that usually people clumped multiple issues together. Instead of dealing with each issue separately, they looked at all of them seeking one solution. When they didn't find the silver bullet to slay all the problems, at once, they got overwhelmed and gave up.

Realizing this was also the way I had been handling my bad days of grieving, I refocused myself on looking at the facts, not my thoughts and feelings. What really was happening? What really was the problem or problems?

I looked at my own struggles as a reviewing of my past and looking at these problems to determine if they were factual or perceived. I found most of them were illusions, merely flaws in my own thinking because I put my feelings and perceptions above the facts. That day was a break through, for me and for a new career in helping others.

As I fretted and strained over solutions, I felt the warmth of the Holy Spirit and He touched me deep in my soul. I felt the Lord was saying to me, "*Collaborate John. Don't try to do it all on your own. I have provided my word. I have provided you with friends and pastors. I have provided you with professional resources, colleagues, friends, family and a wife to help you. You aren't supposed to solve your problems on your own. That is what My church is for!*"

I sat at my desk, stunned. Now it seemed easy. I confessed that my hard work ethic and my pride were getting in the way of God and His resources helping me. I was ashamed and disgusted with myself. *Who did I think I was?* I had been acting like I was the only father who ever lost a son, like no one else ever experienced loss, or death. I was seeing how my pride was taking the blessings of God and turning them inward, as if no one else could understand what we were going through. I had been deceived by my feelings and false wisdom. The enemy had deceived me into believing this grief would stop me from being any kind of a fruitful servant. I confessed that the problem was me.

I collaborated with God, and with friends and family, missionaries and corporate people, pastors and clients. The next step of the process became very evident. I have to analyze the problem, look at alternative solutions and put a strategy in place to bring closure to my grief, or I knew it would eat at me forever. I reverted back to my future direction process at this point.

What was my entrance strategy for solving this self-centered grief problem? What did I need to do to develop a recipe for success? The answers came from the scriptures and prayer as the Holy Spirit revealed them to me. When I stopped and looked at them, they resembled the vision process.

1. Pray and follow the promptings of the Holy Spirit

2. Review the specific issues and concerns separately, instead of all together.

3. Look at the facts, then the perceptions and then your feelings in that order-always.

4. Assemble a team of dedicated and exceptional people. Collaborate.

5. Define and analyze your problems with objectivity, not emotions.

6. Create alternate scenarios for solutions.

7. Define expectations for the team, then get commitment.

8. Seek God to empower your people to succeed.

9. Execute AND Hold everyone accountable to their roles.

10. Communicate effectively.

11. Stay focused on your problem and don't quit until you have brought closure (a solution) and acted upon it.

John Piper had a brilliant quote which helped me get over feeling sorry for myself.

"Develop a wartime mentality and lifestyle; that you never forget that life is short, that billions of people hang in the balance of Heaven and Hell everyday, that the love of money is spiritual suicide, that the goals of upward mobility (nicer clothes, cars, houses, vacations, food, hobbies) are a poor and dangerous substitute for the goals of living for Christ with all your might and maximizing your joy in ministry to people's needs."

No longer did I seek to languish, or stay stuck in my grief. Slowly God created a burning passion to help others in a new ministry of mentoring others. The Greek word, "Paralambano" filled me. It means, to come alongside of and impart; and then for another to receive that impartation and to pass it on to others.

I saw the enemy try to discourage this process and my new found passion. Christians and non-Christians alike, would view the processes and my passion with skepticism, dispelling my learnings as if they couldn't work in the real world. I soon realized that it wasn't me who was wrong, but our culture was wrong. Our culture has influenced our proud American people to think that they should do it all on their own, the "American Way." Be tough, be strong, don't show weakness, pretend there is nothing wrong so you don't appear weak to society and live in freedom, demanding pleasure and comfort and not accepting pain and suffering as part of real life.

What I learned was that nearly everyone has lost something in their lives and will lose much in their future. Whether it be money, identity, friendship, loved ones, careers, ministry, spouse, children, pets, financial independence, comfort, pleasure, property, health, abilities, talents, or freedom, we will all lose. And I am finding through John's death, that there aren't many people who are prepared to handle loss; their own, or others. But by the grace of God, I am devoted to make disciples who can impact others lives and help them overcome problems and find direction while destroying Satan's domain in our society.

Based upon the parable of the sower, I was to work with the fertile soil, plant seed and nurture it for a bountiful crop. I was only to work with those people wired like I was.

I am to focus on only twenty five percent of the people . And I am to mentor those who were seeking new direction or mission or vision in their life, or people who are seeking solutions to life problems, primarily helping executives, business owners, pastors and missionaries.

John's death, the struggles over the past five years and the months leading up to my heart attack and the recovery afterwards have been very difficult, but I thank God for all that has happened. Those events I think, will make my family and me better people. God will utilize tragedy and loss, pain, and suffering to lift you up and draw you nearer to Him.

REFLECTION

What is God doing in your life now that you know will one day be manna for ministry? Do you believe there is a reason for everything? I mean really believe and not simply say it? Perhaps you acknowledge nothing of significance is happening currently. Be assured, something will happen. Will you be prepared? Pray and read His word, then perhaps you will be prepared.

CHAPTER TWENTY SEVEN

What my son's death taught me

As I look back over the past nineteen months, I have seen God up close. He is a teacher and a master, a lover and a forgiver, a deliverer and a protector. He has taught me many important lessons. I read in a book, **Tuesday's with Morrie,** that grieving is like a fire. It flares, roars and leaves a pile of ashes. It begins with a glowing ember and fans itself into a massive conflagration, then quickly burns down, much like a pine tree in a forest fire. The outward appearance of a burnt pine tree is devastating. It appears charred and seared, looking shamefully wasted, but deep in the trunk, there is still life. Death caused me to cry out in my soul. Grief's fire burned my outer appearance and the superficiality of my worldliness. Deep inside there was newness of life.

I cried out in my soul those early days after my son's death, "Shouldn't the world care? Shouldn't someone notice? Will anyone understand? Does it really matter to anyone else but me, right now?"

And I heard God's answers to all those questions in memories of John. The world shouldn't stop and I shouldn't expect it to. Someone will care, but many will not, and my grieving and loss may go unnoticed. But to those who notice, healing and comfort will come. From my pastors Roger and Scott, to my brother Paul, my younger brother Tom and his wife, my missionary friends, David, Ton, Andy, Mark, Anthony, my mother Jean, my wife Beth and my children, Ben, Scott and Adrienne, they all cared.

God didn't want the whole world to notice, but he wanted the people at Berean Baptist Church to notice, the Apple Valley football and wrestling teams, and my board of directors at White Dove to notice. Millions of people die every day, millions of sons and daughters die and millions suffer and grieve. God's sovereign plan had a few people in the world take notice of John's death. My friends and ministry partners Noeline and Samuel in Vietnam, Pradeep and Suneeta in Nagpur, India, Ken in New Zealand; fellow workers and field members from American Express Financial Advisors took notice. They cared. People I never knew from missionary work, churches, businesses and the community kept filling the jar with Elijah's oil. It was those individuals that I couldn't begin to count who loved and showed us compassion. It was an ingredient of Isaiah's oil, the sympathy and caring from others who kept us going.

I would learn that very few people could understand what it meant to lose a child, but more importantly, I knew God wanted me to know what it felt like. And one day God would probably use the experience in not only my life, but in the lives of my wife and children to minister to others. I didn't know when it would happen, or to whom it would happen, but it would happen and we had the experience and authority to minister to others because we were there once.

Now it didn't matter what others or the world thought or did, all that mattered was that my son knew Jesus personally. Now it wasn't a concern how vulnerable or weak I appeared to friends or family or strangers, because my life would never be the same again and I would never be the same. That understanding wasn't positive or negative, it simply just was the way it was going to be. There was joy and love, spiritual joy and peace, because everyone I treasured knew Jesus Christ and would have the same destiny; heaven. Death is our destiny and death is excruciating, but it is a fact of life. The facts are the facts. It doesn't matter what I said, or what they said, all that mattered is what God said. His words count the most.

The surrealism continued, unpredictably. It would happen everywhere and at anytime. A sudden stunned pause. I would descend into total oblivion, "sensory-blocked" to the world around me. John's death never seemed real. Then those moments hit me and I wandered aimlessly in thought, emotion, spirit and body. Those episodes seemed so unreal and I'd look back embarrassed by my complete absentmindedness and concede I had been acting unreal, almost zombie-like. Those times reduced in frequency, but never did they disappear completely.

John's death still doesn't seem real at times. I walk out into my backyard to his tree and memorial stone and stare at it every now and then. I grow saddened, then empty. I look around the backyard remembering the times we played baseball or tossed the football, pitched horseshoes and grilled burgers. I admire the tall maple tree, remembering it as a sapling, now over thirty feet tall, then I look beyond the tree at the screened in back porch. Tears come almost instantly, remembering how we as a family worked with Ray Brown to build that porch. So many reminders of the life John shared with us. So much life now lost. Was it fair? I didn't know and it didn't matter. Whether it was fair or not would be to question God's sovereignty and omniscience. I couldn't bring John back so I didn't try to drag myself into hypothetical scenarios. God knew the plan and I trusted God's timing and wisdom far more than I trusted my own.

I learned that in death there are contrasting stress points, or stressors.

Death is evil and hurtful and cruel, but in contrast, it led to peace and joy and presence in heaven for the believer. During times of grieving, there seemed always to be those diametrically opposed forces attacking each other. The pain of the waves of grief breaking my heart, yet the joy in remembering how much I loved my son so my heart could be broken. A joy and grief, a profound contrasting stressor. The letters and cards from friends and family tore at my soul every time I opened an envelope, but the printed and hand-written words healed the pain, often instantly.

In times of deep sadness, emptiness and loneliness, I learned it was okay to ask the questions, "Does anything really matter? Should I allow myself to be consumed in the flames of grief? Should I quit; just give up?" I battled my logic. My mind would race to 1980 and I'd see this little toddler bouncing off my chest, eager to rough house. I would burst out laughing 21 years later then burst out crying. God showed me that it was okay if I felt useless in my grieving. I learned death is only one aspect of grieving. Living a life continuously in unhappiness was more devastating. I was unhappy. My daily life felt devastating being unhappy. But I knew living a life without God included many more aspects of grieving. To live unhappily meant living apart from God. Living apart from God is sin. The definition of sin to me is being separated from God. *Was I living in sin, unhappy and being apart from God?*

Deep inside each of us is a desire to overcome the grieving, overcome living apart from God and overcome the unhappiness of unhappiness. I learned I wasn't living apart from God. God never left me and I never left Him. I learned feelings cannot always be trusted and I can't rationalize my feelings. So I can't explain certain emotions, nor can I explain the intellectual capacity to judge those emotions. But grieving and feeling lonely wasn't sin. It wasn't being apart from God. It was grieving and loneliness. I learned I can't make stuff up if I don't know the truth, or the facts. I also can't keep searching for answers when there aren't any.

God showed me in the first year that my American culture does not make grieving people like myself, feel good about themselves. I wasn't sure if I had lost my values, my absolute truths, my principles and my beliefs, thus the things I gave up in love and death are the things I now search for the most. There's that contrasting stressor again. My inner voice said, "Don't try to be strong enough to stand for values, truths, principles and beliefs, they aren't important enough to give up my money, toys, fame and success."

But then my deeper soul took over and in purity of motive, I answered my own questions. I don't have to try to be strong or perform or be important or have the right political, spiritual, social and economic status. In the end, it all comes down to you and what you believe in. I chose God and will continue to choose God as the main source of what I believe in. I know it is becoming more and more unpopular to state your beliefs as a Christian, it isn't politically correct and it sounds narrow-minded, elitist, judgmental and old-fashioned. But as I stood looking at the hearse pull away, or the little bush on the banks of the frozen lake, or sat in the dark emptiness of his bedroom, I knew that society and culture and modern thinking didn't have any empirical answers and that most people were searching and they were clinging to ideas and concepts they truly never understood or experienced.

I wasn't sure about them, but I was sure about me. I knew after these past months, that people always act on what they believe in and most people don't know how to act when death comes. So they really believed in nothing because they couldn't act on their beliefs. Life may be up for a vote, but death isn't. Death truly showed me what I believed in, what my loved ones believed in and what many friends and colleagues believed in.

Even in death, so many people tried to comfort us using money and toys as the main ingredient, because they themselves didn't understand nor were willing to learn about the absolute truth of death. I learned first hand that in my culture, Christian and non-Christians alike do not take strong stands on their beliefs, truths and values when each is put to the test. I concluded that that most people handle death one of four ways, much like I handled my heart attack.

The fainthearted seek to understand and to believe in God in a tragic time. They start strong, believing in God, but they grow fainthearted as time goes on. Their beliefs and truths and values wither and shrivel on the vine and they bear no fruit once death occurs to others. There is no love, joy, peace, patience, truth, goodness, faithfulness or self-control, just a sadness and a demand for answers to their questions as to why. Often, I saw and heard of others who were going through the same grieving process, grow restless and angry and bitter toward God. It was because they were fainthearted and could not finish strong. That wasn't a judgment call on my behalf. On two occasions, people told me that is exactly what they did; they refused to finish strong, and just gave up. I confessed, I felt that way momentarily, but fought not to give up.

The second way people handled death was to take on a hardhearted stance. They are the opposite of the fainthearted. They never started to deal with the death. They denied it or pretended it didn't affect them greatly. They were too insensitive, too afraid or too proud to be taught, so the absolute truths never penetrated their hearts and minds and they handled the entire experience without God. Some mourners came to me, only concerned about themselves at the time of John's death, which I found rather bizarre. They weren't interested in me or my family, but totally immersed in their own experience of why God did what He did and they wanted answers. But they wanted their answers, not God's answers. They were so self-absorbed that they forgot they weren't the most important concern during this time.

The third way people handled death was through broken hearts. The brokenhearted came and brought the spiritual fruits. They were meek and poor in spirit, but they knew they had heaven and they would inherit the earth. That was their gift to Beth, my children and me. God used them. Brokenhearted people are teachable, while the fainthearted and the hardhearted seek not to learn, but to be comforted by their own efforts.

But God taught me that the single-hearted, the fourth way to handle death, was where the treasures of God lay. These single-hearted men and women were focused and looked solely to God for the answers. They didn't try to come up with the answers, or the right theology, self-help books, psycho babble or verses. Their eyes spoke more about their hearts than their mouths did. They had only one truth: God loves His children.

I conceded that all of us drifted in and out of those four seasons of grief, but each of us were restored to our most dominant; usually the season we lived in most. I found out who truly believed in what they said they believed in. I learned what I believed in, as well.

In time I learned that it was truly radical to sacrifice the cultural standards for higher standards. If I didn't, I felt that I would remain the unhappiest person on earth. So in John's death, and in grieving, I met absolute truth and defined my beliefs and had to decide how to handle the newly discovered truths. I chose to handle it with God. God wins. God always wins, because He never runs out of time or love. Neither do His single-hearted people who cling to Him as their only true hope.

I learned that throughout my life, I bothered constantly with all the distractions of my simple world and all too often, never got around to experiencing what God had intended for me to experience. I chose to think "It is all about me and not about God." It was always so comforting just to think about me and my gain and my lifestyle. Death taught me that there is no comfort in the worldly sanctuaries of career, money, lifestyle and toys. I needed another sanctuary to think, meditate, ponder, digest, synthesize, innovate and create. God used death to create that sanctuary. I had many sanctuaries I created to escape over the years. I couldn't escape death. I thought for so many years that I didn't need to understand death. It was an event that happened and made people sad, but that was the process we were destined to. So I avoided death and therefore avoided the deeper meaning of life.

I made a determination that I couldn't allow my normal world to create its own sanctuary, a "my world sanctuary" for me so I didn't have to experience the injustice, ignorance, insensitivity and indifference of the world. That was what I did in my daily world of pleasing myself first. My "my world sanctuary" protected me from pain and suffering and death and injustice. It shielded me from the ravages of death and pain, insensitivity and indifference. The "my world sanctuary" also caused me to be unjust, ignorant, insensitive and indifferent. It became my lifestyle trap. I learned I never realized "my world sanctuary" was not the sanctuary God intended for me. I had to allow him to create my relationship and lifestyle with him through experiencing God in His sanctuary in worship, prayer, meditation, and the Word.

For too long I moved in a comatose state, wandering in a meaningless, purposeless life. I seemed out of it, yet was so busy doing what I thought was critically important. Then death came along and I didn't know what to do, because that had not been included in my comatose state. It was total irony. All my life I lived as if I was too busy to contemplate death. In the end, that is all that was left and until John's death I didn't believe it could happen. I thought my life was too important to God. My children's lives were too important. God had big plans for them, so none of us really had to contemplate death. We acted as if we were immune to death. Other children die, not mine. Other people suffer, not me. In my mind I was doing very important things and death was not important. Another trap of the "my world sanctuary."

It was nearly impossible to be insensitive and indifferent during death. I believe God makes us hypersensitive during death and suffering. He gives us insight and wisdom, but we must be willing to be vulnerable. I found it very easy to determine injustice and plead ignorance and escape any experience God intended while living with John's death. The "my world sanctuary" disappeared. I was and still am, very sensitive to death and suffering and very alarmed at the amount of injustice, ignorance, insensitivity and indifference in this world. I doubt if I would have ever been this aware unless I lost a son. I thank God often that I have become sensitive, because John's life and death served at least one purpose: changing my sensitivity and dissolving "my little world" attitude.

I learned I can hear God's voice beyond life and death and when it is all said and done, only our relationships are what are important, first with God, then with our family and then with friends and finally with foes. Ultimately I can then have a better relationship with myself.

I learned worship is more meaningful with broken notes than perfect harmony and all suffering brings you more intimately connected to God than celebration does. I learned that being "ruined for Jesus" was all about gaining and not losing. My life was ruined for Jesus. My "my world sanctuary," my comatose state, my own injustice, ignorance, insensitivity and indifference were ruined. Being ruined by Jesus was a good thing. Those elements of my life that brought conditional words, thoughts, deeds and attitudes were ruined by death. God ruined them. I thanked God for ruining them. I learned that if I lost my love and compassion and passion, I needed to go back to where I last remembered them before they were lost and they would be found there. Often I found them in the ruins.

I wanted to love unconditionally. I wanted to be honest and pure in my motives. When I struggled searching for them, I would go back to an event, or an incident or a relationship where I was embarrassed or angry at what I did or said or thought. Invariably, I would see the ruins and find where I lost my love, compassion or passion. Standing by the "John-tree" and memorial stone in my backyard would emotionally destroy me. And as I stood with my emotions in ruins, God would come.

Defining anguish was a major epiphany for me. Standing near the lake shore where I cried out to God in the days immediately after John's death, I learned how ugly the emotion of anguish felt. I thanked God for that revelation. I never had analyzed my emotions. I would simply act out emotionally and move on, never being accountable for my actions or words. Anguish made me look at all my emotions and define them. Once I could define anguish, I could release it to God and move beyond the intense pain. As I learned to identify my other emotions and release them to God, I found I had less negative emotions and could move beyond emotional incompetence.

Death causes compassion. It equalizes strangers and one can cry for the foreigner, the orphan, the sick, the lame, the hungry, the blind, the widows, the poor and oppressed. I also learned that I could wade deep into the waves of grief and totally immerse myself in what I was feeling, then wade back out again after realizing what the wave was doing to me in my emotions, thoughts, spiritual walk, and relationships. I never thought of myself as a deep person and I shied away from deep thinking people, for I acknowledged my limitations. Intellectually and emotionally, I could never articulate what was inside. I avoided the deep pain and used humor or denial, cynicism or aloofness as if I were beyond emotions.

I was always outgoing in my personality, quick to humor, spew a cynical aphorism or add sarcastic fuel to a dialogue. Again, the contrasting stressor appeared. I learned another portion of my personality was deeply fearful, poorly self-perceived and very defensive. I was so performance based, that I could create an image and hide so well, that people didn't get to see the inner me; they, therefore, never got to know me. I could feign quiet or use humor or change the subject so I could be in control of the conversation. John's death had God show me new truths, and forced me to go deep, not only to understand God, but to understand myself.

If I didn't choose to go deep and experience God through my emotions, thoughts, words and grieving, then I would always compromise my knowledge and experience and pretend that I didn't know what I didn't know. This performance tool allowed me never to be totally committed to anything. I would gauge my audience, determine hot buttons, choose how I could use them to my advantage and choose which position at which I would perform best. This in turn stopped me from knowing God, knowing myself and would increase my fears and doubts. I could change positions, never really take a stand on anything, and laugh it off.

Death changed that approach. I couldn't simply have an opinion about anguish or grief. I had to feel anguish totally, before I could understand it. I had to feel the turmoil in my heart and mind as I anguished. Only then could I recognize what it was and release it to God.

In my daily life I could determine the depths of my involvement and calculate the sequences and consequences. In grief, I couldn't determine the depth nor the sequences and consequences. I learned I could not hold back the waves of grief and that I needed to go deep to understand God and myself. I now know what suffering is, what unconditional love is, what pain is and, most importantly, what contrasting stresses are. I doubt I would have ever learned them if John lived to be 83 years old and I lived to be 108.

By being unconditional in love, I got meaning in life, developed purpose and became devoted to others. My performance now is based on belief; on something just, educated, sensitive and caring. I felt closer to people during suffering than during celebration. Now I could rejoice in celebration mixed with suffering. They were simultaneous experiences and these experiences took me in and out of myself and God. At times I felt close to no one, then everyone, then only God.

One of the hardest things for me to comprehend was returning to work after the time of grieving and realizing how well people got along without me while I was gone. This bothered me greatly when I found it impossible to get along without John because I loved him so much. My new revelation was in my question to myself, "Didn't anyone love me enough to miss me while I was gone?" "Had they felt they could get along without me?"

Maybe it was all in my head and it didn't matter, as people were uncertain how to respond to me. Perhaps, but it didn't matter to anyone but me. This, too, I had to identify for what it was and release it to God. Obviously they didn't love me as much as I loved John, which shouldn't have been a surprise to me, but it was. I wanted to be loved and cared for. My entire adult life was always taking care of others, but death swiftly made me realize I couldn't take care of others, nor could I take care of myself. I didn't want to be treated special, but I wanted to be loved.

I was learning, if I really wanted God badly enough, I could get to Him with love. But I couldn't trust anyone else but God, for only in Him could I get love. In order to love, I had to let love come in and let love go out of me. For unconditional love, I had to allow God to come in and allow Him to go out of my inner self. One day, love will be the only truthful act we will ever think, say or do. One day I will experience that love. For now I was guilty of random acts of kindness and meanness with no rhyme or reason. I learned I was never in control of my motives and acts of unconditional love. Therefore, I was never unconditional.

I often thought about that Friday night, January 21, 2000. I reflected back as I held John on our kitchen floor as he died, realizing he was a baby. To me, that evening, he didn't weigh close to 280 lbs. He wasn't so big. He was a little baby, helplessly a small being in a large world. This giant was a baby. He felt small and he felt light in my arms. He didn't feel like he was 21, he felt like a newborn. I wanted to protect him now as I protected him in that delivery room, twenty-one years ago.

Recently I thought about that death moment. Then I would force myself to think back to the day he was born. As physicians attended to Beth, it was my job to check the APGAR charts to make sure John was progressing from the womb to the world. This little infant, God's creation, was the most important thing that I ever helped create. Holding him in my arms I felt safe. In my arms, he felt safe.

The night of his death as I held John, I could only sense the depth of safety from a living God. I was spiritually stunned as I remembered the creation in Beth's womb, then deliverance from Beth's womb at his birth. The sequence of life continued as I saw the creation of a man, John, on earth. As a dad, I was becoming a man as John was becoming a man. I had so much growing up to do. Then I experienced the death of John on earth and deliverance from death and birth into heaven. All within twenty-one and a half years. In those last horrific hours, I was desperately trying to steal something from death, as if death owed me something but wasn't going to keep its promise. Months later, I could now treasure those thoughts of holding him and hearing God speak in a still soft whisper.

I wanted to look at John as if I were in a different place waiting for John's next steps towards me. Heaven sounded better, more logical, safer, and more real. All I had now was John leaving me for a different place and I was abandoned in a world that wasn't safe, wasn't logical, and wasn't real. Death made living on earth so mundane, yet I had always been fearful of death. Was I substituting living a deeper life with Jesus for a mundane life on earth? It never felt that way until death darkened the present. I had substituted a deeper life every chance I got, because comfort in "my world sanctuary" was my motive. Why go deep? Why answer the difficult questions? No one else had those questions; why should I?

That Friday night I could only look John in the eyes and see death. Again the contrasting stressor, because I learned in his last moments, John looked death in the eye and saw life. Would John have done anything differently if he knew he was going to die on January 21, 2000? I wanted to think so, but God erased those thoughts with the convicting truth that I had often questioned that if this were my last day, would I do anything differently? No, I probably wouldn't if I didn't know the date.

As the earlier days passed after John departed, I would ponder the future. At night when I lay in bed and thought about my day, if I wasn't too fatigued from running around doing things as if death would never come, did it make a difference? Rarely did I ever live as if it were my last day.

I thought with John now in heaven, did he grieve losing his dad and mom, his brothers and sister, and his friends back on earth? What would he do if he could come back with his girlfriend, or his coaches, or pastor? If I were him, would I be sad thinking of all the things I would miss on earth? Would he regret things he had done, like losing control of his emotions in a wrestling match or on the football field? Or what would he do differently about things he had said, or was it all gone and he had no recollection? Did anything on earth that he gained or lost really matter? I wanted to think so, but how would I know?

I also had to realize that I couldn't keep thinking about that which had no answers. If I did, there would be a physically dead, yet spiritually alive son and there would be a physically alive and spiritually dead father. It was a futile mind-game. I recognized the confusion and deep thoughts for what they were, prayed for wisdom and moved on. Destiny was not hidden in death, but in life. I had to be a "spiritually-alive father."

I learned at my near-by lake sanctuary that deeply shown respect and its effect on my relationships were very powerful. This deeply shown respect was one of the most uncomfortable and embarrassing acts I could ever perform. I was ashamed and embarrassed by showing respect, so I sought comfort and pleasure in lauding myself instead of others. Until I grieved I found I was afraid of showing deep respect to others and embarrassed by it. I could make all sorts of self-condescensions about my life, which wouldn't allow God to release his power through my non-respect. Exhibiting deep respect caused me to go deep into my soul and spirit, find the pain, find the words, find the thoughts and find the love of God to heal me and encourage and appreciate others. And God did it through Himself, the scriptures, His church, and His creation. All I had to do was quiet myself and listen.

Another important learning God planted in me through Pastor Roger was that clean grief was like a spring rain shower. The shower was rinsing off the thoughts, confusion, anguish, pain and remorse. Soft rains brought soft-heartedness. Standing in the living water showered down from heaven as unconditional love made clean grieving a difficult, yet much-anticipated movement of God. If "my world sanctuary" had more clean grieving, there would be more compassion and passion for those worse off than myself.

Clean grief caused me not to feel sorry only for myself, but my wife, my children, my friends and John's relationships. I was unable to experience their grief when it occurred, but I learned that I could experience mine, or know when it was happening. At least then I could understand their grieving.

I found the deepest grieving came for me in the early mornings and I wasn't surprised. My most creative, sensitive and constructive time birthed at sunrise. I always heard God in the mornings in my reading, prayer and devotions. So, deep grief came to me each morning. I allowed those times for self-pity. I tried for the rest of the day to fight the self-pity and that is where Elijah's Oil was relied upon. Each morning I was given enough oil only for that day.

"My world sanctuary" never encouraged me to think about death and terminal illness or suffering. Until I visited Vietnam and India on missions trips, I didn't think anyone in the world truly suffered, and I was too arrogant to want to believe differently. My world kept me feeding the flames of ego, family, career, titles, salary, bonuses, mortgage, new toys, paying taxes, being politically correct, voting Independent, and being a Baptist. They were packaged as my world with the hundreds of millions of insignificant deeds I did just to live each day. I didn't want to step back and see the big picture and refocus, or get balanced. I needed someone like God and death to make me step back, refocus and rebalance.

I learned everyone has "my world sanctuaries." For some reason, people create "my world sanctuaries" with the self-help books, television shows, tapes, and seminars. To me those aids didn't have the answers for death as they didn't have the answers for life. There were no clear answers to anything and I was realizing in times of death and pain and suffering, no one knew what to do. Not one person wanted to discuss if there were anything such as absolute truths to believe in.

I learned almost instantly that death makes fools of us all. Death is an absolute truth. And I don't have anything but the absolute truth of eternal life in Jesus, with which to counter death in order to find comfort. I wanted those answers, though. I wanted to know more absolute truths to comfort my pain.

Too often I was a cynical sort and I had to see things to believe things. Death tricked me. I could not believe what I was seeing and I couldn't believe what I was feeling. I had learned in missionary work that God didn't always allow me to see and I had to believe what I felt. I couldn't always understand what I was seeing. I couldn't comprehend with my mind what my eyes were seeing. As I tried to rely on my emotions, I learned a further extreme truth that was not to believe in what I felt. I had to believe in the unfelt and the unseen, the incomprehensible and the inarticulate. Very strange, I couldn't believe what I saw, felt or thought.

I knew if I was ever going to trust God, I had to believe beyond what I could see or feel. I was learning through death. For me to trust God, I would have had to also trust others first and they then would have to trust me. We all learned, in the shadow of the valley of death that we couldn't see and we couldn't feel, and we couldn't rationalize and we had to choose to believe. Then one day, each one of us, as we meet Jesus as John did, will learn that Christianity would be all about trust and nothing else.

I heard the quote so many times but don't recall the originator who said, "Everyone knows they are going to die, but nobody believes it," and it resurfaced in my sanctuary time. I searched my heart for weeks pondering why that quote was true. If John believed he was going to die, he would have lived differently. If I believed I was going to die, I would do things differently. I would live changing the way I spoke, thought, acted and felt. I would seek to love unconditionally. For one thing, I wouldn't minimize the injustice, ignorance, insensitivity and indifference in my life or the lives around me. I knew death was coming, yet I didn't believe it would come soon, so I didn't live differently. I didn't learn about my death when John died, so God showed me through my heart attack what death meant to me.

Another contrasting stressor: I knew death was inevitable and I should be living differently, but I'm not. Can I do anything different to be prepared to die? Yes, but only if I believe it. That is part of my remaining journey.

Would my learning how to die and truly believe in death, cause me to learn how to live? Yes I believe it would and it will. Refocus, rebalance and look at the big picture would be the first things I would need to learn, and I asked God to show me how. It took a very short time to learn that by refocusing, rebalancing and seeing the vision and purpose God had for me, I released emotions, worries, ambitions and lusts. Peace came in the grieving and the anguish was intense but recognizable. Then I would identify it, surrender it, and move on.

I stood on that frozen lake, a day after John died. I couldn't cry, I couldn't speak, and I couldn't pray, but I learned I could be thankful for that moment of complete brokenness and helplessness. There was healing power in brokenness and helplessness. Genuine praise and thanksgiving could only come to me through brokenness and helplessness. It poured forth from me.

God didn't call money, or career, or fame to rescue me and comfort me at John's death. He didn't call the entertainment industry, or the internet. He didn't call Wall Street. For us He called His children to care for His children who had lost a child. Our family knew that nothing could replace a child. But they knew more than I did, that there is a special bond that a friend or spouse cannot replace. There is an energy created from a father and son that can't be created or replicated somewhere else by someone else. There was no deeper relationship apart from God than a parent and a child. There was no greater sense of responsibility and accountability than being a parent. Try as I did, I couldn't find anything in this world to substitute for a son to relieve the pain. Once I recognized this truth for what it was, I quit trying to find a substitute or think I could replace the relationship, the love, the memories and the pain.

Our friends also knew and shared very quickly after I returned to work, that work was not the substitute. I never did believe I could find everlasting joy in work, nor was my personal identity and worth attached to my job or career. But now I recognized what my job and career weren't. They weren't the elements of who I was. They were essentially just a job and a career. I found now I could do my job very well and have a successful career, but they didn't fulfill my purpose, overcome my fears nor spark my passions. Caring relationships were all that mattered, but for so many years I couldn't articulate what mattered most. And if I was able to articulate them, I knew I didn't believe in what I was saying because something was so much deeper. Too deep to put into words. Mourners taught me depth of words and emotions. You simply can't fake grief and agony and you can't hide them either.

The horror, the shock, the terror of death and the scary moments before and after John's last evening would never diminish unless I could see them for what they were and still are. They were of God's timing and perfect plan to take my family and me to a higher level of spiritual maturity. I understood a dimension about God literally, that John's death brought to me. God truly has a sovereign plan for every one of us and He has a time for all seasons. John lived his seasons and was led through those seasons whether I agreed with God's plan or not. The scriptures state: "As for me, being on the way, the Lord led me ..." Genesis 24:27

I must be so one with God that I don't need to ask continually for guidance. John never has to ask for understanding God's will anymore. He is one with God. Sanctification made John one of the children of God. When John was a little toddler, he was very active, but normally he was obedient. As he grew older, at times he would choose disobedience. I was able to relate well to John. As an adult I did the same thing. I guess I never grew up. But as soon as John chose to disobey, you could see in him an inherent contrasting stressor. He was one of those people who always got caught. He was mischievous and rebellious but he had a guilty look that we just knew when he was up to something. At times it was difficult to try to correct him, because he knew and we all knew, no matter what he did, he would eventually get caught.

On the spiritual level, I recognized through John that I, too, always got caught, by God. My contrasting stressor is the warning of the Spirit of God. When He warns me, I must stop at once and be renewed in the spirit of my heart and mind to discern God's will.

We can all see God in exceptional things, like birth and death and miracles, but it requires the growth of spiritual discipline to see God in every detail of life. I felt I always believed there were no such things as so-called random events of life. Life and death and miracles are nothing less than God's appointed order. Now I look forward to discovering His divine designs anywhere and everywhere.

I had to fight for months with what I knew was a weakness, being obsessed with consistency in my own convictions instead of being devoted to God. I couldn't choose God's will for me, yet I tried to and I tried to shed God's will on others as well, as if I had some supernatural wisdom. Reflecting on who John was during his life and now as a being in heaven was a pilgrimage and still is. Mourning doesn't go away. Memories may fade, but are only cooling embers until the winds of events, first times since and the failure of living in "my world sanctuary" fails, then the flames are fanned and I melt in the sudden conflagration of vivid memories. I believe it is God's plan to bring flames as well as cool the embers to grieving loved ones left behind on this planet.

It was a painful plan and painful timing, but it was what God knew I needed most to step away from the self-centered theology I was believing, and I was further developing. God wasn't interested in my theology of how important I thought I was in my partnership with God, or what I had to offer, or how I was working to perfect it all. He didn't need me to live or to die, to build up or tear down. He lovingly revealed that I wasn't the most important element of his creation. Neither was my net worth, tithes and offerings, missionary trips, foundation efforts, ministry, the work I did or the literature I wrote. Again, I always understood it but didn't believe it or I would have changed what I had been thinking, doing and saying.

My sanctuary time allowed me to release everything. At times on the frozen lake, or as I walked the trails or sat on the shaded benches as the seasons changed, I felt as if someone released the Hoover Dam and the surge would sweep me away. Sometimes it did, but the surge was only temporary. The silent moments in my hotel room on a business trip, or at my desk in my house with dawn devotions or the revisiting the football stadium and wrestling room, always built up the pressure for the release. I recognized the anxiety, fear and anguish this pressure caused and it would remain unless I opened the spillway. But God orchestrated the pressure-build up as well as the opening of the spillway. His Elijah Oil lasted as long as it took for the surge to release and subside.

I learned that I wanted to die as John died. With peace, with serenity, with comfort, with the realization that I will see Jesus reach out His hand and take mine as I walk onto the holy ground of the promised land. My heart attack confirmed my ultimate desire, not to see John again, but to see God. I didn't hear John's last words being filled with fright or shame or terror, I heard matter-of-factly, "I see him" and the expression on his face told me he did. What a contrasting stressor that must have been until he clearly saw what he was looking at. I thought how blessed it would be to not only have death so deeply experienced, but deeply articulated so that we would never fear death again.

John had struggled so much in his youth for attention and to be noticed, much like all the rest of us. Despite his accolades and experiences and blessings, it didn't seem satisfying to him. There was always a tension, a frustration of knowing where he was and knowing where he wanted to go, but never knowing how to get there.

The viewing and the funeral brought a satisfaction and fulfillment to me as I knew what he didn't accomplish in life, he had now accomplished in death. I wrestled with the same thoughts and I knew many others did as well. Perhaps this was what God had called me to do-take frustrated people and show them how to get from where they are, to where they want to go. So many people I knew had started out so strong, only to lose their way and wither on the vine, to die and never bear the fruit that was their purpose or calling. I now knew what John had taught me with his death. The fulfillment of a life purpose might not occur during an earthly lifetime, but an eternal lifetime.

Too often I had missed those opportunities to love and to acknowledge his need. Too often I missed the opportunities to show my passion and compassion and so did he. But we both received the same in the end, contentment in knowing I helped him finish strong. John had an insatiable appetite to be understood, to be taken seriously and to know that he mattered in the lives of others. I don't know if it came from his parents missing those opportunities, or if he was simply demanding the maximum love from each of us to know he mattered. I confessed I wanted the same things in my life and I wasn't going to wait until death before it mattered.

John, Jr. and John, Sr. were both men, and we were independent and we were fighters and we weren't going to succumb to reliance upon anyone, until death came. Then the only things we had were each other, our shattered dreams and our sadness. But we saw God and His plan and all along it was never about us being men, or being independent or being fighters. It was about being a warrior of the gospel of light and truth. We stood before our Creator, the only one who could save both of us. It didn't feel like all we wanted it to feel, helpless and inadequate, broken and dependent. But nothing rarely feels the way it's supposed to feel, for we are spectators in life for the most part and do not know the cost, or the pain or the details of playing the game in the trenches. As a spectator I under-appreciated life by being the spectator and under-appreciated those who were living. No longer will I be a spectator.

My culture may define it differently and certainly the media portrayed it differently, but as I fumbled through John's wrestling medals one day and saw his second place medal for heavyweight at States, there were no tears for second place as there were during the competition. There was only a sense of accomplishment. My son came in second in the state championships and he had accomplished greatness. How could I be thirsting for more? He now was with God, how could I not be thankful? How could I be thirsting for more? He had gone beyond good to great and now to the ultimate. He had finished strong.

When he was a toddler and I would roll around on the floor with him, I had great aspirations for him as an athlete. When he got older and competed in elementary and middle school and we'd drive to wrestling tournaments together early in the morning I never felt like it was a waste of time. There was always a sense of purpose in me to make him the best. Never did I realize I would travel with him to the ultimate experience, Holy Ground.

What he craved for his life was what we all craved, being accepted, being loved, and being taken seriously. In his last moments, he found the ultimate desires and needs fulfilled. Jesus. And he knew for sure his parents loved him as Jesus did and we cared. We had a vision painted for life, but not for death. We knew God's will for the short-term and we believed his vision for the long-term, but it was so hard to live what we believed. We always wanted to add to what God was doing.

Once again I think of the story of Abram and Sarah. They heard from God but didn't believe Him. They decided to add to God's plan. Sarah rationalized she was too old to have a baby but Hagar the handmaiden could, so Abram and Sarah had Hagar conceive Ishmael. A substitute, blessed, successful, but still a substitute to the real thing, Isaac. More is not more. More is not necessarily good. More is not necessarily the real thing.

There is no substitute for death. Death is the real thing, no matter how we want to think we can substitute God's plan with ours. There is no more in death. Once is enough. End of story. Death is not a substitute for tenderness, or power, or mercy. When death comes nothing else matters. We think so much matters, and so much is important, but we are caught in the trap of what we need and what we want.

What we want is different from what we need. We get hungry, we need food, but we want ice cream. We get a job because we need money, but we want a higher salary. We find a lover because we need love, but we want the perfect mate. The truth I learned is that what I need is what gives me the most satisfaction. I get satisfaction by offering others what I have to give. I must give more.

If I want respect, I must offer something first. If I want love, I must offer love first. If I want satisfaction and fulfillment, I must commit to give purpose and meaning in another person's life. Too often I thought my wants were my needs and realistically, my needs were offensive and threatening to others. Death brought an end to the brainwashing.

I was worried that people would forget John after he died. I feared forgetting about John as well. I didn't want to forget him, even the details of his life. My real fear was exposed. I was afraid I would be forgotten when I died. God taught me that through love, one doesn't forget. I haven't forgotten anything about John. I am actually remembering more. I learned for me to never be forgotten is to love others with all my heart and I will stay alive in them.

I can hear John's voice at times in my thoughts. It is not to be confused with my voice or other voices. It is not to be confused with God's voice. I learned that if I speak lovingly to others, my voice will not be forgotten, for the world is alive to the voice of love and forgets the voice of power and wealth and fame. I will never forget John's voice. It is a distinctive voice, one calling to a loved one.

I barely slept those first weeks after John died. It was a contrast for me as when I was younger, I used to nod off in class. Sometimes I would nod off in the presence of friends, once in a while, I'd nod off in prayer groups or church services. Often I could fake it. Often I could pretend I was listening to someone and have them totally tuned out. I wasn't present with them. I also learned how to be in spiritual slumber, never really awake to the promptings of the Holy Spirit.

Those moments I spent during the last night with John taught me how to be fully present, totally focused and completely aware. I learned how important it is to be awake. Since then, I have changed my prayer time and devotions and silence. I am thinking and talking to God. I am listening. I am learning to be aware. I am learning to be awake to those around me, including God.

I had always tuned out quickly when something didn't seem as important to me as I thought it should. I often felt so important that I tuned God out and then made up stuff as if I were some holy being in tune with God. I was in tune with myself and never was aware. No time. I heard myself tell others I was too busy, or I had no time, when what I was really telling them was that I was too important to be concerned about what was important to others.

I had no understanding of life as I searched and searched for meaning and purpose, so I kept pursuing what I thought was important and listening to my own inner voice, hoping it was God's voice so I wouldn't have to change what I viewed as important. Instead of slowing down and listening to God, I kept chasing that which had no meaning. I learned that if I could listen to myself and listen to others, I wouldn't have to listen to God. Death changed what I listened to and who I listened to.

I learned how important it was to put value on relationships I took for granted. Another contrasting stressor. That which I thought was valuable I neglected to appreciate and that which I appreciated usually wasn't very valuable in God's eyes.

Grief caused many types of pain. I learned I felt attacked when I grieved, so my initial reaction was to fight back. Then I learned to recognize when I was feeling attacked, release it to God and move on. Feeling attacked would only make me think about myself. I learned to recognize the feeling and release it to God. This brought my thinking to others besides myself. I found purpose and meaning in my life by putting other lives first. Grieving continued to create the stress of pain and the joy of cleansing and ministering to others.

I learned I couldn't run away. It was easy and hard to run away. My first inclination was always to run away from John's death and the fear of suffering. But it was too hard to run away from someone you loved. There were no substitutes for running away. You either did or didn't and I learned I never wanted anyone to run away from me. I needed to love them more so they would never want to run away, but run to me.

As a financial advisor I had always advised clients not to think short-term, but to focus long term on investing, saving, spending and earning. If I am to invest in others instead of John after he died, it would have to be for the long term, for eternity. There was no short-term. And with my wife, my remaining children and loved ones, I learned the short-term thinking and achieving did no good if I didn't think long term. If they didn't know their eternal destiny, it didn't matter what they accomplished or gained short term. The apostle Paul mentioned it in Corinthians, all that he gained he counted as rubbish.

I learned John's death ends life, but not John's love. Jesus taught me that by His example. John taught me that by his experience of dying. In life there is constant competition and negotiation. There is constantly a winner and a loser. In love, there are only winners, only victory, ultimate victory. What enemy hails defeat if their foes show compassion and mercy? There is a winning mentality when all feel loved, no matter how unfair the conditions present themselves. Love bears hope. Loves shows caring, it shows importance and value and appreciation. John's death brought love, appreciation, and value to our relationship and it brought hope in Christ and caring from God, manifested through His people. I learned an important lesson: love is not about caring for my own situation or reputation. It's about caring for another's situation or reputation more than mine.

I also learned about the traditions and rituals of love and death. I wear John's wrist watch. I wear his leather winter coat. I wear his hats and some of his shirts. I have his picture in my office and on my bedroom dresser. I have his memories every time I go into my sanctuary. I have John on my prayer list, a reminder to thank God for the 21 years He blessed me with a son. We have his athletic awards, his game tapes, his football jersey and helmet. We have his high school posters on the playroom walls. Beth has eagles everywhere, pictures, statues, stuffed animals and key chains. Ben drives his car.

I have John's stuffed animal Vince sitting on my desk and his cards, clippings and scrapbooks readily accessible. Our "first times since" have been tributes to our love for him. His first Christmas ornament, his birthday being the same date as the cartoon character Garfield, and his ashes placed at the football stadium and under the stone in our yard, are powerful reminders of relationships, love, compassion and grace. God has been good. We will continue to cherish and invent new traditions and rituals. They are some of Elijah's Oil.

Often I think about how God put my family together. When John was a child, maybe five years old at the time, we had a great Christmas. My parents, grandparents, my brothers and their wives and children and my family got together for a Christmas holiday. A few neighbors stopped by and a number of aunts and uncles and cousins visited as we all congregated at my parent's home. I don't remember all the details, or even if I have the story straight, but I do remember sitting in the living room thanking God in my heart for His plan for our family. We had a lot of fun over the years at Christmas, and I can remember John as being the whirlwind of activity that year. His brothers and sister were active and a lot of fun as well, but there was something about John that made others in our family take notice. The Christmas holiday was one of John's favorite holidays. He knew how to enjoy family and food and holidays.

After spending the entire day at my parent's home, we returned home to a pleasant evening. Beth put the kids to bed and I lit a few candles, put on the tree lights and we sat in the coziness of our living room reliving the day. It was filled with warmth and love. We didn't say much as we sat next to each other, savoring the quiet. I could hear the kids winding down with a toy or a book in their rooms, and I thanked God for the moment. The food, decorations, laughter, conversation, presents and loving fellowship of the day, and hearing our children settling in for the night, gave me a deep afterglow of what God's plan was for us.

A cold winter night surrounded us, but it didn't matter. The love inside the house and the memories of the day took away the chill and darkness. It took away the worries, the uncertainties, the dizzying pace of the holidays and left us together as a special family. I have never forgotten that moment as we reclined on the sofa, listening to a background of Christmas hymns on the stereo and the peacefulness of our household. I didn't want the moment to end. I looked down the hallway and saw the faint mellow orange reflection of the night-lights in the bedrooms. We had prepared a home for our family. This felt like heaven. I wanted to capture the moment and keep it as an ultimate ongoing lifestyle experience. It was just too good to forget.

I don't ever think I'll recapture that moment as it was then. I almost always compare every Christmas since with that Christmas as a benchmark for joy until the first Christmas since John died. I stopped comparing it, as it was too sad for me. I was afraid to celebrate Christmas the same way, because most of those people at the memorable Christmas in Pennsylvania are no longer alive. Each one of those relatives took a piece of that memory from me. John took the most.

If the wings of the dove are simplicity and purity and the wings of the eagle are overcoming power and grace, the broken wings of death are helplessness and anguish. There is a deep pain that lingers at holidays and "first times since." There may be no way to counter it and perhaps God wants us to keep it all as is. But I do know the truth. Combined with each other, my family and I know one day all of our sorrows, death, crying, pain and suffering will be gone. I believe John has that experience now. And with this eagle, and with the dove, or Holy Spirit, we can rest assured that just as the Christmas night where we had a glimpse of the complete memory, the complete family and the complete love of God, in heaven now, we have the complete John, the total John who was born again and finished strong.

I know life goes on and events and people change, but memories don't. I had to make a decision that I couldn't let the past take away from my future. Jesus told us in his words that He must go away to prepare a place for us in his mansion. John's room at the mansion was prepared first. He went to His new mansion. The light in the heavens reflect the love of God in John's new room and we must wait for our room preparations to be finished. We know it will be a far greater reunion when we are all together at the mansion, being complete in Christ and with Christ, face to face as eagles in a nest, with the dove among us.

The bottom line in life and death comes down to where one stands with Jesus Christ, and is He Lord and Savior. I am so thankful John was a believer. That fact never escapes me. And that fact should never escape anyone. Dying without Christ is terror for the dead person and the living. That fact is what has kept grieving tolerable, as difficult as it has been. In the grieving process and now in my mentoring, the witness and testimony of the believer is paramount so God can be glorified, His name magnified and His kingdom advanced.

In the Book of Acts, there is a story of Stephen, the servant, who preached one of the greatest sermons in history and was killed because of it. As he was being stoned he looked up into heaven.

Acts 7:54 When they heard this, they were furious and gnashed their teeth at him. *But Stephen, full of the Holy Spirit, looked up to heaven and saw the glory of God, and Jesus standing at the right hand of God. "Look," he said, "I see heaven open and the Son of Man standing at the right hand of God."*

What impressed me is that in almost every scripture, when Jesus is mentioned in heaven, He is always seated at the right hand of God. But for Stephen, who had shown his love and commitment and willingness to sacrifice for Jesus, Jesus was standing, in reverence and anticipation, because of Stephen's witness. It is my goal that this book will inspire you to live through your loss and be like Stephen. Be true and loyal to Christ and let your witness shine in your heart and on your face, even in the midst of death...for Jesus awaits you.

REFLECTION

Thank you, God, for your love and mercy, joy and peace and for blessing us with a twenty-one year plan so we could learn more about you and your sovereignty. May others like us who read this book know God's love and mercy, joy and peace because of God's sovereign plan for each one of us. I pray this prayer for all people, but especially for those of you whom have lost a loved one, especially a child. May God bless you and grant you peace, in His name. Amen.